# The Palgrave Kets de Vries Library

Manfred F. R. Kets de Vries, Distinguished Professor of Leadership and Development and Organizational Change at INSEAD, is one of the world's leading thinkers on leadership, coaching, and the application of clinical psychology to individual and organizational change.

Palgrave's professional business list operates at the interface between academic rigor and real-world implementation. Professor Kets de Vries's work exemplifies that perfect combination of intellectual depth and practical application and Palgrave is proud to bring almost a decade's worth of work together in the Palgrave Kets de Vries Library.

More information about this series at
http://www.palgrave.com/gp/series/16661

Manfred F. R. Kets de Vries

# The CEO Whisperer

## Meditations on Leadership, Life, and Change

palgrave
macmillan

Manfred F. R. Kets de Vries
Europe Campus
INSEAD
Fontainebleau, France

ISSN 2730-7581                    ISSN 2730-759X    (electronic)
The Palgrave Kets de Vries Library
ISBN 978-3-030-62600-6         ISBN 978-3-030-62601-3    (eBook)
https://doi.org/10.1007/978-3-030-62601-3

This Palgrave Macmillan imprint is published by the registered company Springer Nature Switzerland AG.
The registered company address is: Gewerbestrasse 11, 6330 Cham, Switzerland

# Prologue

*Four givens are particularly relevant for psycho-therapy: the inevitability of death for each of us and for those we love; the freedom to make our lives as we will; our ultimate aloneness; and, finally, the absence of any obvious meaning or sense to life.*
—Irvin Yalom

Sometimes, given my work at the boundaries of organizations and depth psychology, I feel like an invited guest on the Jerry Springer Show—that infamous, confessional TV forum for dysfunctional and dispossessed Americans. At other times, I feel more like "Dear Abbie." In my real life, however, I am a business school professor who has spent many years teaching organizational behavior, the study of human functioning in organizations. But before I was drawn to the field of organizational behavior, I studied economics. And I have since become a psychoanalyst—so the running joke of my professional life is that I try to combine John Maynard Keynes' "dismal science" with Sigmund Freud's "impossible profession."

I decided to become a psychoanalyst because too many management scholars in the field of organizational behavior conveniently left the person out of the equation. Organizational structures seemed to be a much more attractive proposition for most of them than studying the behavior of people in a work setting—far too messy and confusing. I decided that a clinical training would give me a very helpful lens to counter this regrettable trend and acquire a greater understanding of the complexity of human beings. And I have been proved right. Clinical training and practice have provided me with a more holistic understanding of why people do what they do. It has also made me realize that there's no Chinese Wall between people's public and private lives. Working life affects personal life, and vice versa.

Given my work, I am sometimes privy to strange requests for advice. In the past, people would only occasionally solicit my advice but with the rise of social media the barriers to access have disappeared. Nowadays I receive a continuous stream of communications that are often cries for help. But although many of these requests are interesting, they don't make my life any easier. Like Henry David Thoreau, I find myself thinking, "The mass of men lead lives of quiet desperation." Although most people we meet seem completely normal, behind this façade there often lies a very different reality. Quiet desperation isn't difficult to find. For example, what do you make of the following email, which is typical of the sort of thing I get these days. Like every case study in this book, I have anonymized it and disguised the details.

*Dear Professor, I hope that this e-mail will reach you. But let me first introduce myself. I am an executive at a medium-sized IT company where I have been working for many years. Until recently, I kidded myself that I was doing ok. But when I look at my current situation, I realize my life is falling apart. I am not doing well at work or in my private life. My personal worries are affecting my work and my work worries my personal life. My boss recently told me that my performance is not up to snuff. Now I am worried that she is going to fire me. If that happens, it will be a disaster. My salary is my only source of income. There are also lots of deeply troubling issues in my personal life.*

*The reason I am writing to you is that I have read a number of your articles. In particular, your articles about the victim syndrome and greed resonated with me. I also looked at one of your articles about psychopathic behavior. These articles brought me with some comfort, as they helped me understand my present predicament. Thank you for making these articles available. I really appreciate how you wrap up all these threads of human dynamics into a nice, understandable ball. Your articles made me realize that I'm like some of the victims you describe. They helped me better understand why certain things are happening to me.*

*Until recently, I thought I had my life together but that changed when my stepfather died. Since then, things have been falling apart but I'm beginning to wonder whether that started much earlier, to be exact, when I caught my brother in a sexual act with my wife. I forgave my wife but now I'm asking myself why I didn't I see it coming. How long was their affair going on? Was I blind? And since then, my 19-year-old daughter has told me that my brother used to make passes at her. Everything is such a mess. My relationship with my wife has never been the same. There isn't much going on between us.*

*But that's not all. What has upset me even more is finding out that I have been written out of my stepfather's will. Everything will go to my brother. (Our mother died from a stroke a number of years ago.) My brother pulled a fast one on me. He got our stepfather to adopt him and took on his name. He got away with all of this because our family lawyer had died, and his replacement had no idea what my brother is really like.*

*When I confronted my brother with all this, he attacked me, and said terrible things, like that our mother hated me (that was the worst) and made a number of other accusations. The police were called and had to intervene. When they arrived, my brother said I had assaulted him, which is a lie. He started the fight. He also told the police that I tried to run him over in a parking lot, which is completely untrue.*

*The upshot is that I can't go to our family home anymore. My brother has told me to stay away. I am no longer welcome there. He says that everything in the house now belongs to him and if I want any of it, I better contact a lawyer. But a lot of my personal belongings are in that house. Our mother kept things there for me, like the photos from when I was a child, all the family photographs, the school memorabilia and so on. It's terrible.*

*And it gets worse. My brother's girlfriend came to see me recently and said that he owned her money, and could I help her get it back? How can I, the way things stand? She also told me that she'd had a fight with my wife, who was in my brother's apartment. Everything she said about him upset me even more.*

*I keep asking myself what went wrong in our family? I know life was very hard when we were children My mother got pregnant with me when she was very young and put me up for adoption when I was a baby. A few years after my brother was born, my grandfather insisted on getting me back. But I always tried to make the best of a bad thing. As the oldest, I tried to be strong. I was always there for my brother, protecting him when he got himself into trouble, but I clearly didn't do a good enough job.*

*Quite early on, he became an alcoholic and drug addict, but he started to get into real trouble when he was a teenager. He would tell lies, accuse me of things that he had done, and stole money to support his addictions. That period was hell for me. He went to jail when he was around 19 for hitting someone in a bar with a baseball bat. But as he is a very good talker, he only got probation. Personally, I think, he's got psychopathic tendencies.*

*Looking back, I realize that I couldn't have had the same relationship with my mother as my brother (in secret) had with her. Otherwise, why would he scream at me that my mother hated me? I never felt that was the case but on the other hand, why he would say such a terrible thing? What he's said, and the financial mess I'm in now I'm not going to inherit anything, make me wonder whether my mother and stepfather ever really loved me. All in all, my family background is a mess but your articles about family dynamics made me realize I'm not alone. Reading them was like a lightbulb going on.*

*I'm sure you can understand that my personal situation is affecting my work. Like I said, I'm worried I'll get fired. I've always had a difficult relationship with my boss. She isn't an easy person. She is very manipulative and self-centered, although I have to admit that she can be quite charming. I think she's a flaming narcissist. She claims that she cares about me, but I wonder if that's really true. Her words sometimes sound very hollow. And she's always taking credit for my work. It makes me furious, but I find it hard to stand up to her.*

*In spite of it everything, I feel sorry for my brother. I think he is lonely. Although he's very good looking, he's never been capable of stable relationships. He's been married and divorced several times and he has very poor relationships with his children. I don't think that he has any real friends. But although I feel sorry for him, the way he's treating me kills me.*

*What do you advise me to do? Should I sue my brother for my part of the estate? Do you think it's worth the fight? What am I going to do about my relationship with my wife? Should I start looking for another job? As things are now, I am just muddling along. I'm just trying to survive. And while all this is going on, I'm trying to be the best father I can to my daughter, hoping I can leave her with good memories of me.*

Quite some email to get out of the blue. A lot went through my mind as I read it.

## You Cannot Not Communicate

Sometimes, the loudest cries for help are silent. Often, when people communicate, many things remain unsaid. Bearing this in mind, this particular cry for help has an *Alice in Wonderland* quality to it. The writer seems to have been drifting through life for far too long not seeing the dramas playing themselves out around him. Of course, as a defensive maneuver, it may have been less painful for him not to see them but now he can't shut his eyes to them any longer. Maybe reading the articles he mentioned caused some imbalance in his usual modus operandi. They may have helped him take a few steps toward understanding what's going on in his family and his life in general. But will self-diagnosis be enough?

I am not saying that a light bulb, or "Aha!" moment can't have an enlightening effect. Understanding psychological dynamics can be therapeutic, and after all, diagnosis is the first step toward taking greater control of your life. Most of us look ceaselessly for some kind of order in a very baffling universe and try to make sense out of mystifying things. But even assuming the author of this email has a modicum of self-understanding, will he be able to untangle all the strands of his very troubled life on his own? Does he see what's really there? Does he realize what he is up against? Is he aware how toxic his present situation is? Does he understand the motivations of the people he's dealing with? In other words, will his diagnoses be enough? Is it enough to label people as depressed, paranoid, obsessional, bipolar, narcissistic, or psychopathic?

I am always hesitant to categorize people myself. I have always been wary of making fixed diagnoses, although, I admit, I have never been exactly a saint in the matter. I've done it many times. The fact is that the more I get to know individuals, the harder I find it to assess what they are all about, and to make sense of what drives them, which makes classification redundant. Frankly, I am far more interested in the "scripts" that drive an individual's inner theater—what's going on inside them. At the same time, I am fully cognizant that the "other" will never be fully knowable. With this in mind, I wonder whether the sender of this email was helped by labeling the behavior of the people around him (his "narcissistic" boss, his "psychopathic" brother). It might have given him the illusion of having a degree of control over a very messy situation. It might make him feel a bit better.

Dramatic though this email is, I get the impression that a lot of the drama (whether consciously or unconsciously) remains unstated. This raises the question of what this person isn't seeing? What has been left out of this story? Also, given how ignorant I am about his situation as a whole, what help can I realistically provide? And while I am at it, can I deal with not knowing? Realizing how handicapped I am, in light of my ignorance, should I just ignore this communication? At the same time, I always tell myself and others that the capacity to tolerate a large amount of uncertainty is a prerequisite for an effective executive coach or therapist. It is what the poet John Keats called as being "capable of being in uncertainties, mysteries, doubts, without any irritable reaching after fact and reason."[1]

My clients may have a fantasy that I guide them systematically and sure-handedly toward a known goal, but I have to admit that the reality is very different. The journey is much more of an emerging process, during which I improvise and feel for direction. I also have to tolerate not knowing—to accept the isolation, anxiety, and frustration that are inevitable parts of the work I do.

---

[1] Li Ou (2009). *Keats and Negative Capability*, London: Continuum Literary Studies, p. ix.

This email made me wonder how effective I can really be when attempting to provide psychological "containment" from a distance. Dealing with emails is very different from dealing with clients face-to-face. Taking a dispassionate view of this person's predicament, the question was whether I should even try. Do I have the ability to manage this person's troubling thoughts, feelings, and behaviors? Should I make his problems my problems? After all, he came into my life uninvited.

In a more professional setting—not this kind of long-distance communication—I always try to absorb my clients' feelings. I try to reframe whatever they are experiencing in a more manageable way. In my various roles as coach, psychotherapist, or consultant,[2] I try to take on my clients' anxieties, sadness, and pain. I try to be empathic. Also, I try to create a safe space that can help my clients to model healthier ways of dealing with their life challenges. What's more, I remind myself continuously that, as an executive coach or psychotherapist, I have to make myself obsolete. I want my clients to become their own caretakers. I want them to reach a point when they can take care of their issues by themselves.

All these thoughts were going through my mind while trying to deal with this email that came out of the blue.

Although this email was unsolicited, it was not the kind of communication I felt I should simply put aside. I couldn't ignore it. Troublesome as it was, it was a life drama that stuck with me. I kept thinking about the person who wrote it. After giving it further thought, I decided that the author deserved a response. So, I wrote back briefly that I appreciated his email. I told him that it would be very important for him to have the strength to own his own life. He should ask himself whether he wanted to be the product of circumstances or the product of his own decisions. If he decided to choose the latter, he might want to take a few action steps.

I explained that while reading my articles may have helped him understand his predicament better, reading by itself might not be enough. More work might be needed to put together the various strands of what was clearly a

---

[2] Generally speaking, I have never been a purist in using the terms coach, psychotherapist, or even consultant. Although there is substantial literature about the differentiation between the terms, I have learned from experience that many people in the helping professions move quite easily between these roles. In the way that I work, I tend to be more of a lumper then a splitter, that is, as a lumper, I take a more gestalt-oriented view of things. I like to group things into broad categories, assuming that differences are not as important as similarities. Splitters, on the other hand, are into precise definitions, making distinctions, creating new classifications. Of course, now I have made this comment, you (the reader) may have realized that while the splitter in me just divided people into two kinds—lumpers and splitters—the lumper in me now is confusing you, saying that we are all mixtures of both. For the sake of simplification, however, I usually refer to myself as a psychotherapist or coach. On occasion, I also use the term psychoanalyst.

terribly confusing life situation. Given the extent of his difficulties, I questioned whether he would be able to do this by himself. He might consider seeking out the help of a psychotherapist or coach to help him untangle what was happening to him.

As a starter, I suggested that something should be done with respect to his relationship with his wife. He might want to explore whether they have enough in common to continue to stay together. Living parallel lives did not seem to be a solution. What's more, it could negatively influence his daughter—about whom I knew very little. With respect to his tenuous work situation, it could very well be that coaching could help him clarify his relationship with his boss. In any case, whatever he planned to do, it would be a good idea to contact a search consultant to see if he had other options, workwise. I also told him that a greater understanding of his various troubles could very well lead to further insights and actions. It could even give him the strength to contact a lawyer to become better informed of his legal position vis-à-vis his brother.

The question that stayed with me was whether this individual would be able (and prepared) to untangle his messy past. Would he regress? Would he prefer to continue not wanting to see? Would he have the courage to deal with some very unpleasant realities? It begged the question of how much "truth" he would be able to handle. Would he continue to act out some of his dysfunctional behavior patterns? Would he be able to accept the idea that moving forward implied letting go of certain illusions?

Sometimes, damaged people, if they want to move forward, have to relinquish the fantasy of having a better past. In many instances, their challenge is to let go of a number of illusions, as they need to work on how to make the best of the future. But moving forward also implies that they have to forgive themselves for the mess they find themselves in. Therefore, I ended my reply by applying to the "oxygen mask first" principle. We all know that when a plane is in trouble, we need to put on our own oxygen mask first, before helping others. Likewise, it is essential that we love ourselves before we can love another. Although my correspondent might not have much control over his current situation, he did have some control over himself. Perhaps that's where he should start. Only by taking greater care of himself would he be able to take care of others, including his daughter.

That's where I left it, but his story still kept me in knots, wondering how I could have been of greater help. I was curious about how the situation would end. Would he be able to take the actions needed to improve his situation? Would he find ways of dealing with his demons of guilt, self-justification, and self-destruction? And would he be able to overcome his sense of despair—the price that we usually pay for a greater sense of self-awareness?

## Wandering and Wondering

Receiving communications like this makes my life quite challenging. These life dramas keep me on my toes. I get a constant stream of requests for advice, not just emails of this kind that come out of the blue, but also WhatsApp, FaceTime, WebEx, Zoom, and Skype exchanges, through which I try to help my clients solve knotty problems. And, in my role as a consultant, I see people in my office, and in their offices. Every time, there is the expectation that I can help them untangle complex situations. Then again, as a professor, I give talks at conferences, and I give a great number of lectures about my work. Many of these presentations lead to intense dialogues, in which I am asked to respond to difficult issues. All these activities require much travel. These trips take me to unusual places—in reality and in fantasy. They also lead to many strange encounters, providing me with exciting new learning opportunities.

Sometimes I feel like the cartoon character Mr. Magoo, who bumbles around the world, and, due to his extreme nearsightedness, constantly finds himself in messy situations. Like Mr. Magoo, I do "wander" around a lot, "wondering" what is happening to me. But Mr. Magoo always manages to untangle himself, ending up unharmed. This is a fantasy ending for me. Emotional labor always takes its toll.

As a wanderer, I have always been intrigued by the wanderer who graces the cover of this book. Caspar David Friedrich's iconic painting, *Wanderer Above the Sea of Fog*, is one of the greatest works of Romanticism. It shows a lone man, dressed in boots walking clothes, steadying himself with a cane, and standing on a precipice overlooking a cloudy, inhospitable landscape. As he looks over the sea of fog, he seems to be in a state of self-reflective introspection.

The emotion I always experience when I look at this painting is intensified by the fact that we see the figure in the foreground from behind. This presentation is known by the German term *"Rückenfigur"* (figure from the back). The composition enables the observer to identify with the figure and see what the painter is trying to see. In Friedrich's words, "The artist should paint not only what he has in front of him but also what he sees inside himself."[3]

---

[3] Golding Notebooks (2019). *Wanderer Above the Sea of Fog by Caspar David Friedrich Journal*, Independently Published.

Looking at this painting, I identify with an individual comfortable with an ambiguous, psychic landscape, wondering at the fog but ready to explore it and find clarity. I see it as a metaphor for the kind of work I do. As a wanderer I try to bring clarity in an unknown psychic landscape, all the time wondering what's going on. I try to help people to find their way through the fog of life. During these guided journeys, I put on my clinical hat to understand better the micro issues that emerge from the fog but also try to make sense of the societal conundrums at work.

I like to be empathic and helpful during these explorations but at the same time, I don't want to get completely lost in my clients' pain. That would make me less effective as a coach or psychotherapist. I also need to resist the temptation to be a know-it-all consultant. I constantly remind myself that I don't have all the answers. I am not the one who should fill all the voids in the encounter with my own version of meaning. On the contrary, it should always be the clients who steal the show. They should be able to find the answers by themselves. My role is to ask the right questions. I can only create tipping points. I often ask myself, what do I really know? In fact, the older I am, the less I seem to know. And I am no longer young enough to know everything.

In my work, it is essential to appreciate the uniqueness of the other. All my explorations of individual and societal issues should be seen as a co-creative process from which unique "goals" emerge, often as surprises—a process through I arrive at "truths" that I could never have known beforehand. My ultimate objective is to give my clients more freedom of choice—to help them stretch their minds, because, to quote Oliver Wendell Holmes, "[a] mind that is stretched by new experience can never go back to its old dimensions." The aim of the kind of work I do should never be an illusory "cure." What I aim for is to help people change and grow. Whatever happens, it is always a work in progress.

This is a book of meditations on leadership and life that I have written for executives and the people who deal with them. I make observations on what it means as a therapist or coach to help these people to become more effective in what they are doing. I reflect on what it takes to become a better leader. Also, I present many situations in organizational and political life—being it micro or macro issues—that can lead to various forms of derailment. I point out numerous pitfalls of leadership—including loneliness, meaninglessness, hubris, and greed—and discuss how leaders can manage disappointment, deal with regrets, and detect the dangers of closed minds or toxic corporate cultures. I also comment on the developmental challenges executives face, including the human life cycle—aging being an important concern. I look at talent and culture management and discuss how to create—something that is always top of mind—best places to work. Other themes are cult-like organizations and the danger of creating false prophets in the helping professions; the leader-society interface—how leaders can (and do) take advantage of historical moments to affect societal trends, for good or for bad; the consequences of societies moving from a "we" to an "I" focus; and the implications of living in the cyber age.

This is also a book of very personal reflections on how to live a fulfilling life. And the coronavirus pandemic with its many regressive and paranoid strands, has made the theme of self-exploration even more urgent. Drawing on a number of events in my personal history, I try to explain why I do what I do and what makes me feel at my best. The ancient Greek philosophers struggled with this theme, trying to discover the supreme good for mankind, the best way to lead our life and give our lives meaning. For Aristotle, in his *Nicomachean Ethics*,[4] this supreme good is best understood by looking at its purpose, or goal. Aristotle introduced the term *eudaimonia*, arguing that the goal of life is to maximize happiness by living virtuously. To achieve this, we need to fulfill our own potential as a human being, and engage with others—family, friends, and fellow citizens—in mutually beneficial activities. But there is also *hedonia*, the pursuit of subjective well-being—seeking pleasure, avoiding pain, searching for the fundamental pleasures afforded by food, sex, and social interactions, which are central to our survival. Both hedonic and eudaimonic pathways play a crucial role in leading a fulfilling life. This is what this book is all about.

Along the way, I try to provide insights into the way I work to help the reader see what people in the helping professions can do to help others change. My reflections come from different angles. Not only do I have to think about how I experience the other, I also have to pay attention to the other's perspective. The work I do always implies building bridges. It means giving in without giving up; it means staying openminded when things aren't always what they seem to be. While operating in this complex interpersonal field, I realize that our intrapersonal relationships define our interpersonal and group relationships. In more than one way, everything that happens in our lives is a reflection of what we experience within ourselves.

---

[4] https://oll.libertyfund.org/titles/aristotle-the-nicomachean-ethics

# Contents

# About the Author

**Manfred Florian R. Kets de Vries** brings a different view to the much-studied subjects of leadership and the psychological dimensions of individual and organizational change. Bringing to bear his knowledge and experience of economics (Econ. Drs., University of Amsterdam), management (ITP, MBA, and DBA, Harvard Business School), and psychoanalysis (Membership Canadian Psychoanalytic Society, Paris Psychoanalytic Society, and the International Psychoanalytic Association), he explores the interface between management science, psychoanalysis, developmental psychology, evolutionary psychology, neuroscience, psychotherapy, executive coaching, and consulting. His specific areas of interest are leadership (the "bright" and "dark" side), entrepreneurship, career dynamics, talent management, family business, cross-cultural management, succession planning, organizational and individual stress, C-suite team building, executive coaching, organizational development, transformation management, management consulting.

The Distinguished Clinical Professor of Leadership Development and Organizational Change at INSEAD, he is Program Director of INSEAD's top management program, "The Challenge of Leadership: Creating Reflective Leaders," and the Founder of INSEAD's Executive Master Program in Change Management. As an educator, he has received INSEAD's distinguished teacher award six times. He has held professorships at McGill University, the École des Hautes Études Commerciales, Montreal, the European School for Management and Technology (ESMT), Berlin, and the Harvard Business School. He has lectured at management institutions around the world. *The Financial Times*, *Le Capital*, *Wirtschaftswoche*, and *The Economist* have rated Manfred Kets de Vries among the world's leading management thinkers and among the most influential contributors to human resource management.

Kets de Vries is the author, co-author, or editor of 50 books, including *The Neurotic Organization, Leaders, Fools and Impostors, Life and Death in the Executive Fast Lane, The Leadership Mystique, The Happiness Equation, Are Leaders Made or Are They Born? The Case of Alexander the Great, The New Russian Business Elite, Leadership by Terror, The Global Executive Leadership Inventory, The Leader on the Couch, Coach and Couch, The Family Business on the Couch, Sex, Money, Happiness, and Death: The Quest for Authenticity, Reflections on Leadership and Character, Reflections on Leadership and Career, Reflections on Organizations, The Coaching Kaleidoscope, The Hedgehog Effect: The Secrets of High Performance Teams, Mindful Leadership Coaching: Journeys into the Interior, You Will Meet a Tall Dark Stranger: Executive Coaching Challenges* and *Telling Fairy Tales in the Boardroom: How to Make Sure Your Organization Lives Happily Ever After, Riding the Leadership Roller Coaster: A Psychological Observer's Guide* and *Down the Rabbit Hole of Leadership: Leadership Pathology of Everyday Life* and the eBook, *Journeys into Coronavirus Land: Lessons from a Pandemic.*

In addition, Kets de Vries has published more than 400 academic papers as chapters in books and as articles (including digital). He has also written approximately 100 case studies, including seven that received the Best Case of the Year award. He is a regular writer for various magazines. Furthermore, his work has been featured in such publications as *The New York Times, The Wall Street Journal, The Los Angeles Times, Fortune, Business Week, The Economist, The Financial Times* and *The Harvard Business Review.* His books and articles have been translated into more than thirty languages. He writes regular blogs (mini-articles) for the *Harvard Business Review* and *INSEAD Knowledge.* He is a member of seventeen editorial boards and is a Fellow of the Academy of Management. He is also a founding member of the International Society for the Psychoanalytic Study of Organizations (ISPSO), which has honored him as a lifetime distinguished member. Kets de Vries is also the first non-US recipient of International Leadership Association Lifetime Achievement Award for his contributions to leadership research and development (being considered one of the world's founding professionals in the development of leadership as a field and discipline). In addition, he received a Lifetime Achievement Award from Germany for his advancement of executive educa-tion. The American Psychological Association has honored him with the "Harry and Miriam Levinson Award" for his contributions to Organizational Consultation. Furthermore, he is the recipient of the "Freud Memorial Award" for his work to further the interface between management and psychoanalysis. In addition, he has also received the "Vision of Excellence Award" from the Harvard Institute of Coaching. Kets de Vries is the first beneficiary of INSEAD's Dominique Héau Award for "Inspiring Educational Excellence." He is also the recipient of two honorary doctorates. The Dutch government has made him an Officer in the Order of Oranje Nassau.

Kets de Vries works as a consultant on organizational design/transformation and strategic human resource management for companies worldwide. As an educator and consultant, he has worked in more than forty countries. In his role as a consultant, he is also the founder-chairman of the Kets de Vries Institute (KDVI), a boutique strategic leadership development consulting firm.

Kets de Vries was the first fly fisherman in Outer Mongolia (at the time, becoming the world record holder of the Siberian hucho taimen). He is a member of New York's Explorers Club. In his spare time, he can be found in the rainforests or savannas of Central and Southern Africa, the Siberian taiga, the Ussuri Krai, Kamchatka, the Pamir and Altai Mountains, Arnhemland, or within the Arctic Circle. Websites: www.ketsdevries.com and www.kdvi.com

# 1

# The Rot at the Top

*Be not afraid of growing slowly, be afraid only of standing still.*
—Chinese Proverb

*If you think you are too small to be effective, you have never been in bed with a mosquito.*
—Betty Reese

My interest in the lives of executives goes back a long way. CEOs in particular, have always fascinated me. You might ask, why? Why do I study CEOs? Why don't I focus on other people? Is it that I'm attracted to power? Do I get vicarious satisfaction from dealing with powerful people? I've no hesitation in stating that power isn't the reason. Power has never been important in either my personal or professional life. I believe my curiosity about people in leadership positions has other sources.

Of course, figuring out why we do what we do is always a challenge. We easily confuse *Dichtung und Wahrheit* (poetry and truth)—the title the writer and statesman Wolfgang von Goethe gave to his memoirs. As the clock of time ticks merrily along, we're likely to mix up narrative truth with historical truth. Memory can never be wholly reliable and self-reports can be particularly misleading because there is always the risk that our defenses will go into overdrive. So, when we take a deep dive and try to understand our motives, we might not always like what's revealed. We might prefer to push the things we don't like to see out of conscious awareness. Whenever I wear my psychoanalytic hat listening to my clients, I am very aware that specific events can become confusing viewed through the telescope of time.

I have a very early memory of poring over newspapers with my grandfather, looking at pictures of famous people, including political leaders. While we looked, my grandfather made it quite clear to me that the rot starts at the top—as the saying goes, "fish start to rot from the head down." Even though I was so young, he thought it was important for me to understand that if attention isn't paid to what's going on at the top, trouble was likely to follow. My grandfather also told me that knowing that something is rotten at the top is one thing but doing something about it is something else. It can be very hard to stop the rot, especially as most human beings are wary of change. They might want other people to change but changing themselves is a very different proposition. Even if they have the will to change, they may not have the skill to do so. With hindsight, I realize that if he had had the chance, my grandfather would have liked to be a lawyer or politician. Perhaps he thought that having a public or professional role would have given him the credibility to put things right in a world where he believed things were very wrong.

This was a short time after World War II ended and of course I was only a child, so although I took in what he was saying it didn't make much sense to me. Later on, when I had become an aficionado of detective stories, Sherlock Holmes' famous statement, "You see, but you do not observe," rang a very loud bell.[1] Detecting the strange dynamics that occur at the top of organizations—and how they affect the lives of others—has formed a significant part of my work.

Generally speaking, we aren't very good observers. Nevertheless, what we need to know is often staring us in the face. As Goethe put it, "the hardest thing to see is what's right in front of your eyes." His words remind me of a story I heard about Professor Louis Agassiz, the founder of Harvard's Museum of Comparative Zoology. Agassiz was well-known for his observational skills and he liked to transfer these skills to others. He gave one particular student an assignment to study a fish preserved in alcohol. After ten minutes, the student thought he had seen all there was to see but when he looked for Agassiz to tell him his findings, the professor was nowhere to be found. The student had no choice but to spend more time studying the fish. When Agassiz finally returned, and after the student reported what he had seen, the professor's response was that he hadn't looked anywhere near carefully enough and had missed "one of the most conspicuous features of the animal. Look again; look again!" In the words of the student, "he left me to my misery. And so, for three long days, he placed that fish before my eyes, forbidding me to look at anything else, or to use any artificial aid. 'Look, look, look,' was his repeated

---

[1] Arthur Conan Doyle, *A Scandal in Bohemia: The Adventures of Sherlock Holmes*. Amazon Media.

injunction." Frustrating though it had been, the student, after many hours studying the fish, learned how to look. He said later: "What I gained by this outside experience has been of greater value than years of later investigation."[2]

Like my grandfather, my father also took pride of place in my inner world. He was CEO of a mid-sized company and I used to be fascinated by the way people responded to his ideas. If an idea resonated with him, he was masterly at ordering people about. And to me, a young child, his business exploits seemed magical, not least because of his many travels. He would come and go from the kinds of faraway places that I could only dream of. My brother and I were kept informed about where he was from colorful postcards, always with the terse message "Greetings from Papa." These messages were even more charismatic because we didn't live with him. My parents were divorced and in my fantasy world my father was larger than life. This, and his position as a captain of industry, no doubt contributed to my interest in what happens at the top of organizations.

When I was little, the contrast between my grandfather, a lowly craftsman who was often victimized by decisions made by people at the top, and my father, who was a real mover and shaker, must have been baffling. How could I reconcile their respective positions in the world of work? Why was one successful, and the other a failure—not from a personal but from a work perspective? Now I am at a late stage in my life, I wonder how far my life's work has been based on the fantasy that if I could modify the behavior of the people at the top—making them change for the better—it would have a trickle-down effect on their organizations (at least for people at lower levels). Who knows, it might even help to make their organizations better places to work. Throughout my life, this desire, based on my early life experiences, has guided many of my activities in different ways.

In my various contributions to the management literature, I have pointed out the relationship between leaders' personalities, their decision-making practices, and the way their actions affect organizations and societies.[3] I have been privy to many situations where the leaders of both public and private organizations have had a devastating effect on their surroundings. Because I was born during World War II, I was highly attuned to dysfunctional leadership practices taking place on a grand scale. I knew from my mother that many members of my family had been killed by the Nazis. Most people now accept that political leaders like Hitler, Stalin, and Mao murdered tens of

---

[2] http://people.morrisville.edu/~snyderw/courses/Natr252/agassiz.html.

[3] Manfred F. R. Kets de Vries and Danny Miller (1984). *The Neurotic Organization*. San Francisco: Jossey-Bass; Manfred F. R. Kets de Vries and Danny Miller (1988) *Unstable at the Top*. New York: Signet.

millions of people. But who doesn't find Stalin's observation that "a single death is a tragedy; a million deaths is a statistic" an indication of a very sick mind? Yet it is very disturbing—if the present political landscape is a signifier—that so many seem to have forgotten what has happened in the past, increasing the likelihood of repeating the same mistakes. In my experience, only by mourning the past do we have a chance to start genuinely new beginnings.

Perhaps it was unusual for a child to be shielded so little from knowing what was happening in those early postwar years. Certainly, I remember being totally captivated by radio reports of the Nuremberg trials, when the senior German war criminals were brought to justice. At the time, their crimes against humanity were far too horrifying to comprehend. But as I grew older, and I became more aware of the gruesomeness of it all, I was deeply troubled by the realization that these despotic leaders were not exceptions. They didn't commit those atrocities on their own. They had many willing henchmen. It is a sad truth that our inner wolf doesn't need much encouragement to be set free and start devouring everybody who stands in its way.[4] Later in life, I saw similar dynamics taking place in the world of organizations, albeit on a much smaller scale.

My awareness of the devastation that leaders can bring about compelled me to ask what motivates these people? Why do they behave the way they do? What happens to their values? And, most importantly, is there anything that we can do to preempt or tackle it?

These are not just historical questions. In present-day society we once again see too many second-rate hucksters in the limelight, manipulating the masses to foster their own narrow self-interests—the coronavirus pandemic not being an exception. Many contemporary world leaders behave like the Lorelei—the enchanting, mythical siren whose song lured seamen to their death. Gifted in the art of make-belief, they relate fantasies to an unwitting public, while their reality is steeped in mendacity. They exploit humankind's wish to believe in magic, with disastrous consequences. As the philosopher Bertrand Russell noted, "The whole problem with the world is that fools and fanatics are always so certain of themselves, and wiser people full of doubts."

---

[4] Manfred F. R. Kets de Vries (2005). *Lessons on Leadership by Terror: Finding Shaka Zulu in the Attic.* Cheltenham: Edward Elgar.

# 2

# A Leadership Laboratory

*Be yourself; everything else is already taken.*
—Oscar Wilde

*The true laboratory is the mind, where behind illusions we uncover the laws of truth.*
—Jagadish Chandra Bose

These disturbing childhood memories have been a major catalyst for my desire to work with C-suite executives and my interest in leadership education. How can leaders be prevented from going astray? How can they be made thoughtful? These questions motivated me to create a somewhat unusual leadership seminar at INSEAD, the world's premier global business school. Building on the success of that seminar, I initiated a master's degree program on change management at the school. It also led to my designing many leadership team coaching programs for executives all over the world.

## Character Building

I wanted to find ways to create more reflective leaders who would retain their sense of humanity whatever challenges might come their way. I wanted to develop the kinds of leaders who would recognize the power of self-observation and critical thinking—individuals who would have the ability to evaluate themselves, face their strengths and weaknesses, and critique their own experiences in order to build new understandings. I was also looking for individuals

© The Author(s), under exclusive license to Springer Nature Switzerland AG 2021
M. F. R. Kets de Vries, *The CEO Whisperer*, The Palgrave Kets de Vries Library,
https://doi.org/10.1007/978-3-030-62601-3_2

who were prepared to take other people's perspectives, who were skilled at deciphering meaning and had the ability to listen and observe. More than anything, I wanted to create leaders who were interested in creating best places to work for their people. Someone once facetiously suggested that I seemed to be looking for leaders who have the wisdom of a Socrates, the drive of an Alexander the Great, the political skills of a Machiavelli, and the patience of Job. But that was way off the mark. I prefer to keep my feet on the ground. I like to be pragmatic. And I believe that it was a far from idealistic decision to take up this educational challenge. I thought that what I was setting out to do was achievable.

In leader development it is important to engage in character building. Much of our understanding of being human hinges on what we call "character," the particular combination of qualities that makes someone who he or she is—the behavior patterns that make each of us distinct from others.[1]

Lumpers tend to use the terms character and personality interchangeably, but splitters take a more nuanced view of both, suggesting that personality refers to the outer appearance and behavior, deriving as it does from the Latin *persona*, which means mask. They maintain that personality is easier to read: we might judge people as funny, introverted, conscientious, energetic, optimistic, confident, overly serious, lazy, negative, or shy. Character, on the other hand, refers the hidden traits of an individual that reveal themselves only in unexpected or acute circumstances, what someone is like inside. Character cannot be easily judged, because it is made up from someone's moral qualities and traits, like honest or dishonest, trustworthy or shady, kind or unkind, generous or mean. In everyday use, character is more likely than personality to indicate evaluation, for example, when someone is said to have a "good" of "bad" character. But I am a lumper, as I've said before, and I find the distinction between personality and character artificial. Whichever term is used out of expedience, for me it means the same.

I see character as something indelible or deeply etched in our being. Character is the most precious thing we have; it determines our true north and sets limits that we will not cross. The word derives from the Greek verb *charassein*, meaning to mark with a cut or furrow. Our character helps us to live life in a specific way, defining how we treat or behave consistently toward others and ourselves. Of course, character is shaped by the environment around us. It is molded by antecedents—by existing economic structures, political life, community and family relationships.

---

[1] Manfred F. R. Kets de Vries & Sidney Perzow (1991). *Handbook of Character Studies: Psychoanalytic Explorations*. Madison, Conn. International Universities Press.

From my observations in the seminars and programs I run, leader development can make a modest contribution to character building. Clearly, at this critical junction in the history of humankind, given the many devastating forces plaguing our Planet, leaders that are proficient in magical thinking aren't going to solve our problems. We need a very different kind of leadership—leaders who can resist the calls of regression; whose outlook is firmly based in reality. What's needed are quality driven leaders. And to list some of these qualities, I'm using a simple acronym. I suggest that these leaders should subscribe to what may be called a seven C leadership model. Or to be more specific, I am referring to leaders who possess the qualities of **C**omplexity, **C**onfidence, **C**ompassion, **C**are, **C**ourage, **C**ritical thinking, and **C**ommunication.

As a starter, given the state of the world, I suggest that we should be looking for leaders who have the capacity to deal with *complexity*; who possess a long-term, systemic outlook in dealing with problems. Such leaders will be true merchants of hope, given their visionary but reality-based outlook to things. Also, these leaders should have a solid sense of self-*confidence*. Possessing a sense of inner security will contribute to better decision-making. Thus, insecure, immature leaders, please don't apply. Furthermore, having *compassion* enables leaders to approach the people they lead with humility, respect, appreciation and empathy. I am also referring to leaders with a reflective capability, who possess emotional intelligence. In addition, such leaders need to *care* passionately about whatever they are doing. In more than one way, here passion and inspiration will go hand in hand. These leaders also need to have the *courage* of their convictions. They need the personal integrity, the moral values, and the persistence to make tough decisions. Also, such leaders will be skilled in *critical* thinking. They have a deep understanding of what they are doing—and they know how to tap other people's brain. Finally, they need to possess good *communication* skills—the ability to present their ideas concisely, coherently and (particularly in crisis situations) repeatedly.

I could have chosen to work with selected individuals, small groups, executive teams, or embark on major organizational transformation programs to turn these educational ideas into reality. Instead I decided to do all of these. I wanted to cast a very wide net and reach as many executives as possible. The question was how? It soon dawned on me that creating a small, intense workshop for C-suite executives who had the power to push change down through their organizations would be a feasible way to start.

As many have found out the hard way, changing yourself is a journey full of resistance. It is entirely human not to want to be pushed out of your comfort zone. When you are faced with change, the question that always springs to mind first is how it will personally affect you. Given this, I decided on a modular design for the leadership program. A stepped structure might help develop more thoughtful, reflective leaders and also give me the opportunity to test what kind of design was going to be most effective. My intention was that the people who participated in the program would learn something about themselves by working with each other (participating in a co-creative process). They, they would have the opportunity, between modules, to practice what they had learned in the workplace and at home.

I had no illusions about the risk involved in this structure. I knew that after the participants went back to their homes and offices, many were likely to revert to their old habits. Established routines, as we all know, are very hard to break. We are pretty malleable when we are young, but in later life change is much more difficult. Although I found myself up against resistance, I knew that there was going to be a further module, and then another one. I have learned from experience that follow-ups are essential. Most New Year's resolutions end up as dismal failures—too many good intentions, too little action—but follow-up makes defeat less likely. As time passed (and with some nudging from me and the other participants), I hoped to see most of them making baby steps toward constructive change. And "as you are what you repeatedly do," the acid test for me was how the participants behaved after they had completed the program.

Although I hardly expected it when I first designed this program, the experiment was an eye-opener. Gradually, the program transformed into a highly effective learning laboratory in which executives, encouraged to take part in a unique "life" case study methodology, were able to deal not only with superficial problems, but could also address deeper, underlying concerns.

## "Life" Case Studies

Although I have written more than a hundred case studies, in my work with executives I rapidly realized that there is a great difference between "life" case studies related in class and more cerebral, written cases. Written cases will always be a pale reflection of what's really going on in an organization. Although I am a multiple graduate of the Harvard Business School—and thus well indoctrinated in the case study method—I have always felt that it requires a high degree of narcissism to claim that you can put down on paper, in a very short space of time, the essence of what goes on in an organization, let alone come to solid conclusions about what should be done about it in subsequent class discussions. I strongly believe that to capture the essence of why people do what they do you need to be some kind of anthropologist and need to spend a lengthy period of time observing the interactions between the various players in the organization.

Written case studies can be useful pedagogical tools, but in terms of developing a different approach to personal and organizational transformation, I was fortunate in having live case studies sitting right there in the classroom. Their active participation in what was happening in their organizational and personal life greatly expanded everyone's perspective and made the interpersonal, group, and organizational dynamics so much richer. Given the narcissistic disposition of many of them, it came as no great surprise that they preferred talking about themselves to having more cerebral, abstract discussions. The "life" case study approach creates a very different learning experience, with exceptional immediacy: you can observe how the "case studies" unburden themselves of deeply troubling issues; how they struggle to tell their specific narratives; how they try to work out what to say and what not to say. This deeply experiential process has a very powerful impact, compared to the traditional, didactic case learning approach.

One of the attractions of the case study method (whether a written or a "life" case) is that experiential learning has far more impact on understanding and change than lecture-based teaching. People like to be exposed to material that resonates with them and to feel involved.

Getting participants in this program to present their life situations made me realize how effective the simple activity of storytelling can be. I saw clearly how these stories affected listeners, and that listening to these stories could have a life-changing impact. It could even dent their "character armor." Every time a story was presented, the listeners realized that they were not the only ones with problems, that they were not alone in their confusion—that there is no human action that isn't recognized by other people. Understanding their personal history, they also became aware of why they were doing what they were doing—but that their behavior was no longer effective at this stage of their life. Also, they realized that, whatever our cultural history, we are all part of the human race, with similar behavior patterns. A school like INSEAD has no national identity, which made it a unique learning laboratory. Within its culture of communality, sharing stories became a great way to unite participants and create an intense learning community. What they learned from these stories became a great way to help each other to undertake baby steps toward change. After all, there is an altruistic motive deep inside all of us.

# What's Missing?

Interestingly, many of the executives who enrolled in these developmental programs felt that something was not right in their life. Often, this was the catalyst for enrolling in my programs in the first place. While they seemed to be quite content on the surface, having everything that really mattered—health, family, friends, and a good job—they had an uncanny feeling that there was something missing from their life. It seemed they were experiencing a kind of existential vacuum. In moments of contemplation, they would wonder whether their life could be made different, but they didn't know how. There was a deep, intense longing for a nameless something more.

I came to realize that this sense of alienation and despair had to come from their recognition of their fundamental aloneness in what seems to be, at times, a very indifferent universe. Many of the people I dealt with experienced a lack of meaning and purpose in their life. Although this void might have been felt for some time, they had reached a point in their life when they were experiencing a greater sense of urgency. They no longer wanted to let it be. They wanted greater control over their life. At the same time, they had no idea of how to change the situation they found themselves in. Their reason for enrolling on the program was to figure out what they thought was missing.

## The Energy Barometer

While these participants were wondering what to do with their life in the future—and feeling somewhat mentally paralyzed—I made it clear to them that they didn't have to be passive spectators in the theater of life. They had choices. They could try to live a life more aligned with what made them really feel alive; they could focus on the activities that energized them. They could make an effort to create greater congruence between their inner and outer theater. But it was important to become more aware of the things that would really be worth their energy and the things that they should put aside because they were draining them of energy. They should try to live according to what I refer to as a self-created "energy barometer." They should start a diary, listing the energizing and draining situations they found themselves in. A tangible record could help them figure out what kinds of activities made them truly feel alive.

If we could live our lives in alignment with our authentic self, we might well have more energy and feel much better. However, this would imply giving ourselves permission to dive deep into our inner world and be willing to rely on our own wisdom and power. We need to recover the untapped potential deep within us. We need to give ourselves the space to listen to our own voice and identify the things that are really important to us. Too often I have observed that we tend to listen to the noises of the external world, only to get lost in the crowd. We need to be truer to ourselves. To quote Confucius, "He who conquers himself will be the mightiest warrior."

## Team Building: Vision without Action Is a Hallucination

The realization that storytelling helped create an intense learning community gave me the courage not only to work with executives who came from different organizations but also to experiment working with executive teams. I knew from my consulting experience that many of the teams I had dealt with were dysfunctional and operated at cross-purposes. I've often found myself describing top executive teams as "unnatural acts." So, I decided that as well as helping individual executives to be more effective, I would try to do the same for teams.

Of course, one way of simplifying team processes is to hire people who look and act alike and reject people who appear to be different. Teams made up of people who think alike create a more predictable environment and speed up decision-making. The general rule is that if you want quick decisions, you'd do better to hire clones. However, I have learned from experience that if you want to make more creative decisions—if you want to unblock blocked situations—you do much better if you aim for diversity in gender, culture, age, educational background, industry experience, and so on. Of course, managing very different and diverse people brings many challenges, as the possibilities for misunderstanding increase dramatically. Differences can trigger paranoia and suspicion, which cause havoc in any organization, and help explain why many organizations take the easy way out and hire for similarity. If you want to hire for diversity—as I have learned through much experimentation—the team coaching intervention technique, using the "life" case study methodology, can be highly effective.[2]

Whatever the extent of diversity, it will always be an organizational challenge to get everyone, from top to bottom, on board to make their organizations work and implement decisions. But I have seen over and over

---

[2] Manfred F. R. Kets de Vries (2014). Vision without action is a hallucination: Group coaching and strategy implementation, *Organizational Dynamics*, 44 (1), 1–8.

again that, without the presence of a well-functioning team, it is highly likely that individual executives will do things their own way, often resulting in uncoordinated, even conflicting, decisions and actions. If executives behave like ships that pass in the night, they may act in ways that are not in the best interest of the organization or themselves and the implementation of strategy can be expected to suffer. I found out that the group coaching technique, incorporating the life case study approach, is an excellent methodology to get executives singing from the same hymn sheet, to break down silo-like behavior, and to accelerate execution. Group interventions create greater organizational alignment, which helps to get things done. They also make lateral and virtual communication more effective, which is vitally important when dealing with complex matrix structures and virtual teams—virtual learning after the coronavirus pandemic having become more important than ever before. Furthermore, group interventions can be a buffer against paranoid thinking and scapegoating, both far too prevalent in too many organizations. Fear never brings out the best in people and I always tell the people I work with that they would be wise to monitor carefully the fear-safety axis in their organizations. Feeling that you work in a safe environment will enhance productivity and creativity; working in a climate of fear will do the opposite. Gratifyingly, I have found that these interventions create a true learning environment, and that through them the term "knowledge management" becomes a reality, not just a meaningless slogan. After all, if your colleagues remain strangers, why share what you know with them? It is very hard to remain a stranger using the life case study methodology. In the world of storytelling, there are no strangers.

# 3

# The Clinical Paradigm

*All ideologies are idiotic, whether religious or political, for it is conceptual thinking, the conceptual word, which has so unfortunately divided man.*
—Jiddu Krishnamurti

*Above all we have to go beyond words and images and concepts. No imaginative vision or conceptual framework is adequate to the great reality.*
—Bede Griffings

I have found many conceptual models helpful guides my interventions. When I work with executives, however, I have always tried to be non-ideological. I've seen too often how ideology can kill creativity and I've learned from experience that creative work always happens at the boundary of different fields. So, when helping people change, I will do anything that works. I will apply any theoretical framework that can be helpful in the situation where I find myself.

In my approach to complexity, I have drawn on ideas from evolutionary theory, developmental psychology, neuroscience, family systems theory, cognitive psychology, motivational interviewing, paradoxical intervention, existential psychology, appreciative inquiry, and positive psychology. This has informed a psychodynamic-systemic orientation to understanding puzzling situations that I call the clinical paradigm. This particular way of looking at things has proved a highly effective change methodology.[1]

---

[1] Manfred F. R. Kets de Vries (2011). *The Hedgehog Effect: The Secrets of Building High Performance Teams*, West Sussex, UK: John Wiley & Sons; Manfred F. R. Kets de Vries (2018). *Down the Rabbit Hole of Leadership: Leadership Pathology in Everyday Life*. London: Palgrave Macmillan.

# Taking a Clinical Perspective

So, what is the clinical paradigm all about? First, it presupposes that there is a *rationale behind every human act.* I argue that there is always a logical explanation why people do what they do, even if, at first glance, what they do seems highly irrational. All behavior, how strange it may seem at first, will have some kind of rationale. But because the explanation may be elusive—inextricably interwoven with our unconscious needs and desires—we have to do some detective work to tease out the clues that underly perplexing behavior.

The second premise is that a great deal of *mental life—feelings, fears, and motives—lies outside our conscious awareness* but still affects our conscious reality—and even our physical well-being. However, we aren't always aware of *what* we are doing, much less *why* we are doing it. Though hidden from rational thought, the human unconscious affects (and in some cases even dictates) conscious reality. Like it or not, even the most rational among us have blind spots, and even the most honorable have a shadow side—a side that they don't know and may not even want to know. Therefore, to maintain our psychic equilibrium, we resort to a variety of defensive mechanisms, from very primitive ones like splitting, projection or denial, to more sophisticated ones, like intellectualization.[2]

The third premise is that we are influenced by our basic human needs. These needs determine our character, creating the tightly interlocked triangle of our mental life, the three points being cognition, emotions, and behavior. To influence behavior, both cognition and emotions have to be taken into consideration. But emotions, in particular, determine many of our actions and emotional intelligence plays a vital role in the leadership equation. We are defined by the way we *regulate and express our emotions.* Emotions give our experiences positive and negative connotations, creating preference in the choices we make and the way we deal with the world. Emotions also form the basis for the internalization of mental representations of how we experience the world—and the experiences we have of others—memories that guide our relationships throughout our lives. Of course, the way we perceive, and express emotions may change as the years go by, influenced by life experiences.

The fourth premise is that human development is an inter- and intrapersonal process. We are all *products of our past experiences,* and those experiences, including the developmental experiences provided by our early caregivers, continue to influence us throughout life. The past is part of our present

---

[2] George Vaillant (1992). *Ego Mechanisms of Defense: A Guide for Clinicians and Researchers.* Washington, DC: American Psychiatric Press.

consciousness—it is the lens through which we view and experience the present. Like it or not, the past influences our present and future.

Over the years, I have discovered that using the clinical paradigm in leader development can be a highly effective way to explore the hidden rationales for emotions, thinking, and behaviour, often related to my clients' search for meaning, belonging, competence, control, or other major existential concerns. Taking the premises of the clinical paradigm into consideration has helped me understand the out-of-awareness behavior patterns that are part and parcel of the human condition.

## The-Snake-Under-the-Carpet Syndrome

I always try to make clear to my clients that unless they deal with the underlying issues of their problems, there is a high probability that those problems will re-emerge, that nothing will change, that things will go back to the way they were before. I explain this using the metaphor of the snake under the carpet. Imagine you walk into your house and there's a bump under the carpet. You try to straighten out the carpet to get rid of the bump. And you do. But a bit later, the bump comes back, because there is a snake under the carpet. You won't get the carpet really straightened out until you get rid of the snake. When you deal with a problem, it's important to remember that what you see is not necessarily what you get. Submerged issues need to be dealt with before you can arrive at real solutions. Don't try to hide from reality; don't just straighten out the bump under the carpet. Symptom suppression is not the prescription.

The snake-under-the-carpet syndrome explains why relationships can become so miserable. It helps us understand why organizational life is often so difficult to comprehend. It explains why working relationships, in particular executive teams, are frequently so dysfunctional. Most of the answers to these conundrums lie in our human nature, our ability to trust one another just so far, and perhaps not far enough, and our inability to see past our own needs to understand that richer benefits, both psychological and material, may be easier to obtain through the collective efforts of a group rather than as individuals.

The snake-under-the-carpet syndrome also explains why many organizational activities fail to live up to their promises. Putting on my economist's hat, the answer lies in the obstinate belief that human beings are supposedly rational entities. But we should know better. Every individual can have a different rationale. That's why using the clinical paradigm can be so helpful. Too many traditional organizational designers fail to take into account the subtle, out-of-awareness behavior patterns that are part and parcel of the human condition. Meanwhile, the personality quirks and emotional lives of the people who work in organizations continue to divert them from their specified tasks. Many executives fail to appreciate the complexity of interpersonal relationships, teamwork, and organizational culture and that they are acting out unconscious scenarios.

Organizational leaders need to accept that many subtle psychological forces lie below the surface of human rationality and can sabotage the way they and others function. But irrational as these behavioral patterns might be, there is always a rationale to them, if we know how to disentangle the threads. Individuals run numerous real risks when working in organizations, arising from their fear, anxiety, and uncertainty about the exercise of influence and power in the workplace. If these concerns are not addressed, the anxiety generated by these risks becomes too great and cannot be contained by simple leadership actions or facilitating structures. Instead, individuals will mobilize social defenses to protect themselves.[3] These defenses, expressed through rituals, processes, or basic hidden assumptions, displace, mitigate, or even neutralize emerging anxiety but also prevent real work from being done. The result is preoccupation with dysfunctional processes and inhibiting structures that reinforce vicious circles, preserving the status quo.

Whatever the situation leaders of organizations find themselves in, they need to realize, when trying to motivate their people, that there is always more going on than meets the eye. Organizations are forums in which sensitive interpersonal issues are dealt with discretely (and often indiscreetly). Thus, if people are to function non-defensively in the face of performance pressures in the workplace, they need the kinds of leadership and supporting conditions that convert the prevalent anxiety into productive work. Unfortunately, too many executives are largely unaware of concepts from psychodynamic psychology and systems theory. Instead, the rational-structural point of view usually dominates. Too many executives fail to acknowledge the unconscious dynamics that affect human behavior. Too many executives treat their organizations as rational, rule-governed systems, perpetuating the illusion of the economic man as an optimizing machine of pleasures and pains, while ignoring the multifarious peculiarities that come with being human.

We need to get used to the idea that there is no such thing as a Holy Grail of rational management. The rational-structural view of organizations has not

---

[3] Alistair Bain (1998). Social Defenses Against Organizational Learning, *Human Relations*, 51 (3), 413–429.

delivered the promised goods. It has only created much economic chaos and lots of grief. Thus, organizational designers would do well to become familiar with the language of the clinical paradigm—although I accept that doing so can be uncomfortable. It can be disturbing for people from a traditional background in management or economics. But creating and maintaining an effective work environment necessitates a dedicated focus on both the structural and the human aspects of organizational life—a daunting challenge, to say the least. We have to hang on to the knowledge that most of what happens in our mind is unconscious and that communicating with that mysterious part of who we are will be a real challenge. Carl Jung put it very simply: "Until you make the unconscious conscious, it will direct your life and you will call it fate."

# 4

# An Existential Dive

*Man is nothing else but what he makes of himself. Such is the first principle of existentialism.*
—Jean-Paul Sartre

*The single biggest problem in communication is the illusion that it has taken place.*
—George Bernard Shaw

One of the participants in my leadership workshop (I'll call him Peter) was experiencing some form of existential anxiety and questioning the meaning of his existence. Too many changes were happening simultaneously and contributing to his low state of mind. The first change was the death of his father, with whom he had many unresolved issues. Peter realized that his father's death made closure difficult, complicating the mourning process. He was also retiring as CEO and taking on the position of Chairman of the Board. It was beginning to dawn on him that the role of Chairman was very different from running the day-to-day operations of the company. All of a sudden, he had much more time on his hands and he really didn't know how to deal with it. One unhappy result of this was realizing how far apart he and his wife had grown. They seemed to be living in parallel universes.

Having more time available may seem like a luxury, but for some, idle time can become the devil's playground. It may force them to reflect on things that before were more easily pushed out of conscious awareness. Given his present situation, it was difficult for Peter to transcend his previous state of constant

© The Author(s), under exclusive license to Springer Nature Switzerland AG 2021
M. F. R. Kets de Vries, *The CEO Whisperer*, The Palgrave Kets de Vries Library,
https://doi.org/10.1007/978-3-030-62601-3_4

busyness—no longer being able to resort to the "manic defense."[1] This describes a pattern of behavior whereby we try to distract our conscious mind from uncomfortable thoughts or feelings with a flurry of activities or try to avoid them by resorting to opposite thoughts or feelings. Being locked into our own mind—unable to find any mindless escapes—can be extremely uncomfortable. For many of my clients, many inner demons come to the surface when they no longer can rely on this manic defense.

## The Nightmare

In Peter's case, his existential anxiety had been triggered by two painful transitions, but his present state of anguish had flared up following a nightmare about one of his best friends, a very successful businessman. When I asked what this friend meant to him, Peter said that he had always looked up to him as a role model, someone he wanted to emulate. In his nightmare, a large, admiring crowd was standing on the front lawn of his friend's house waiting for him to show up. But instead of making a grandiose appearance, his friend stayed out of sight. Eventually, he slipped out of the back entrance to the house, to avoid being seen by the crowd. After his escape, he walked up to Peter, looking unwell. When Peter asked what was going on, his friend told him that he wondered whether all the effort he had made to be successful had been worth it. He was exhausted by maintaining a façade of success. Yes, he knew he had a several imposing houses and flashy cars; he even had a yacht. But the houses were empty. There was nobody there. The cars were just sitting idle in the garage. And he very rarely used the yacht. Why was he hanging on to them? What was the point of having them? The he asked Peter if he could borrow some money and use his phone. Peter went to help him, but then couldn't find his wallet or his phone. This made him feel very panicky and he woke up.

At first, Peter brushed the nightmare aside, saying to me that all dreams just random noise in the neurological system. But he changed his mind when I told him that in dreams, we often see the things we don't want to see in daily life. Dreams can be indicators of major personal concerns. Nightmares in particular should be seen as very strong warning signs—like someone is talking to you, but you don't want to hear what's being said. And a dream that isn't interpreted is like a letter that isn't opened. I explained that, like it or not,

---

[1] Melanie Klein (1935). A contribution to the psychogenesis of manic-depressive states. *International Journal of Psycho-Analysis*, 16, 145–74.

he was the director, producer, and scriptwriter of his dreams. He created all the images himself. He owned them and was best placed to recognize the associations that would help him to figure out what was really going on— there is usually residue from the preceding day that triggers a dream. Dreams can have multiple meanings and can be confusing because they use highly symbolic language. For children in particular, dreams are like safe rehearsals for difficult situations they might have to face in the future. Dreams tend to slip away from us quickly because when they become too vivid, we get confused between what's reality and what's fantasy. But this is also the reason why dreams can be such great help in the creative process. Many important creations have been instigated by dreams. And we could think of nightmares as dreams that have failed in their role as the guardians of sleep. Instead of neutralizing the anxiety associated with their content, as dreams are meant to do, they compound it.

I encouraged Peter to think about the associations he could make with his nightmare. One of the first was futility. Here was his highly admired friend who told him that all his efforts to be successful had turned out to be pointless. All his life, he had been trying to get people's admiration but for what? Wasn't this the same question Peter was asking himself? Did his friend represent another version of himself? The nightmare made Peter question why he had always tried to emulate his friend. Those thoughts led him to question what he had really accomplished in life. In his dream the things that were precious to him (money and his phone), the latter symbolizing all his important contacts, seemed to be lost. Were these the only things that should be important? Then Peter wondered why the house in his dream had been empty. Why was there nobody there? Was there anybody who really cared about him? Where was his wife? What did an admiring crowd on the lawn matter? Those people were merely strangers.

Existential anxiety is related to difficulties in adapting to change—when we find ourselves in situations that take us out of our comfort zone. When we are faced with significant life transitions, we can lose the security and safety of a familiar context and structure. If that's the case, we can start to question the whole point of living. Why bother to carry on doing what we're doing, if we have to accept the fact that we are going to die? Why bother to make all this effort? It is pointless to go through all these motions, if it's only going to end in death. And as is to be expected, these thoughts will come more top of mind as we age.[2]

---

[2] Irvin Yalom (2011). *Staring at The Sun: Being at Peace with Your Own Mortality.* New York: Piatkus.

## Death Anxiety

I knew that both the aging process and exposure to death (the recent death of his father) had contributed to Peter's experience of death anxiety—heightened existential anguish related to death. Like many of us in the same situation, he was becoming more aware that death is the shadow that follows us wherever we go. From a neurological point of view, we have to thank the development of our frontal lobes (the last part of the human brain to develop) for these experiences. This part of the brain has given us the ability to conceptualize the future—and a part of that future is the knowledge that death is inevitable. Given our biological architecture, death anxiety is a universal and seemingly exclusively human phenomenon. It is always lurking under the surface of our consciousness, making it hard to adapt to the reality of our own finiteness.

Death anxiety was making Peter feel anxious about everything, although he was unable to articulate exactly why he was feeling this way.[3] As we spent some time together reflecting on his mental state, I pointed out that self-awareness is a very precious gift but it can also be toxic. Increased self-awareness can be a fertile ground for anxiety. Self-awareness makes us human, but it also makes us aware that we will grow, blossom, and, inevitably, diminish and die. But I added that this kind of anxiety can also become a path toward greater self-insight and wisdom.

## A Sense of Disconnection

As if death anxiety wasn't enough, Peter also experienced strong feelings of disconnection. Associating with the lost phone in his nightmare, he questioned his relationships to everything and everyone. As things stood, he felt completely alone and lost, in spite of having a family and friends—and in spite of having a very successful career. These concerns about death and about belonging meant that he had become preoccupied with how to deal with life's big questions—how to create new meaning in his life. What should be his future focus? Where did he fit in the greater scheme of things? The question whether he had really fulfilled his full potential added to his anguish. He wondered whether he had made the right choices throughout his life. For most of us, the most important choices we make will be our choice of partner and choice of career. But we will also question how our life might have evolved if we had made different choices. Although Peter's unhappiness was far from

---

[3] Manfred F. R. Kets de Vries (2014). Death and the executive: Encounters with the "Stealth" motivator, *Organizational Dynamics*, 43 (4), 247–256.

ideal, I saw his current struggle as a very natural, human way of discovering what was really important to him.

I pointed out to Peter that while we have the luxury of freedom of choice, having to make choices can be very stressful. With freedom of choice comes the responsibility to make good use of it. There is always the nagging question of what choices to make? Having to decide between several choices can be paralyzing. I suggested that Peter should reflect on the choices that would provide him with most meaning. Some people have a hard time dealing with the guilt (and regret) of not living as fully as they believe (or know) they could have lived. These feelings can become really troublesome when they think they may have made the wrong choices. Fear of dying is one thing, but what about the fear of having lived a meaningless life?

## Finding Meaning

Peter's case illustrates the significance of meaning. When you grow older and realize that the way you are living your life is providing very little meaning, focus, or structure, the likelihood increases that you will look start to back at your life. However, if you become preoccupied with dissecting your past, the possibility of existential despair is increased. You may obsess about losses, mistakes, and bad choices. Unfortunately, you will never be sure whether the choices you have made have been the right ones. But you also realize that the alternative is no longer a realistic option. You may start to brood about what your other life could have been, in particularly relating to your choice of partner. The more you feel that you have "unlived" your life, the greater your death anxiety will be. For some people, the thought of death will mean all their activities are increasingly experienced as meaningless.

Existential despair is the theme of an early film, *Ikiru* ("to live"), by one of my favorite directors, the late Akira Kurosawa. His film dramatizes the affirmation of life through an exploration of death. Starting with an X-ray of a diseased stomach, it tells the story of Watanabe, a Tokyo bureaucrat, diagnosed with terminal cancer, who comes face-to-face with the emptiness of his existence. He will die soon but he has never really lived. Wallowing in his own misery, he tries to find escape in nightclub life, but these diversions don't bring him much pleasure. Eventually, inspired by a lively young woman who has a very positive outlook to life, Watanabe realizes that it is not too late to do something meaningful. He remembers a group of women looking for help to clean up and transform a boggy wasteland in their neighborhood into a play park for children. The group has been shuttled from one bureaucratic office to another with no result. Watanabe decides he will take on their cause and support their lobbying for the playground. He knows exactly how the city bureaucracy works and uses this knowledge to make the playground a reality. The sad truth of the film is that Watanabe only starts to reflect on life when faced with the imminence of his death. Wouldn't his life have been much better lived, if he had realized how brief his time on earth would be?

Existential anxiety can be very painful, as the stories of Peter and Watanabe show, but it can also stimulate us to find new meaning in our lives. In Peter's case, I tried to reframe his situation by pointing out that his concerns about having led a meaningless life could also be a sign that he was in a position to really appreciate life. Perhaps he should stop looking forward and back and make a greater effort to be in the present—forget the goal and enjoy the journey. Too much self-absorption could trap him in a highly neurotic spin of future-based thinking that could cause a great deal of anxiety about meaninglessness. Perhaps he should be less preoccupied with material things like houses, cars, and yachts and make a switch in perspective that could enable him to live more fully and passionately in the present. A different outlook might help conquer his anxiety. He should give up his maladaptive coping strategies, which were making it impossible for him to live an authentic life. Too many people go through life with their "eyes wide shut," never looking at the big picture—never considering the activities that would provide them with meaning. The most effective response Peter could make to his existential crisis was to have meaningful relationships and engage in meaningful pursuits. Human beings are meaning-making creatures. Whatever situation we find ourselves in, we will always try to create meaning. When we can't, we become prone to existential dread and anxiety. Peter's challenge would be to discover the kinds of activities that would provide him with meaning on a daily basis.

I suggested that it would be good practice for Peter to regularly remind himself of the things he should be grateful for. Were his feelings of gratitude related to his family, to his friends, or other people? Perhaps he could look for patterns among the things he appreciated and start to keep a balance sheet of the activities that made him feel truly alive. It would be good for his mental health to spend more time getting involved in these kinds of things. We all need to be able to identify the activities that energize us and give us pleasure and create a sense of flow—a feeling of being at our best.[4]

As time went on, Peter came to accept that existential anxiety is part of the human condition but that this didn't mean he had to live with constant stress,

---

[4] Mihaly Csikszentmihalyi (2004). *Flow: The Psychology of Optimal Experience* New York: HarperCollins.

worry, and fear. The challenge for each of us, when dealing with life's big questions, is to find our own ways of meaning making. It is our responsibility to find ways to make life livable. When we live a life that provides us with meaning, our existential anxiety is likely to abate. I told Peter that he should understand that it isn't the future that's so frightening; on the contrary, it is the inability to have some control over it that makes us afraid.

I pointed out to Peter that he was fortunate in having so many options—an observation he found reassuring. There are always things that will be out of our control but many of Peter's concerns were self-inflicted. Fortunately, our self-determination and free will gives us the freedom to make choices about the things that we can control. Peter shouldn't see himself as the victim of circumstances. He should make the effort to be the master of his own fate.

# 5

# The Self-Actualizing Equation

*The two most important days in your life are the day you are born and the day you find out why.*
—Mark Twain

*In any given moment we have two options: to step forward into growth or to step back into safety.*
—Abraham Maslow

Death anxiety has been referred to as a fear of nonexistence or nonbeing. Although we might be conscious of the fact of death, and even imagine we are prepared for it, we are always shocked when death threatens us, or when someone dear to us dies. Although at a rational level we know that death is part of the cycle of life, at an irrational level, we look at it very differently. The idea of disappearing into a void—of having to confront the disintegration and decay of our body—is not easily worked through psychologically. The anticipation of a state of nothingness, in which the self has ceased to exist, is unacceptable. Symbolically, death can be seen as the ultimate humiliation, the ultimate narcissistic injury. Consciously or unconsciously, we interpret our pending annihilation as a devastating blow to our sense of self. As the unconscious does not deal with the passage of time and doesn't calculate the amount of time we have left in our life, we act as though death will occur to everyone—except ourselves. It explains why we are always looking for solutions to cope with this unacceptable idea. And one way of dealing with death anxiety, is to find reassurance and comfort in a variety of immortality systems.

© The Author(s), under exclusive license to Springer Nature Switzerland AG 2021
M. F. R. Kets de Vries, *The CEO Whisperer*, The Palgrave Kets de Vries Library,
https://doi.org/10.1007/978-3-030-62601-3_5

# Transcending Death

The natural world, and our need to find our place in it, can be seen as a major immortality system. We tell ourselves that everything that lives comes from the body of the Earth, and everything that dies will go back into it. On Earth, all living organisms interact with their inorganic surroundings, being part of a self-regulating, complex system that perpetuates life on our planet. All living organisms and inorganic material are part of one single living planetary being called Gaia—a dynamic system that shapes our biosphere and maintains the Earth as a fit environment for life. Thus, our perceptions of nature and immortality are intimately connected. Setting out into mountains, valleys, and forests, and onto rivers and oceans, is a very basic human urge and a form of communion with life and death for many of us. Many people feel they have a special bond with nature and view death as a transition rather than the end. They may even experience "*unica mystica*," an "oceanic feeling" of out-of-body boundlessness in which they merge with the universe. No wonder that, for many, global warming represents a particularly terrifying eschatological possibility, and, as a signifier of total annihilation, raises massive denial reactions. Of course, the coronavirus pandemic has only added to our concerns about the ways we have been dealing with Mother Nature.

Apart from this *unica mystica*, there are other ways of coping with death anxiety. Identifying with a religious, political, or cultural immortality system has always been a very attractive way of assuring us of continuity. These belief systems represent our most ingenious solutions for dealing with death. Religion has always been our most resourceful ally in alleviating our fear of death and the annihilation of the self. All the major world religions hold out the promise of an afterlife, providing a consoling function and playing an integrative role in society. Moreover, with heaven as the ultimate destination, religions provide an obvious incentive for living a virtuous life, conforming to a set of high-minded values.

Modern science has added new ways for us—or part of us—to biologically transcend death, through organ donorship, sperm banks, and cloning. But taking an evolutionary perspective, our children will always be our major immortality project. The philosopher John Whitehead said, "Children are the living messages we send to a time we will not see." We project our own aspirations and achievements on our children, hoping they will perpetuate our beliefs and values. Children help us to see death as a transition that we can survive through others' memories. After all, isn't it true that the dead are never dead to us until we have forgotten them? We trust that our children will carry not only our genes but also our memory. We imagine that the passing of memories from generation to generation will amount to continuity. Thus, our symbolic immortality continues after our death as our spirit lives on through our children, grandchildren and family, emphasizing history, memories, stories, and our philosophy of life.

When we are creative—through art, literature, scientific discovery, or an act of kindness toward someone in need—we also create a kind of symbolic immortality. In this way, we not only deal with our death anxiety but also "escape" death by living on through our actions and accomplishments, which may be remembered for generations or possibly centuries. Creating some form of legacy becomes a major driving force to transcend death. Artists hope that their work will live on after their death. Creation gives them meaning in life and their work may benefit future generations. Scientists are motivated to build cumulative knowledge. They hope that someone else will carry their research work forward—another expression of creative immortality. Creativity as a way of combating death anxiety can also become an integral part of our search for meaning. In a similar way, actors and athletes can make history through extraordinary performances or by breaking longstanding records, a unique opportunity to "leave one's mark." All these symbolic immortality activities are means of transcending death and living on in the memory of others. From the perspective of the world of work, I have often seen how executives attempt to confront reminders of their mortality by creating a tangible legacy—an organization, buildings, awards, and so on. Creating a business that will be continued by family members is an obvious way of ensuring some form of immortality. This conscious or unconscious wish of immortality lies at the core of many family business dynasties, informed by the illusion that people are not really dead while their names are still spoken. Another way is to build large buildings or stadiums to be named after them, literally concrete representations of their enduring existence. Many corporate leaders are motivated by the semblance of immortality that this provides. You can even find a psychological parallel between making a mark on the landscape (for example, with a building) and the exercise of power. However, as well as giving a false sense of permanence, impressive buildings can also be signs of corporate pathology—a signal that the organization might be on its way toward decline.

# The Essentials

The term self-actualization has always sounded rather whimsical to me, but it's not a concept we should brush aside. To the best of my understanding, self-actualization has to do with the full realization of our creative, intellectual, or social potential. Most of us try to be the best that we can be. Trying to self-actualize can help us to create good memories for ourselves and others. I also believe that the ability to self-actualize can be an effective antidote to existential anxiety, including the fear of death.

According to Abraham Maslow (who popularized the concept), "What a man can be, he must be. This need we call self-actualization."[1] I would add other important ingredients, including self-discovery, self-reflection, self-realization, self-exploration, meaning, belonging, control, and competence. I have noticed that self-actualized people are less dependent on the opinion of others. They are more secure about themselves. From what I have observed, if you have these self-actualizing qualities, you are more likely to feel better in your skin.

## Maintaining our Equilibrium

As a way of dealing with our inevitable demise, we like to work toward something larger and more important than ourselves. Most of us, unless we invest in something larger than ourselves, will be more susceptible to depressive thoughts. But it is our fear of death that incentivizes us to leave some kind of legacy, however small. A major way of doing this and creating meaning is not necessarily to build a grandiose monument but to make a difference in the life of others. There are many ways of transcending the self.

This proposition seems to be valid in all dimensions of our lives, including the world of work. For example, in an organizational setting, if you can connect your personal goals with the goals of the organization, you will be much more committed and feel more authentic. And if you have others buy into your vision—if you are able to build these kinds of connections—you will feel even better. People work for money but die for a cause. Conversely, if you don't understand, or are unable to sign up for, the "bigger picture" you're likely to become disengaged and demotivated at work.

---

[1] Abraham H. Maslow (1943). A Theory of Human Motivation. *Psychological Review*, vol. 50, no. 4, 370–396, http://psychclassics.yorku.ca/Maslow/motivation.htm.

This touches on the sense of belonging, which is a basic existential need, just like our need for food and shelter. Our evolutionary heritage means that all of us have an inherent desire to belong, to be part of something. We are a social species. We like to belong to a group—whether that's our family, friends, co-workers, religion, or something else again. From an evolutionary psychological perspective, our need to belong has helped us to protect and define ourselves. For paleolithic humans, being part of a community was protection against ever-present dangers. When we experience a sense of connection—when we feel valued, needed, and accepted by others—this feeling of being part of a greater community will improve our motivation, health, and happiness.

This fact is very well illustrated in the famous Harvard longitudinal study of adult development (the longest study of this kind ever done). The researchers found a strong correlation between people's flourishing lives and their relationships with family, friends, and community.[2] How happy we are in our relationships has an extremely powerful influence on our health. Tending to our relationships becomes a critical form of self-care. In other words, there are going many occasions when we need "the other" simply to feel good in our skin. We don't want "the other" to fix anything, or do anything in particular, just to let us feel that we are cared for and supported.

Control is about the need to direct our own life and work. To be fully motivated, we must be able to be in charge of what we do, when we do it, and whom we do it with. Self-efficacy means our ability to succeed in different situations,[3] that is, the extent to which we believe we have control over the forces that govern our lives, how much trust we have that our actions will influence the outcomes of various situations, and how far we believe that we have choices. However, the quest for control over our life—the confidence that we can handle any difficulties that come our way—is a never-ending challenge. But if we manage it, not only will we feel safe, we will also feel that we have options. Unfortunately, my own observations indicate that many people live with the lingering fear of not having enough control. In particular, they wonder whether they have made the right choices, most significantly the choice of life partner and the choice of work.

Competence is the ability to do things successfully and efficiently, feeling and knowing that "I can do it!" When we feel competent, we have a sense of ourselves as capable of tackling any task and challenge that comes our way.

[2] https://news.harvard.edu/gazette/story/2017/04/over-nearly-80-years-harvard-study-has-been-showing-how-to-live-a-healthy-and-happy-life/.

[3] Bandura, A. (1994). Self-efficacy. In V. S. Ramachaudran (Ed.), *Encyclopedia of Human Behavior* (Vol. 4, pp. 71–81). New York: Academic Press.

The sense of competence also implies fostering ongoing personal growth and development, the ability to explore, and the capacity to handle critical feedback. The feeling of personal competence helps us persevere when faced with challenges, which makes it an important ingredient for a positive sense of self-esteem.

In my efforts to develop leaders, the challenge has always been to nurture these important themes. In Chap. 2, I referred to the 7Cs—characterological patterns that are important in making us the way we are—and to that equation I would add searching for meaning, obtaining a sense of belonging, having control, and competence. I tell my clients that the difference between dreams and reality is action. Sitting on their hands and waiting for something to turn up will get them nowhere. It is important to believe (illusory though it sometimes seems) that it is up to them to own their own lives.

In your journey through life, you will have moments when you feel beaten up, and broken. At these moments you should tell yourself that often the places that have been broken, become much stronger once they heal. Sometimes, the bad things that happen to you turn out for the better. You could call these moments of truth, moments when you really learn. Your challenge is to see these moments as learning opportunities and take advantage of them. In fact, it's your responsibility to do so.

Let me give you a personal example from the beginning of my academic career. When I was a visiting professor at the Harvard Business School, my dream was to be offered a permanent position at the school and I duly applied for one when it became available. At the time, I was giving the highest rated course at the Harvard Business School (an institution where teaching is very important), something I was proud of, and which gave me added confidence in my application. My sponsor, Abraham Zaleznik, was a senior member of the HBS faculty (and a psychoanalyst) who had "split" from the Organizational Behavior (OB) department because he thought the departmental approach to human behavior left a lot to be desired. Looking back, I realize that I was very naïve when it came to academic politics. The OB faculty was unlikely to welcome a disciple of Zaleznik. Basically, I had backed the wrong horse. They turned me down and one of their main reasons was that a senior "visionary" member of the department reckoned that I was "never going to write anything"—words that have stayed with me ever since. At the time, I experienced this setback as a serious narcissistic injury. I felt the decision was deeply unfair—as it probably was. But now, so many years later, I wonder what my life would have been like if I had got the job? Would I have had the same opportunity to be so independent in my work? Would I have been able to self-actualize? Challenged as I was by the criticism of that particular faculty member, would I have written so many books and articles? And would I really have enjoyed living in the United States, given my attachment to Europe and its great cultural diversity? I can't really answer these questions. But what I do know is that this setback motivated me to do many things. It made me decide to become a psychoanalyst, a decision that, I think, has made me more effective in my work, and it encouraged me to spend much of my time writing. It also made me realize that it is easy to deal with success but how you deal with failure is what shows true character. This dramatic setback (as I experienced it at that time) made me more philosophical when dealing with the vicissitudes of life. It probably also made me a better psychotherapist and coach. And it taught me to be more realistic about human nature.

As a psychotherapist and coach, I have learned how I can help people to find answers to their quests. But I also have become aware of my many limitations. I can only do so much. Metaphorically, I can open doors for my clients, but they have to choose to walk through those doors themselves. In the words of the Buddha: "No one saves us but ourselves. No one can, and no one may. We ourselves must walk the path." A self-actualized person may not be perfect, but he or she is always perfectible. Wherever you are in life—whatever your character—you are always going to be a work in progress.

# 6

## The Power of Storytelling

*We tell ourselves stories in order to live.*
—Joan Didion

*We are, as a species, addicted to story. Even when the body goes to sleep, the mind
stays up all night, telling itself stories.*
—Jonathan Gottschall

Once upon a time, long, long ago, in a small village, deep in the mountains
of a faraway land, there lived a master potter. He was renowned far and wide
for his craftsmanship. Nobody in the land was able to make pottery like him.
Never had there been a person who possessed such artistic genius. It made
him a living treasure. Because of his remarkable craftsmanship, his workshop
grew and grew, drawing visitors from far and wide. But the incessant pressure
to produce new masterpieces made work increasingly stressful for the potter.
His energy was waning. The continuous pressure he was working under began
to show. And as the potter's fingers became bent with arthritis, it became
increasingly difficult for him to model the clay. With his failing health, his
creative spark began to diminish. As he realized that his time on Earth was
coming to an end, he wondered how much longer he would be able to continue as before. What would happen when he was no longer there? Would his
children be able to continue his work? Was anyone of them good enough to
be his successor?

The potter had three children, two sons and a daughter. The sons were the
apple of his eye. He thought they were sensible lads. He looked on his daughter, however, as a bit of a simpleton. Like her husband, the potter's wife loved

© The Author(s), under exclusive license to Springer Nature Switzerland AG 2021
M. F. R. Kets de Vries, *The CEO Whisperer*, The Palgrave Kets de Vries Library,
https://doi.org/10.1007/978-3-030-62601-3_6

her sensible sons very much. She couldn't do enough for them and gave them all the good things in life. In contrast, she paid very little attention to her daughter. She dressed her in rags, made her do all the hard work, and she would give her only the leftovers from the dining table to eat.

As the potter drew close to death, he summoned his three children, and told them: "Go forth into the great, wide world. Find and learn from other artists. Use this knowledge and what you have learned from me to perfect your craftmanship. The one among you who will bring me the most creative piece of work will be my heir." Having had their father's blessing, the children went on their way, travelling to the far corners of the Earth to find another master craftsman who could help them create the finest pieces of pottery.

This is a classic way to start a fairy tale. It sets up our expectations for what comes later: how the children will go about their quest, what kind of quest it will be, the challenges they will face, and the obstacles they will have to overcome during their journey. And as we are pretty fairy tale literate, we know this is a Cinderella-type setting—two favorite sons and a mistreated daughter—and that, in many fairy tales, the least favored person usually comes out on top and everyone lives happily ever after.

Let's see what happens next.

The potter's three children soon came to a crossing with two signs: one read "Ever Ever Land," and the other "Never Never Land." The two sons decided Ever Ever Land seemed the better and easier option. They told their sister not to come with them, but to take the other road. They hoped she would get lost—or even eaten by wild beasts. So, they separated. Not long after, the two boys met an old, crippled woman, who begged them for food. But the two boys laughed at her, saying, "Why give good food to beggars?"—upon which the old woman turned into a troll and put them in a dungeon.

Meanwhile the girl followed the path toward Never Never Land. After a lengthy struggle through the undergrowth, she too met an old, crippled woman, who asked her for something to eat. The girl said that she had only few crusts of bread but would be very happy to share the little she had. When she untied the bag that she carried on her back, instead of stale crusts she found pies, delicious roast meats, and a bottle of fine wine. The old woman explained that because of her kindness, the girl now had a magic sack that would help her to make the most imaginative pottery. The old woman also told her what had happened to her brothers. When the girl heard of their sad fate, she cried, and begged the old woman to forgive their rudeness, and to set them free. The old woman warned her that this was not a very good idea, but agreed, nevertheless. However, when her two brothers were set free and saw the beautiful pottery their sister pulled out of her sack, they became green with envy. What happened next is another story.

Doesn't the story of the potter sound very familiar? It's really a story of two transfigurations: the human one and the business one—a story of growth, decline, and possible rejuvenation. But there are many other themes in the story, including one we all have to deal with, the fact of growing older, of diminishing capabilities. It is also a story of sibling rivalry, jealousy, and envy. Furthermore, it is a story of parent-child relationships. How effective have the potter and his wife been in developing their children? Have they properly assessed what their children are capable of? Why did they treat the two boys so differently from their daughter?

It's safe to bet that the daughter will become her father's successor, simple though she seems. But how will this affect the others in our tale? After all, sibling rivalry and parent-child conflict can be extremely toxic. What may seem, at first glance, to be a very simple fairy tale, is actually the beginning of very complex labyrinth of human relationships. And as you read the story, I'm sure that many associations crossed your mind and that a number of these themes resonated with you.

Storytelling has an ancient history. The earliest evidence can be traced back to the Lascaux caves found in the French Pyrenees. Dating from 17,000–15,000 B.C.E., the 600 paintings, mostly of animals, are believed by historians to be inspired by "hunting magic"—a ritual practice by prehistoric people to magically foretell successful hunts. The artwork may have been the earliest form of storytelling. It's likely that the most ancient of our myths, legends, archetypes, traditions, and symbols have their roots in the stories our Paleolithic ancestors told around their fires.

By telling stories, Homo Sapiens has been able to hand down learning and knowledge, stories being our way of understanding and making sense of the world in which we live. Stories connect us to a larger self and to universal truths. Stories are an entry point to the understanding of different ways of looking at the world. Furthermore, through telling stories—this treasury of unique memories possessed by all of us—our personal memories will not be lost. Transitory as our lives are, stories create the illusion of permanence. Stories allow us to understand what we are all about, because rich narratives engage our curiosity, emotions, and imagination. Stories connect us to others by sharing our passions, our sadness, our hardships, and our joys. Generally speaking, sharing our stories makes us more effective in dealing with life's challenges.

When we tell stories, or recount our experiences, we will realize that we aren't alone; that others have had similar experiences; that others have been able to overcome the challenges with which life has confronted them. Through storytelling, we understand how things work, how we make decisions, how we justify our decisions, how we persuade others, and what our place is in the world. Also, when we are asked to tell the story of our life, we are more likely to reflect what we are all about. Stories help us to solidify our identities. As I have discovered, having listened to a very large number of stories, when someone's narrative catches the audience's attention and engages them, we make our own story more understandable to ourselves.

## Neurological Mirroring

Storytelling is associated with the evolution of our brain. We could say that we are hardwired for storytelling, because it has a neurological dimension: listening to a story when it is told or read out to us activates specific parts of our brain, triggering our imagination. Therefore, it's fair to say that every time we hear a story, our neural activity increases. It is as if the switchboard of our mind is turned on, setting a mirroring process in motion.

Mirroring was first observed in research done with monkeys that mimicked each other's behavior. As an explanation of this mirroring behavior, the existence of "mirror neurons" that ignite the parts of the brain responsible for our emotional reactions was hypothesized. This mirror neuron system is involved in diverse processes such as understanding speech, understanding the meaning of other people's actions, and understanding other people's minds. According to this theory, our neurobiological makeup explains why we rapidly form relationships with others and how we empathize by observing the actions of others. We automatically internalize the movements and mental states of others—something that is thought to have evolved when our prehistoric ancestors lived in groups, as these mirroring processes would help them to be more alert to the ever-threatening predators.[1]

Interestingly, imagined experiences seem to be processed in a similar way to real experiences. Merely by listening to stories, a process of imagination is put in motion, contributing to creativity and self-discovery. Due to the presence of these mirror neurons, stories affect our brains, as listening to them changes our brain chemistry, influencing our beliefs, attitudes, and behaviors. Stories

---

[1] L. Carr, M. Iacoboni, M. C. Dubeau, J. C. Mazziotta and G. L. Lenzi (2003). Neural mechanisms of empathy in humans: a relay from neural systems for imitation to limbic areas, *Proceedings National Academy of Science U S A, 100(9)*, 5497–502; M. Iacoboni (2009). *Mirroring People: The Science of Empathy and How We Connect with Others* (1st ed.). New York, NY: Picador; Christian Keysers (2011), *The Empathic Brain*. Social Brain Press.

that are personal and more emotionally compelling will have a greater impact on our brains. Haven't we all experienced how stories linger in our memory far more than facts? Actually, the only thing that can replace a good story appears to be another good story. This explains why rich, compelling narratives have such a powerful impact.

The mirror neuron system helps explain our capacity to identify with storytellers. The intricate processes that occur within our brains demystify how we establish relationships with strangers through listening to their story—where they come from, what they do, and what we may have in common. Dramatic stories, in particular, have a remarkable capacity to spur empathy and cooperation, rather like a form of neurological microsurgery on our neural networks. For social animals like us, this evolutionary gift is very powerful, as it allows us to quickly assess whether the person we are dealing with is angry or kind, dangerous or safe, friend or foe.

The effect of the mirroring process on our power of imagination means that we're not only spectators in the story, as listeners we're also active participants. While sorting out the various themes of a story (like in the fairy tale that opened this chapter)—while our brain is trying to make sense of the experience—we are also looking for lessons learned. We get angry when our favorite characters are angry. We're sad, when they're sad. We're happy, when they're happy. No matter what form of storytelling is used, our brain networks are activated, making us resonate with the storyteller's intentions, motivations, beliefs, emotions, and actions. Furthermore, by telling our own personal story, others are able to walk in our shoes, an interpersonal dynamic that inspires empathy and motivates us to help others.

## Oxytocin

At a biochemical level, while we listen to stories, our brain synthesizes a neurochemical called oxytocin, enabling the empathic response.[2] Oxytocin is sometimes called the "love drug," because it contributes to emotional attachment and makes us more sensitive to the social cues around us. Its presence is associated with sociability, and its absence with feelings of isolation. Thus, when the brain synthesizes oxytocin, people will be more trustworthy, generous, charitable, and compassionate. As a matter of fact, the amount of oxytocin released by the brain at any given time seems to predict the degree to which people are willing to help others.

---

[2] https://www.frontiersin.org/articles/10.3389/fnins.2018.00512/full.

As is to be expected, higher levels of oxytocin are released when people listen to very emotional stories. We can hypothesize that the brain cells of the storyteller and the people listening to the story, will mirror each other, stimulating the release of oxytocin. This interface of mirror neurons and oxytocin explains why we are compelled to relate stories to our own experiences. A part of the brain called the insular cortex plays a significant role in this interface. The insular cortex is responsible for pain perception, social engagement, empathy, emotions, and numerous other vital functions. Neurologists suggest that we can change our behavior by changing our brain chemistry—in other words the neurobiology of the brain plays an important role in any change process.

## Emotional Resonance

When I began using story telling in my work with clients, I realized how powerful the resonance between narrator and listeners can be, how stories can have a curative effect, and how the narrative process can have a positive effect on our mental health. I became aware of the degree to which the "life case study" methodology promoted psychological growth and helped transcend psychological problems. From what I could see, the storytelling approach encouraged presenters and listeners to really deal with their issues and pursue what was meaningful to them. They would be encouraged to find ways to change their life situation.

The group "life case study" methodology provides a context for cathartic experiences. I have experienced how it allows executives to get things off their chest; to bring repressed feelings, fears, and covert conflicts to the surface, helping them to better understand why they do what they do. Also, while listening to executives' life stories and challenges, I have seen other participants come to realize that they are not alone in their confusion. Mutual identification with specific problems helps to bring the team together. It offers opportunities to jointly discuss more effective ways of dealing with the knottier issues of life. Understanding the "whys" of old patterns of interaction can help them unpack dysfunctional behavior, increasing the chances of change. Such reflections can lead to a willingness to experiment in doing things differently—and by doing so, create new scenarios for the future. In more than one way, the group setting offers the opportunity for vicarious learning. Participants come to appreciate that learning does not only occur through direct participation in dialogue but also through observing and listening to other people's stories. Through the group coaching process, the participants become a real community. I have observed over and over again that this feeling of social belonging becomes a very powerful catalyst for change. The group setting is also an opportunity for collective learning. Explanation, confrontation, clarification, and even direct advice about how to do things better can reduce anxiety and establish a sense of control over troublesome issues. Executives can draw from their own rich experiences to share information about major issues in life and recommend different approaches. Finally, I have seen how the altruistic motive can be a very positive force for change. The stories that are presented invite help from others who have found themselves in the same boat. Where possible, they provide guidance and encouragement for dealing with the challenges each of them faces. We know that, from an evolutionary perspective, we are hardwired for cooperation. The altruistic motive is ever-present and the desire to help others by offering support, reassurance, and insights will have a therapeutic effect, contributing to each executive's level of self-respect and well-being. And in that respect, paradoxically, altruism has quite a selfish aspect.

# 7

# "Rewriting" Stories

*Stories create community, enable us to see through the eyes of other people, and open us to the claims of others.*
—Peter Forbes

When I guide my clients in their personal journey, I aim to bring some structure into the process. When they tell their stories, I encourage them to explore the intrapersonal dimension of their lives. I want them to say something about their emotions, motivations, beliefs, attitudes, the way they make decisions, and how they set goals. I also want them to reflect on the interpersonal dimension of their lives, emphasizing that we are all social beings—that many of our issues concern our interactions with others. Then again, I want them to pay attention to their developmental side. I want them to acquire greater awareness of the fact we are on a journey from birth to death, a journey that has many peaks and valleys. I want them to reflect on some of the critical incidents on their developmental journey. Finally, I want them to think about the existential dimension—the realization of the limitations of our existence and that of others—the way they find themselves existing in their world. I push them to ask themselves what gives their life meaning. However, it is up to each one of them to decide who and what they are through their own actions. I want them to reflect on the meaning of life considering free will, choice, and personal responsibility. Are they really living with a purpose, and if so, is that purpose their own, or is it something that has been sold to them by someone else?

© The Author(s), under exclusive license to Springer Nature Switzerland AG 2021
M. F. R. Kets de Vries, *The CEO Whisperer*, The Palgrave Kets de Vries Library,
https://doi.org/10.1007/978-3-030-62601-3_7

What makes the methodology of the "life case study" story telling approach so powerful, in comparison to the more traditional case study orientation used at business schools, is the fact that the participants are able to question the live case who is presenting about issues stirred up by their narratives. Afterwards, the individual storytellers, having reflected on their presentation with the others—and encouraged by them—often have the courage to take the first successful steps toward change. They learn to write a new story about themselves—a story of renewal. They come to realize that the alternative to being able to create a new story about themselves is despair. It's the loss of hope.

Furthermore, they realize that they cannot simply unlearn many behavior patterns by themselves. They will need the others to help them "rewrite" parts of their stories. Enlisting the help of others is a highly effective method of probing why they were doing what they were doing and to find alternative ways of dealing with whatever difficult situations they were in. In this "rewriting" process, they also discover that group pressure can be an extremely powerful tool for change. The "editing" of these narratives by the others turns into a very helpful prompt in changing the storyteller's outlook on the world. And as I became more proficient in this narrative intervention technique, I could see that this group (or team) coaching methodology was remarkably powerful in achieving positive personal and social change.

Applying concepts from the clinical paradigm (explained fully in Chap. 3) to decipher knotty issues turned out to be very helpful in discovering connections—finding out why people were doing what they were doing. The narrator and listeners would recognize how often family re-enactments were responsible for seemingly irrational behavior patterns. As I helped my clients understand better the major themes within these narratives, I would point out the significant impact of the unconscious on behavior, creativity, and development. I would tell them that if they wanted a better understanding of their deeper motivations and their resistance to change, they needed to pay attention to the roots of dysfunction rather than simply deal with its surface manifestations. To help get them to this point, I would explore with them how past experiences contribute to behavior in the present, how they tended to repeat behavior patterns that once were important for reasons of survival, but in their current phase of life had become highly dysfunctional. I would also make them aware how a greater awareness of their emotions, conflicts, and blind spots would allow them to live a much fuller life. While I helped them unravel the patterns that made up their life, I always kept in mind the systemic context in which they would be operating.

# Times of Trouble

Of course, group interventions are not for everyone. Some people are better off in a one-to-one situation. For example, people who have problems with reality testing, or have identity issues, or resort to primitive defense mechanisms, may be unsuitable candidates for such a reflective program. Therefore, a key question to me, in selecting executives for such a program, was their psychological readiness. Were they prepared to undertake such a challenging journey? Were they courageous enough to do so? To get a sense what they were all about, I would ask them a number of simple questions. Why did they apply to this specific program? Why did they think this program would be useful to them? What kind of "fantasies" did they have about the program? What did they want to get out of it?

Many of the executives that I met in my work wanted to make adjustments to their leadership style. They wondered how effective they were, given changing societal and industry circumstances. Might there be better ways to manage the people they had to deal with? What should they do to create a high-performance team or culture? Some of them were the "crown princes" or "princesses" of their organization, but how well would they do after having been the leader in waiting? Would they be able to hack it? Would they be afraid to find themselves at the top of an organization? A number of the participants were looking for ways not only to reinvent themselves but also to change their organizations. How could they create a better place to work? Some of these very senior executives even admitted they were bored doing what they were doing. Obviously, boredom can have dangerous consequences for both executives and their organizations. It can lead to risky decision-making. Other executives struggled with where they were in their career. Their life trajectory and their career trajectory no longer seemed to be aligned and they wanted to do something about it. What could they do differently? What could they do next? They wanted to avoid the fear that they had made the wrong choices.

Some executives said that they were aiming for a better life balance. When I asked them to elaborate, they would say that they wanted to be more effective in priority setting. Clearly, saying no was not their strongest point. Many didn't seem to know the difference between working hard and working smart. They didn't know how to identify the important activities, those where they really could add value. Dealing with seemingly endless information flows made them feel stressed out. Whatever they tried to do, they were always running. They never had enough time to complete all the things that they were supposed to do. Given the stress they were experiencing, what they wanted most was to have a life. They wanted to feel better in their skin. They wanted to feel more authentic, not always having to wear a mask. In addition, some of them felt that they were stuck in routines, "measuring out their lives in coffee spoons," like T. S. Eliot's Prufrock. Many wanted greater excitement in their lives, to reinvent themselves, to learn how to play.

A number of executives were able to say upfront that they were trying to cope better with their darker side, although they found it more difficult to describe what this darker side looked like. I inferred that they were referring to the inner "demons" that were blocking them from progressing the way they wanted. Some "confessed" that destructive forces like spite, envy, and vindictiveness colored much of their behavior. But they also realized that these negative emotions didn't make their life easier. For these people, forgiveness had no part in their repertoire. Their life was made up of stark blacks and whites, with nothing in between. They categorized people, putting them into boxes. This made them behave very judgmentally. They were notably lacking in empathy. They all needed to work on their emotional intelligence.

A major concern was how to deal with their children, spouse, and other family members. In particular, they worried that their children might experience the same problems they had had at their age. Was it possible to prevent this unfortunate intergenerational transmission? For a large proportion of participants, the empty nest syndrome loomed prominently, and many struggled with how to put new life into their marriages.

The search for meaning was a very important issue for many executives. Although most had more than the means to live, when it came down to it, they often seemed to have very little to live for. Some of them were only now beginning to realize that meaning was important to them. Finding meaning in whatever they were doing, would make them feel more alive—make them feel more complete. Some of them understood, however, that meaning would be an ever-changing target. Nevertheless, something had to be done, particularly as they were getting older, and time was running out. Although they realized that it might be late in the game, they still wanted to make a difference. Of course, death anxiety, as I describe it in Chap. 4, was hovering overhead. The sense of immortality that comes with being young was long gone. With the older generation disappearing, as well as some of their cohort, death had become more of a reality.

My work with executives has often been a difficult ride. Changing people's behavior can be very hard work, not without its disappointments. It requires tackling people's character armor—their deeply ingrained patterns of behavior. Many of us are very attached to our chosen defenses. Sometimes, trying to progress with clients felt like treading in quicksand. It could be hard to get a grasp on things, as the original issues that brought these executives to me would morph over time into something very different. All too often, there were many issues behind the presenting issues, creating confusion in me. But my experience of having to work in this twilight zone, made it clear to me that (consciously or unconsciously) all of us are on a quest for answers about our origins, our destiny, and what brings meaning.

Reflecting on leading a life of significance and meaning, you may come to realize that the value of living is not about fame or money or resources, it's about people and the way you can improve other people's lives. Now as I am older myself, I know that it is not enough to have lived; I need to live for something. To me, helping clients in their life journey became a very meaningful endeavor. Their willingness to put their trust in me was inspiring.

Eventually, many of my clients realized that their wellbeing would be enhanced not by measuring their successes in terms of their personal gains, but by what they had contributed to the greater good. When you help others, you also help yourself, a highly successful prescription for better mental health. The Dalai Lama has put this very succinctly: "Our prime purpose in this life is to help others. And if you can't help them, at least don't hurt them."

The altruistic motive can be extremely powerful. Altruism activates reward centers in the brain. And as neurobiologists have found out, when engaged in an altruistic act, the pleasure centers of the brain become active.[1] Paradoxically, as I mentioned before, when you help others, you seem also to help yourself. Personally, I have found that the most fulfilling moments in my life have been the times when I helped others, when I felt I was making a difference. Like others, this prosocial behavior—this kind of "selfishness"—makes me feel good. I do what I do because I don't want to live in the kind of world where people don't look out for each other. I'm not referring only to the people who are close to me, but to anybody who needs a helping hand, as I have also been helped by acts of kindness from strangers. I remind myself that what we do for ourselves alone dies with us, but what we do for others and for the world remains.

---

[1] Megan M. Filkowski, R. Nick Cochran and Brian W. Haas (2016). Altruistic behavior: mapping responses in the brain, *Neuroscience and Neuroeconomics*, 5, 65–75.

# 8

# Our Inner Theater

*Happy people build their inner world; unhappy people blame their outer world.*
—Chinese proverb

*Each of us harbors in our inner universe a number of "characters," parts of*
*ourselves that frequently operate in complete contradiction to one another, causing*
*conflict and mental pain to our conscious selves. For we are relatively*
*unacquainted with these hidden players and their roles. Whether we will it or not,*
*our inner characters are constantly seeking a stage on which to play out their*
*tragedies and comedies.*
—Joyce McDougall

"John, can you tell me what gets you out of bed in the morning? What makes you feel alive? What drives you?" What followed these fairly intrusive questions was a long silence. Obviously, John found it difficult to respond. Eventually, after some prompting, he came up with a number of rather clichéd answers. His inner drivers remained a mystery, however. His rather convoluted responses made me wonder whether he himself knew what he was all about. Was he one of those people who remain strangers to themselves? Did he allow himself time to reflect on the challenges he faced in life? Or was he playing ostrich, just pushing unpleasantries aside? When I met the members of his team—in trying to get a better sense of him—I asked them what they could say about John. How would they describe him? What did they think drove him? Their hesitant responses suggested that they were also at a loss. They didn't really seem to understand him. To them, John appeared to be a blank page. Clearly, he was the kind of person who kept his distance. I

**49**
M. F. R. Kets de Vries, *The CEO Whisperer*, The Palgrave Kets de Vries Library,
https://doi.org/10.1007/978-3-030-62601-3_8

wondered why? Why was he so hard to approach? Why was he such an enigma to others? At the same time, I wondered whether there was something that held his people back from talking about him. Were the people who reported to him afraid to speak their mind? Eventually, one of them remarked that although John was quite reserved, he didn't mind being the center of attention. There were times when he would seek out the limelight. When I asked her to elaborate on this comment, her response was vague. But her observation about John's need for attention stayed in my mind. In the short conversation I had with him, I'd also noticed contradictory forces of standoffishness and self-centeredness. All in all, he was not a person you easily warmed to.

Generally speaking, if we want to get the best out of ourselves and others, we need to understand why we do what we do; what motivates us to make specific choices. What can be said about the "scripts" people follow? I have always liked the idea of the inner theater, a conceptualization introduced to me by my first psychoanalyst (and later friend), Joyce McDougal. She wrote in one of her books: "[That] 'All the world's a stage,' and that all the men and women in it are 'merely players' expressed Shakespeare's deep conviction that we do not readily escape the roles that are essentially ours. Each of us is drawn into an unfolding life drama in which the plot reveals itself to be uncannily repetitive."[1] According to Joyce McDougal, if we want to understand the other, we have to make sense of their inner scripts.

A point Joyce made very clear to me during the many sessions I had with her was her belief that "*Le rôle du psychanalyste est d'aider chacun à découvrir sa vérité*" ("The role of a psychoanalyst is to help each person to find his or her truth".)[2] I still remember sitting in her office, full of paintings by her artist-psychoanalyst husband—a survivor of the World War II Bataan death march and Japanese captivity, hearing her say this. Joyce gave me his highly praised memoir, *Give Us This Day*, an account of the intense suffering of these prisoners.[3] This book about the painfulness of the human condition made a deep impression on me. Now, many years later, I must confess that I very much miss our sessions. When she became my supervisor many years after I had my first analysis with her, she not only gave me a better understanding of my clients and myself, but also gave me many insights into the history of psychoanalysis—and how to live life in general.

Joyce helped me to become more sensitive to people's inner theater—to identify their major "scripts"—and she made it quite clear to me that finding

---

[1] http://www.academyanalyticarts.org/mcdougall-prologue.

[2] https://www.cairn.info/revue-le-carnet-psy-2001-7-page-20.htm#.

[3] Sidney Stewart (1999). *Give us this day*. New York: W.W. Norton.

these scripts is difficult. Homo sapiens is a very complex animal. It is not always easy to make sense of a person like John. As there are many people like John who find it hard to respond to my questions about their drivers, and as a way of nudging them a little bit, I sometimes ask them what values they would like to impart to their children. I also ask them what kind of people they admire, and the reasons why? What makes those people so special to them? With respect to their values, I ask what kind of behavior they find unacceptable? Is there a red line that would them make quit their job? And why?

I find the responses to these questions helpful, as they encourage people to identify what's really important to them. In addition, I sometimes ask them who, during the course of their lives, have been their major "scriptwriters"; who has had a significant influence in their lives—and why do they think that's the case? Not surprisingly, when I ask the last question, the most common responses are intimate relationships with parents, grandparents, brothers and sisters, uncles and aunts, teachers, spouses or partners, and even some of their bosses. Sometimes, however, the chosen role models are less personal. They might be historical and contemporary figures. I might also ask them sometimes what kind of "hedgehog" they are: the point is to try to gauge from their answer how close they can get to people? The reactions to this question give me an understanding of their developmental history.

## Attachment Behavior

You may well ask how hedgehogs come into it. Imagine this: on a very cold winter's day, a few hedgehogs are searching out other hedgehogs to huddle up with to keep warm. But because of their prickles they are forced to make a choice. Get close, stay warm, and get stabbed; or keep away, stay safe, and freeze. The pain from the mass of spines makes the hedgehogs separate, until the cold forces them back together. So, they keep on shuffling moving back and forth until they find the appropriate distance for both warmth and comfort. Of course, this story is a metaphor for the challenges of human intimacy. It is a way of describing a dilemma we all face, as we simultaneously crave and are wary of connection. Although we may intend to form close reciprocal relationships, this may not happen, for reasons that can have a long history.

The hedgehog dilemma was first outlined in 1851 by the German philosopher Arthur Schopenhauer, who concluded that the hedgehogs "discovered that they would be best off by remaining at a little distance from one another."[4] In other words, the hedgehogs realized that while they wanted to be close, the only way to avoid hurting one another would be to avoid getting too close. But the degree of closeness is case specific. It all depends on the kind of attachment pattern you are comfortable with.

Attachment patterns turn out to be a key theme of the scripts and scriptwriters who help define our inner world. The nature of connectedness between human beings is very much dependent of how our parents respond to our needs while we grow up. The kind of interface we are exposed to will have a deep impact throughout our life. Fortunately, attachment theory helps explain how early parent-child relationships emerge—how it influences a person's subsequent development.[5] Here, our attachment pattern—based on our earliest life experiences—is the approach we will use to manage and maintain relationships, with respect our partners, or at work. While adult attachment patterns may not exactly correspond with early childhood attachments, there is no question that our earliest relationships with our caregivers play an important role in its outcome. By understanding better our attachment patterns, we will gain a greater appreciation of how the earliest attachments in our life have a fundamental impact on all our adult relationships.

There are three main attachment styles: secure, anxious, and avoidant. Generally speaking, securely attached people have had a healthy childhood, thus becoming better equipped to deal with intimate relationships. For anxious and avoidant people, however, intimacy will be more of a struggle, the main reasons being difficult experiences in early life, such as neglect, poor parenting, or abusive relationships. These attachment styles can be summarized as follows:

Avoidant: I am not very comfortable coming close to others. Usually, others want to be closer to me than I am prepared to accept.
Secure: It is quite easy for me to get close to others. I am comfortable having people depend on me or having me depend on them.
Anxious: I find it difficult to accept that others are reluctant get as close to me as I would like. Unfortunately, my need to get closer to people sometimes frightens them away.

---

[4] Arthur Schopenhauer (1851). *Parerga und Paralipomena*, Volume II, Chapter XXXI, Section 396, London: Oxford University Press, 1974.

[5] John Bowlby (1969). *Attachment. Attachment and loss: Vol. 1. Loss.* New York: Basic Books; Mary D. S. Ainsworth, (1991). Attachments and other affectional bonds across the life cycle. In C. M. Parkes, J. Stevenson-Hinde, & P. Marris (Eds.), *Attachment across the life cycle* (pp. 33–51). London: Routledge.

A secure attachment pattern is found among roughly half of us. The other patterns are more problematic. But before you start blaming your parents for relationship problems, keep in mind that they, like you, are just common mortals who had their own issues with their parents. Also, remember that attachment styles formed during early childhood are not necessarily identical to the patterns that come to the fore later in life. Much can happen between infancy and adulthood, so intervening experiences also play a large part in the creation of adult attachment patterns.

## Attachment Styles and Life Anchors

This very brief summary of various attachment styles suggests that John's is likely to be avoidant. Although this helps explain how he relates to others we would also benefit from understanding other aspects of his inner theater—his values, beliefs, and attitudes—which I identify as life anchors. Understanding our own life anchors will provide us with greater insight into what drives us, why we do what we do, and we you interact with others. It will make us less of a stranger to ourselves.

Our *values*, a set of abstract and general ideas and principles, form the core of our life anchors. Generally speaking, values underlie our judgments and guide our opinions on social, political, or religious issues. They are the foundation of our beliefs, attitudes, and behavior. For example, in France, where I live, you don't have to go far to find the words *liberté, égalité, fraternité* ("liberty, equality, fraternity") inscribed on all government buildings. These principles dictate what's supposedly important in the lives of French people and shape their standards of behavior and guide their action. They can be defined as moral choices that they try to use consistently in life.

In contrast, *beliefs* are the ideas we generally hold to be true regardless whether or not they are supported by hard, factual, and empirical evidence. Our beliefs grow from what we see, hear, experience, read, and think about, creating the assumptions that we make about the world. They are more specific than values, as they are shaped by the successes and failures that we experience in everyday life.

*Attitudes* are our states of mind, feelings, or dispositions about certain issues. Our attitudes determine whether we think a specific situation or thing is good, worthwhile, valuable, or bad. Thus, when we "like" or "dislike" someone or something, we are expressing an attitude. I must emphasize, however, that attitudes, like values and beliefs, are mental constructs. They are inferred from the things we say or do.

These life anchors set the stage for our inner theater, with our attachment style providing the scenery. This inner theater will be colored by the things we learn from our parents and other significant figures while growing up. As far as this inner theater influences our thoughts, it has no external consequences. It does have consequences, however, when the scripts invite some form of action, subtle though those actions may be.

Our life anchors can be a shortcut to helping us understand what we are all about and how we see ourselves and perceive others. They underlie all our interpersonal relationships and lifestyle choices. They drive our behavior and give meaning to our life plans and designs. But identifying our life anchors can be a challenge and is not always to do alone, however. We might need the help of others. And to aid in this process, I have developed an instrument that helps identify some of our major motivational themes: The Inner Theater Inventory (ITI™).[6] In this assessment instrument, I describe twenty-two life anchors that represent the most dominant drivers in our lives. The more prevalent of these are meaning, achievement, recognition, meaning, power, money, vengeance, learning/exploration, and lifestyle quality.[7]

*Meaning.* Meaning is probably our major existential concern, making it an essential life anchor. I have met many executives who only felt truly alive when they felt they had a purpose. They wanted to be connected to something larger than themselves. If they couldn't find meaning in what they were doing, life became empty, leading to boredom, dissociation, and even feelings of alienation.

*Achievement.* People for whom this life anchor is important always try to meet or exceed specifically defined standards of excellence. They set challenging goals, taking calculated risks, and like to get results. Most likely, taking a developmental perspective, they were brought up by parents who also emphasized achievement. Working hard was the way to obtain their parents' approval.

*Recognition.* People for whom this life anchor is important want to stand out and be admired. From early childhood, their sense of self is shaped by positive recognition and acknowledgment of their existence. Whether the interpersonal relations in their youth were characterized by under- or over-stimulation, the end result was to make them crave attention. For example, recognition was John's life anchor. It explained his self-centeredness and narcissistic disposition and was complicated by his avoidant attachment style.

---

[6] M. F. R. Kets de Vries (2009). *Inner Theatre Inventory: Instruction Manual,* INSEAD; https://www.kdvi.com/tools/18-inner-theater-inventory.

[7] For a full list of the various life anchors, I recommend that you test the ITI™ for yourself.

*Power.* For people for whom this life anchor is important, power is essential for their self-esteem. Their need for power will vary, however, depending on their experiences with authority and control during their formative years. Some people might be strongly driven to control other people's lives as a way of compensating for feelings of inadequacy. Other power seekers may have a more constructive outlook. But when people become obsessed with power, the ending tends to be miserable for themselves and for others.

*Money.* Growing up in a household where money is scarce can create feelings of anxiety, helplessness, and dependency. For some people, the acquisition of money represents deliverance from misery, triumph over helplessness, escape from a gray existence, pathway to independence and security, and a boost to their self-esteem. Predictably, this particular life anchor has a flip side, when it becomes of overriding importance. Instead of bringing satisfaction, a preoccupation with limitless wealth may contribute to a sense of emptiness and even end in depressive reactions.

*Vengeance.* According to a Chinese proverb, "He who seeks vengeance must dig two graves: one for his enemy and one for himself." The desire to inflict punishment in return for injury or insult is a natural human tendency, a form of defense against feeling wronged. But for some people, wanting to get even becomes a major life anchor. Fantasies of vindictiveness and revenge are often fed by the desire to restore personal integrity and recover from feelings of helplessness, violation, and injustice. The challenge for people blinded by revenge is to bury the hatchet and move on. Forgiveness and reparation are the cornerstones of a much more fruitful way of looking at life.

*Learning/exploration.* The love of learning can be an intense, life-long pursuit. People for whom this life anchor is important only feel truly alive when tackling new challenges, obsessed as they are by a love of understanding, the urge to "figure things out," and their need to explore and inquire. Far too quickly, the tried and tested become boring to them and they often pursue one seemingly crazy idea after another—the entrepreneur and innovator Egon Musk, who belongs to a clan of Musk entrepreneurs, comes to mind.

*Lifestyle quality.* When lifestyle quality is a life anchor, executives prioritize finding a satisfactory balance between work, friends, and family. Often, this implies having a measure of control over when, where, and how they work. It's likely that their experiences of family life when growing up—the absence of their busy parents from significant events—make them determined that their and their children's lives will not be the same.

# What Makes You Feel Alive?

In your journey of self-exploration—in your search for your most significant life anchors—it will always be a challenge to obtain a better understanding of your own impulses, desires, opinions, and subjective reactions. Only when you become more familiar with the hidden scripts in your inner theater will you begin to act in ways that are congruent with your overall value and belief system. When you understand your life anchors better, you will find out how you are perceived by others and how you can help others to better understand what drives you. You will be more aware of what is happening within and around you—how your inner world affects your outer world. You will be more conscious of your actions and behavior. Also, when you recognize the cognitive dissonance between your inner and outer worlds, you may be motivated to close the gap.

When you pay attention to your own life anchors, and those of others, you may also realize the richness of the interior lives of the people you deal with. You need to get away from the fallacy of thinking that everyone else thinks like you. Everybody's story—in spite of the inevitable similarities—is unique. If you don't make an effort to dig deeper, you may discover that your perceptions of others are completely wrong. And even when you do get to know them better, you may be only scratching the surface of what they are really all about. This observation reminds me of the words of the Irish poet John O'Donohue: "Each one of us is the custodian of an inner world that we carry around with us. Now, other people can glimpse it from [its outer expressions]. But no one but you know what your inner world is actually like, and no one can force you to reveal it until you actually tell them about it."

# The Inside-Outside Axis

Identifying your attachment pattern and life anchors will help you to make greater sense of your inner world. Although you may be in a hurry to change your outer world, having a better understanding of your inner world will help you to put things in greater perspective. Attachment patterns and life anchors will help you decipher your inner theater, your relationships with other people, how you work with others, and what can go wrong while doing so, if you don't pay attention. But while you have a better understanding of the complexity of your inner theater, you should bear in mind that your inner world is always a work in progress, and that when things change inside you, they will also change around you.

From a work perspective, understanding your inner theater and that of others will make you more effective in interpersonal relationships, leading your teams, and help you to create the kinds of corporate cultures where everyone feels at his or her best. After all, the main challenge of leaders of organizations is talent and culture management—having an understanding of what makes people "tick" and giving them the opportunities to be the best that they can be. It will make you more effective in deciphering what motivates others. This approach is what differentiates run-of-the-mill from high-performing organizations.

# 9

## Caveat Emptor

*Beware of false knowledge; it is more dangerous than ignorance.*
—George Bernard Shaw

*Since I was not able wholly to subscribe to any one set of beliefs advanced by any "guru" I had to fall back on my own, however derivative.*
—Anthony Storr

As I stress throughout this book, the journey to understanding your inner theater is not easily undertaken alone. You will need some guidance, and for that you need a guide who can be genuinely helpful and steer you in the right direction. Unfortunately, that's not easy either. The Greek stoic philosopher Epictetus said, "A guide, on finding a man who has lost his way, brings him back to the right path—he does not mock and jeer at him and then take himself off. You also must show the unlearned man the truth, and you will see that he will follow. But so long as you do not show it him, you should not mock, but rather feel your own incapacity." Always be careful whom you ask for help. *Caveat emptor*—buyer beware.

Although I often have given guidance to people undertaking major life changes, I never promise them a quick fix. Not that I wouldn't like to. It would be very nice if I could. I have no illusions about what I am capable of doing but being a magician is not part of my repertoire. I have learned from experience that quick fixes—in spite of the miraculous transformations promised in the self-help sections of bookstores—tend to be non-fixes. Instead, I tell my clients: if you want to learn something about yourself that will make you more effective in your relationships at work and at home, I may well be

© The Author(s), under exclusive license to Springer Nature Switzerland AG 2021
M. F. R. Kets de Vries, *The CEO Whisperer*, The Palgrave Kets de Vries Library,
https://doi.org/10.1007/978-3-030-62601-3_9

of some help. But if you want miracles, I'm not your man. I have no magic wand.

Sadly though, I don't always succeed in getting my point across. People looking for help and comfort are always susceptible to what is called the "idealizing transference."[1] To explain why this is the case, we have to go back to our childhood experiences. How often did you run to a parent for comfort after falling and hurting yourself? How often did you turn a grownup for protection? This search for a comforting, protective other person continues into adulthood. We like to associate with people we perceive as calm and soothing, who can take care of us, particularly if we cannot comfort ourselves. Thus, without my wishing it in the least, as a psychological helper, there is always the chance that my clients will be inclined to over-valuate me. And although this admiration may make feel me good, I also know I will never be able to live up to their exaggerated expectations. Because I am aware of these transferential patterns, which are part of the human condition, I am always on my guard against the idealized projections of others so that they don't go to my head.

Although I don't have a magic wand, I can still help the people I deal with to change. However, I try to set realistic expectations. Most changes (as I have learned repeatedly) are incremental. I have also discovered from my work in organizations—cynical as it may sound—that it is far easier "to change people than to change people." Change is hard work and it can be painful. I tell people that if they are prepared to change, they must realize that it will be an *inside* job. You can't change what's going on around you, until you change what's going on inside you. And if you change nothing, nothing will change. You have to *want* to change. I can only take on the role of facilitator.

But in spite of this, many people I meet, who say they want to change aspects of their life, look for short-cuts and I have to disappoint them. Short-cuts leave you short. People don't like it when I tell them that I'm not the person for quick fixes. They find it difficult to accept that change is painful and takes an incredible amount of commitment, time, energy, and effort.

## *Homo Mirabilis*: The Rise of the Miracle Workers

The unwillingness to make an effort is the reason why many people fail to change. It also explains why the self-help industry remains so robust. Partly, it's due to our gullibility: if one formula doesn't work, there's always another

---

[1] Heinz Kohut (1971), *The Analysis of the Self.* New York: International Universities Press.

one around the corner we can try. Of course, if quick, self-help cures did work, why is there a never-ending stream of self-help books? If there were such a thing as a magic formula, shouldn't there be one very, very rich and messianic person around somewhere, living the high life off the proceeds?

## The Triumph of Hope Over Experience

As things are now, big business has been built on the myth that you can become infinitely wealthy and happy by taking a variety of magical "cures." And given our strong wish to believe, I'm afraid that people will continue to line the pockets of the prophets of the self-help industry, in perpetuity. It is difficult to let go of the notion that "I can have everything I want without any effort." It is difficult to let go of the idea that it's possible to make a million dollars, be madly in love, have remarkable sex, look like a film star, and spend each day full of happiness. It is difficult to give up the fantasy of being extremely successful, happy, rich, slim, sexy, and loved. The price you pay for hanging on to these ideas is that you let go of reality. It is so much more pleasant to indulge in wishful thinking, particularly if a myth fits our expectations.

As well as the countless self-help books, there are also coaches galore, and other self-appointed miracle workers in the helping profession, ready to tell you that what you wish for is readably obtainable. People sign up for their services when they hear a convincing story of how others have achieved miraculous change. If something sounds good and is easy to understand, our default position is to expect it to be true. This explains why so many false beliefs persist despite the existence of hard facts. We are too ready to search out dubious information that supports our pre-existing beliefs—the result being that feelings overrule facts.[2] Our naivety when it comes to dealing with our emotional health explains the endless supply of therapists, coaches, and consultants who trot out exaggerated promises. Frankly speaking, I am amazed by the disingenuousness and downright dishonesty of many of these self-help gurus/coaches and the bullshit they offer as services and products.

## "Psychic" Circuses

Many of these pseudo-professionals, often driven by monstrous egos, are highly persuasive. They are extremely talented in the use of idealizing

---

[2] Carol Tavris and Eliot Aronson (2015). *Mistakes Were Made (but Not by Me): Why We Justify Foolish Beliefs, Bad Decisions, and Hurtful Acts*. New York: Mariner Books.

transference. When they are the recipients of unrealistic projections from their clients, they do not push back. On the contrary, they encourage idealization; they want to be perceived as miracle workers.

They also know how to disrupt people's mental equilibrium. I have seen how motivational self-help gurus and coaches assault their victims' (not clients') senses by using rock concert and cult technology in their interventions. They create "psychic" displays (including drumming, dancing, jumping, and shouting) as ways of fooling their naïve targets. But high fiving, hugging people, or daring them to go on fire walks or tightrope walking is not going to solve their psychological problems. It will not benefit their mental health. Instead, they might like to consider the words of the great showman and circus impresario, P. T. Barnum: "There's a sucker born every minute."

## Healer, Heal Thyself

Many of the people who are attracted to these types of mental health gurus and coaches lack critical reasoning skills. They are naïve and quickly seduced. When they undergo this kind of shock treatment, they may believe that they are experiencing transformative change, but they will later regret the exhibitionist behavior they are led into.

From what I have seen, many of these psychological miracle workers fail to recognize the great complexity of the human animal. I have frequently seen how, without presenting a shred of scientific evidence, they claim to know what's wrong with their clients, to have all the answers. In their attempts to come across as experts, they resort to pseudo-scientific approaches, although many of them have no formal education in psychology, psychiatry, or psychotherapy. In fact, they have very little idea what psychotherapy is all about, as they have never been exposed to personal therapy, a *sine qua non* to becoming truly effective in the helping profession. They have no idea what life is like on "the other side"—that is, the client's. They don't know that to fully relate to another, it is imperative that they first relate to themselves, not using the other to shield their own neuroses.

Granted their circus workshops might improve their clients' spirit, at least temporarily. But will they make them feel better in the long run? Implying that there are no constraints to our ability to become our best self, to live our best live, to embrace our own truths, is very attractive, but it is also quite naïve.

I also find it paradoxical is that scores of these "helpers" fail to practice what they preach. I have seen many self-proclaimed "health" or life coaches who have unhealthy relationships with food, exercise, and their body image. The sad truth is that many of these coaches lead rather empty lives. Many "relationships coaches" turn out to be lonely and afraid of intimacy. Many high-powered consultants aren't able to train their dog. The motto "Physician, heal thyself" comes to mind. Many "helpers" don't recognize that they're actually very troubled themselves, even as they try to be everyone else's anchor. Perhaps, instead of giving all and sundry advice about how to live to, they should find a psychotherapist or coach themselves. I know I sound unfriendly, but many people in this sector don't understand themselves (and consequently, don't understand others). However, they are very good at blurring the line between reality and fiction by offering oversimplified band-aid solutions to clients whose problems lie at a much deeper level.

Promising miracles can give you a temporary "high." But what happens after you reach this "high?" How many "quick-fix" gurus ever bother to do a follow-up? How do their clients feel after the euphoria has subsided? There are no simple solutions to feeling unsuccessful, rejected, lonely, or inadequate. Self-limiting beliefs that hold you back cannot be easily changed. You need to accept that whatever the wished-for change, there are going to be many hurdles in the way, ranging from disturbing emotional baggage and ingrained habits, to environmental forces that will reinforce the status quo and are hostile to change. As Sigmund Freud said, "From error to error, one discovers the entire truth."

# 10

## The "Freudian" Trajectory

*The first human who hurled an insult instead of a stone was the founder of civilization.*
—Sigmund Freud

My skepticism about self-appointed miracle workers doesn't mean that people in the helping profession can't make a difference. On the contrary, if we forget about magic, they can be extremely helpful. I know from personal experience that if you want to make changes to your life, it is always better not to do it alone. Helpers, in the form of well-trained therapists, coaches, or consultants, can provide you with guidance and greatly facilitate the journey. However, I also realize that asking for help can be a big step to take, as executive coaching, psychotherapeutic, and psychoanalytic interventions are shrouded in mystery for many people.

Many people decide to ask for help when they reach a point where they are forced to acknowledge that they are not doing so well. The reasons vary. They might be unable to sleep; they might have a recurring bad dream; it could be an unexplained somatic symptom that doesn't seem to have a physical cause. Whatever is bothering them, it seems to be all in their head. They may have sexual problems; they may be haunted by bizarre, intrusive thoughts. They might exhibit self-destructive behavior at work. Any of these or similar disruptions to their normal way of being make them realize that something is going very wrong.

There are people, however, who still find the idea of asking for help unpalatable, even though they recognize that there's something wrong with them.

© The Author(s), under exclusive license to Springer Nature Switzerland AG 2021
M. F. R. Kets de Vries, *The CEO Whisperer*, The Palgrave Kets de Vries Library,
https://doi.org/10.1007/978-3-030-62601-3_10

Like the movie tycoon Samuel Goldwyn, they consider that "anyone who goes to a psychiatrist ought to have his head examined." Eventually, the disturbing psychological intrusions they experience become so disruptive that they are forced to take some form of action.

## Secondary Gain

In my roles as a psychoanalyst, psychotherapist, executive coach, or consultant, I know that for many people, asking people like me for help can be very scary. Humans have a natural fear of the unknown. It explains why you, as a client, might be very reluctant to spill your guts to a perfect stranger. You might wonder whether that person is going to be empathic, or will judge you, or think you're completely crazy. It won't help that, although you may deny it, your reluctance to ask for help might means that you don't truly want to deal with your problems. Digging deeply into your own psyche is a very scary idea. Who knows what you might find buried there? Will you be able to bear looking at what you may find? To find out that you are controlled by seemingly unconscious forces could come as a nasty surprise. You may even experience the idea that you may not know why you are doing what you're doing as a form of narcissistic injury. And even if you have the courage to see someone, you might also ask yourself whether other people will reject you once they find out about the "real" you. Will they be horrified? What's the use of all this digging, finding out who you really are, why you do what you do? Wouldn't it be better to let sleeping dogs lie? Or, to take a very different perspective, what if you happen to like your neuroses? What if your discomfort—strange as it may sound—gives you pleasure? This idea may sound strange, but it is a concept that psychologists have described as "secondary gain."[1]

Secondary gain can be defined as the advantage that occurs as an accessory to a stated or real problem. It refers to the paradoxical psychological benefits derived from suffering from certain symptoms. Secondary gain may be the reason why many people remain stuck in dysfunctional behavior patterns and are unwilling to change their behavior. Let's take Lisa, one of my clients, as an example. During our consultations, I give her a lot of encouragement and caring comments. The sympathetic attention she gets from me might encourage her to remain distressed. Without her being consciously aware of it, instead of feeling better and moving on, remaining troubled gives her a reason

---

[1] David A. Fishbain (1994). Secondary gain concept: Definition problems and its abuse in medical practice, *APS Journal*, 3 (4), 264–273.

to continue to ask me for help. As a coach or psychotherapist, I had better be aware of this dynamic, otherwise, our relationship could become interminable. Secondary gain, it should be stressed, is not something a person is consciously aware of. Generally speaking, people who use secondary gain to their advantage are not consciously manipulative or faking it. It doesn't mean that their distress or impairment isn't real.

Secondary gain aside, for many people, it is overwhelming to open yourself up and become vulnerable. But if you decide to take this step—which can be momentous for some—bear in mind that you are not alone. Many people have made this journey before you. In saying so, I am well aware that in many cultures seeking professional help remains taboo. There is a tendency to pooh-pooh all this psychotherapy or coaching nonsense. The people who ask for help, and their helpers, are often figures of fun. Yet all of us will need help at times. We are only human. And a large number of us will visit a helping professional at some point in our life. (Estimates range from ten to thirty percent in the Western world.)[2]

Psychoanalysts in particular, have been popular subjects of ridicule. Just think of movies such as *Analyze This*, in which Hollywood makes fun of the silent, bearded psychoanalyst who is asked "to cure" a mobster. I guess such a scenario is to be expected, as movies need drama and conflict to keep audiences engaged. It may also explain why the behavior of people with mental health problems is often presented in such extreme ways in the media. The problem is that this creates a large credibility gap between what's seen in popular films and what really happens. Unfortunately, too many films that deal with mental health issues play to our worst prejudices.

In the media, psychoanalysts are often depicted as retro-figures with heavy beards, a Viennese-sounding accent, a strange, aloof manner, and the inability to say anything more than "Hmmm." In the meantime, their clients squirm on their couches, seemingly abandoned. Unfortunately, such characterizations do little to help the general public grasp what really occurs in therapeutic or coaching situations. But I can assure you that it is quite different from the pyrotechnics of the quick-fix miracle workers I described in Chap. 9. The magic worked by these helping professionals is supported by a large body of research in human development.

---

[2] https://www.mentalhealth.org.uk/statistics/mental-health-statistics-people-seeking-help
   https://www.who.int/whr/2001/media_centre/press_release/en/

# The Enigma of Sigmund Freud

Sigmund Freud, the founder of psychoanalysis, laid the groundwork for what happens in the field of mental health interventions. In spite of his remarkable original ideas about mental functioning, for many people he has remained a controversial figure, due to his disturbing ideas about sexuality and aggression. The negative biases about Freud's ideas detract from the remarkable impact they have had on Western civilization. Nobody else has made such an effort to encourage us to spend time on self-reflection for the purpose of better self-understanding and greater wellbeing. Nobody more than Freud has made such an effort to point out the existence of the inner demons that can prevent us from leading a full and fulfilling life.

Listening carefully to his patients, Freud discovered that our conscious thoughts are just the tip of the iceberg. He made us aware of the massive psychic structure that lies underneath, pointing out how appearances can be extremely deceiving. All too often, according to him, rationality was only a veneer, covering a large, seething cauldron of primitive sexual and aggressive drives and contradictions. And while he explained that most of our activities take place at an unconscious level, Freud also suggested that they exert a powerful effect on our conscious activities.[3] Furthermore, he maintained that emotional and psychological problems such as depression and anxiety are often rooted in conflicts between the conscious and unconscious mind. Due to the presence of these complex psychological dynamics, many of us are really strangers to ourselves.[4] Freud also asserted that rational decision-making is actually an illusion, although we can always find "rational" reasons why we engage in certain activities. However, some serious detective work is needed to figure out the reasons why.

If these insights aren't troublesome enough, Freud also gave voice to other matters that many of us prefer to push away from our conscious mind, such as infantile sexuality, our "neo-sexualities" (another word for perversions), and the impact of the forces of love and hate—our life and death instincts. His theories about the psychosexual stages, defensive structures, transferential processes, and dream symbolism, were troubling. Freud was the first to determine that personality is heavily influenced by the events of early childhood—something that we now take for granted—and that childhood experiences

---

[3] Sigmund Freud (1933). New Introductory Lectures on Psycho-Analysis *and* Other Works, Volume XXII, *The Standard Edition of the Complete Psychological Works of Sigmund Freud*, London: Hogarth Press and the Institute of Psychoanalysis.

[4] Timothy D. Wilson (2004). *Strangers to Ourselves: Discovering the Adaptive Unconscious*. Cambridge, MA: Harvard University Press.

have an enormous impact on adult behavior. Long before it became voguish, Freud studied the development of character and noted that leaders would do well to examine their own drivers, their narcissistic disposition, and their prevalent neuroses. He pointed out the multitude of inner forces that can lead them astray. He also identified the strange urge to keep on repeating the same mistake—the concept of repetition compulsion—a psychological phenomenon by which some people repeat an event or its circumstances over and over again. People suffering from repetition compulsion seek comfort in the familiar and predictable, even if this means searching out self-defeating situations or people who are emotionally or physically abusive. These people are trying to rewrite their history, hoping to change the outcome, while telling themselves that this time they will get it right. Presenting these kinds of situations gave Freud the opportunity to point out how we rationalize dysfunctional behavior, and how we get stuck in dysfunctional activities because of psychological dynamics that occur under the surface and block us from moving forward.

## Bald Men Fighting for a Comb

Although psychoanalysts can offer people a great deal of help to feel better in their skin, their public relations skills have been sorely lacking. They have frequently been their own worst enemy. Obsessed by theoretical "purity," too many psychoanalysts have been dismissive of other methods of intervention. All too often, they like to see themselves as superior to others in the helping profession: due to the length of their training, they tend to portray themselves as members of a highly exclusive club. As Freud himself described them in his 1930 essay, *Civilization and Its Discontents*, they are "communities with adjoining territories, and related to each other in other ways as well, who are engaged in constant feuds and in ridiculing each other."[5] There is always the uncomfortable truth of too great a resemblance. To alleviate this narcissistic injury, we may be inclined to downplay our similarities with others and emphasize our differences—which can lead to seemingly insoluble disagreements.

The fact that much psychoanalytic training takes place in specialist institutes contributes to many psychoanalysts' sense of feeling special. Wanting to have more control over the discipline, its leadership decided to move their

---

[5] Sigmund Freud (1930). Civilization and its Discontents, James Strachey (ed.), *The Standard Edition of the Complete Psychological Works of Sigmund Freud*, Volume XXI, London: The Hogarth Press and the Institute of Psycho-analysis.

educational programs out of university settings. But this unfortunate decision cut many psychoanalysts off from a broader intellectual environment. Its image hasn't been helped either by the fact that psychoanalytic treatment tends to be highly intensive and long term, not very attractive in our day and age, when people (and insurance companies) look increasingly for shorter-term solutions. Acceptance of psychoanalysis was made even more difficult (particularly for American psychologists) because of its pessimistic view of human nature. Psychoanalysis is not exactly an exercise in positive psychology. Freud himself famously declared that the goal of psychoanalysis was the transformation of "neurotic misery into common unhappiness."

## The Contemporary Relevance of Psychoanalysis

It has also been said that some of Freud's propositions are outdated. True enough, developments in neuroscience and cognitive, developmental, and evolutionary psychology have advanced theories of human development, departing from a number of Freud's concepts. But these critics should note that some of the propositions that shocked people so deeply were very much colored by the time in which Freud lived. Numerous follow-up studies have shown that many of his ideas have remained valid into contemporary society. Recent reviews of neuroscientific work confirm that many of Freud's original observations, not least the pervasive influence of non-conscious processes and the organizing function of emotions on our thought processes, have been confirmed in experimental laboratory studies.[6] These studies have also demonstrated the considerable efficacy of psychoanalytically oriented treatments. Psychoanalytic psychotherapy is just as effective as other forms of psychotherapy. There is also considerable evidence that the effects last longer—and even increase—after treatment ends.[7]

Although the more classical forms of psychoanalytic treatment are on the decline, this does not mean that the psychodynamic perspective is dead. Despite its many critics, psychoanalytic concepts have played a seminal role in the general development of psychology as a science. I find it ironic, that

---

[6] https://psycnet.apa.org/buy/2006-05420-001; Mark Solms (2018). The scientific standing of psychoanalysis, *British Journal of Psychiatry International*, 15 (1), 5–8.

[7] S. de Maat, F. de Jonghe, R. Schoevers, et al. (2009) The effectiveness of long-term psychoanalytic therapy: a systematic review of empirical studies. *Harvard Review of Psychiatry*, 17, 11–23; J. Shedler, (2010) The efficacy of psychodynamic psychotherapy. *American Psychologist*, 65, 98–109; Steinert, C., Munder, T., Rabung, S., Hoyer, J., & Leichsenring, F. (2017). Psychodynamic Therapy: As Efficacious as Other Empirically Supported Treatments? A Meta-Analysis Testing Equivalence of Outcomes. *American Journal of Psychiatry*, https://doi.org/10.1176/appi.ajp.2017.17010057

secondary sources in psychology and most contemporary textbooks, while not explicitly crediting Freud, have integrated many of his ideas in their texts. In spite of all the criticism, Freud's ideas continue to influence our approach to the treatment of mental health issues and still exert a very significant influence on psychology. It is interesting to note that while some psychology departments typically treat psychoanalysis as a purely historical artifact, scholars of art, literature, history, and general humanities are more likely to teach psychoanalysis as an ongoing and relevant subject of study.

At the risk of sounding defensive, I repeat—that Freud's approach to therapy was revolutionary given the time in which he lived, something many of his critics prefer to forget. His suggestion that mental illness is treatable, and that talking about our problems could bring relief, was truly visionary. Psychoanalysis opened up a new view on mental illness—that talking about problems with a professional could help relieve symptoms of psychological distress. It was, after all, called the "talking cure." Narration can be a very powerful tool. Telling stories can be life changing. Many people in the helping professions have come to realize that the self-examination technique used in the psychoanalytic process can contribute to long-term emotional growth.

Another one of Freud's insights is that bringing information from the unconscious into consciousness widens an individual's area of choice and gives people greater control over their destiny. But Freud also pointed out that acquiring this self-knowledge can be difficult, as we have to counter a number of defense mechanisms that exist to protect us from disturbing information contained in the unconscious. There is no such thing as a quick fix. Dysfunctional behavior patterns need to be worked through. And it takes time to practice different ways of doing things.

## Know Yourself

My argument in this very cursory review of the history of psychoanalysis and its various spinoffs is that many of us would do well to take another look at the helping professions and how beneficial they can be in improving our mental health. Bearing in mind the *caveat emptor* theme of Chap. 9, many people would nevertheless benefit from asking for their assistance. As a psychoanalyst, psychotherapist, and coach myself I am unavoidably biased, but a truth I have learned through my practice is that people who have the courage to do so realize that asking for help can be the greatest gift they give to themselves. The maxim, "Know thyself", inscribed on the Temple of Apollo at Delphi, is as valid today as it was in ancient times. Unravelling the narrative of our life, and embarking on such a personal journey, can be a highly effective way to resolve problems as wide-ranging as self-esteem issues, persistent anxiety problems, stress symptoms, sexual dysfunction, feelings of depression, envy, jealousy, and lack of purpose, as well as many other issues that will trouble us at various stages of our life.

While psychotherapy and executive coaching can awake the demons of the past—reminding people of previous traumas and unhappiness—the process also can be greatly empowering. Asking guidance from a trained professional help us acquire greater insight about troublesome issues, change difficult life situations, and prepare for future challenges. These kinds of interventions can also foster the creative process, encourage psychological risk-taking, help us develop deeper levels of emotional intelligence, and contribute to a greater sense of realism about the vicissitudes of life.

I sometimes ask my clients what they would prefer: having some form of control over their life, or being controlled by unknown forces? Do they prefer to take a passive position, and just see how things unfold, or do they prefer taking actions that enable them to create outcomes of their own choice? Unsurprisingly, most of them express a preference for the former. True freedom is having control over your own life. If you don't, somebody else will.

# 11

## The Rollercoaster Ride of Change

*A Twice-Born person pays attention when the soul pokes its head through the
clouds of a half-lived life. Whether through choice or calamity, the Twice-Born
person goes into the woods, loses the straight way, makes mistakes, suffers loss, and
confronts that which needs to change within himself in order to live a more
genuine and radiant life.*
—William James

*Everyone thinks of changing the world, but no one thinks of changing himself.*
—Leo Tolstoy

In Roman mythology, Janus was a king of Latium (a region of central Italy),
who had his palace on the Janiculum, a hill on the western bank of the River
Tiber. He was proudly venerated as a uniquely Roman god, not one adopted
from the Greek pantheon. The Romans pictured him as having two faces, one
looking forward, the other looking back, so that he could see in both directions simultaneously. All gods of antiquity had a specific purpose, and Janus
was the god of a threshold or gate (the name Janus is etymologically related to
*ianua*, the Latin word for door). Janus himself was the *ianitor*, or doorkeeper,
of the heavens. He oversaw all forms of transition: beginnings and endings,
entrances, exits, and passageways. He held a staff in his right hand, to guide
travelers along the correct route, and a key in his left hand to open gates. His
job was to keep evil spirits out of homes, buildings, shrines, schools, court-
yards, and wherever there was a doorway or gate. Romans took a minute each
day to pray to Janus and thank him for keeping their homes safe from evil.

© The Author(s), under exclusive license to Springer Nature Switzerland AG 2021
M. F. R. Kets de Vries, *The CEO Whisperer*, The Palgrave Kets de Vries Library,
https://doi.org/10.1007/978-3-030-62601-3_11

Janus is also associated with the transition between peace and war. Numa, the legendary second king of Rome, famed for his religious piety, is said to have founded a shrine to Janus Geminus ("two-fold") in the Roman Forum, close to the Senate House. This temple was known for its large, ornate doors, the Gates of Janus. King Numa intended the shrine to be a signifier of peace and war. The doors would be open when Rome was at war and closed whenever it was at peace. For a leader, it was a significant achievement to be able to say that he had closed the gates. Under King Numa, the Gates of Janus are said to have stayed closed for 43 years. But they rarely remained so thereafter.

The ability to deal with transitions, and arrive at some form of conflict resolution, is an essential leadership characteristic. It is also essential for people in the helping profession. The ability to create peace of mind for their clients and help them through transitions is high on their agenda. Like Janus, they try to protect their clients from evil, whatever form it might take.

But as Freud pointed out, helping people through transitions—getting them to change—is never easy. You may need some Janus-like qualities, as change can be a very confusing process. Homo Sapiens is a messy, dynamic, imperfect creature with very rough edges, so if you decide to embark on change, there will be many days when it looks like you are stuck. There will be many times when you will feel low and wonder why you are doing what you are doing. To enable change, you may have to look both backward and forward.

There are many reasons why you might want to change. For example, there may be friction in your relationships with the people close to you. You may have trouble at work. Your children may not be growing up the way you would like them to. You might have conflicts with your partner. You may have unexplained physical problems. Any of these problems will affect your mental state. They make you feel worthless; they make you apathetic. You may end up telling yourself that life is hopeless, that you feel helpless, that you might as well give up. Alternatively, you might say to yourself, I cannot continue living this way. I should do something about it. I need to take control of my life. I need to close the Janus gate.

If you are serious about personal change, the choice is up to you to do something about it. But the armor that fits your personality is not easily penetrable; your character has been formed over many years. Although you may have been quite malleable as a child, by the time you reach adulthood you are pretty well set in your ways. As a grownup, your brain will be more hardwired. You have developed more patterned ways of doing things; you have acquired very specific and habitual methods of dealing with the stresses and strains of your daily life. But although you aren't as malleable as you used to be, this doesn't mean you can no longer change. The mere fact of staying alive means you will be changing constantly, without your realizing it.

## Incremental or Quantum Change?

Of course, there will always be exceptions to this observation. Change can sometimes take a much more dramatic form. I usually differentiate between two forms of change: incremental and quantum-like. Most changes are incremental and linear, but although they may be small, and take place over time, they can add up to very big changes—as you may have discovered yourself. What might appear to the outside world as dramatic change could be the result of an extended series of small adjustments.

Although incrementalism may be your default mode, I have also seen how change can happen in a much more discontinuous and nonlinear fashion. This kind of change should not be dismissed as wishful thinking or a passing delusion. Some of us have been in situations where we were the subject of quantum-like change, when we experienced a sudden personal metamorphosis. In these instances, a dramatic transformation can occur within a relatively short time span, characterized by a deep shift in values, feelings, attitudes, and actions. Some clients have described this process to me in terms of "a bolt from the blue" or "seeing the light." But most often, such a dramatic transformation occurs when a traumatic event or major life challenge has shaken someone's worldview. I have noticed that some kind of turbulence precedes such a change, a rupture in the knowing context or a misalliance of ordinary patterns of perception. Consciously and unconsciously, it impels whoever is subjected to such a change to look for alternative ways to carry on living.

### Being Twice-Born

In my experience, this kind of sudden transformation—these quantum changes—happen to individuals who have had life-threatening experiences—people who have become (to quote the famous psychologist William James) "twice-born."[1] Actually, James went one step further in describing this phenomenon. He noticed some overlap between mystical, religious experiences, and these quantum-like changes. Most often, however, religion excluded, people who are "twice-born" experience a strong sense of renewal after a tragic

---

[1] William James (2013). *The Varieties of Religious Experience*, Full Text of 1901 Edition. Amazon Kindle.

event, such as death, illness, an accident, or another out-of-the-ordinary experience. I have seen how certain challenges and tragedies—and the need to make sense of them—become instrumental in stimulating some people to reach out for a more meaningful life. In light of their personal experiences, they acquire a greater awareness of the fragility of life, the tragic transience of our existence. Whatever setbacks they have had, they come to realize that their time in this world is limited. There is only so much that they can accomplish. The illusion of unlimited power and progress to which they subscribed when they were younger is shattered. This comforting illusion evaporates, however, following a traumatic or life-threatening experience. Nothing confronts us more potently with the finiteness of our existence than the imminence of our own death.

This recognition compels people to stop wasting time. They are left with a greater sense of urgency. They determine to make the most of the time that's left. Given the feeling that time is running out, they are willing to take more risks and step into the unknown. They are ready to change the parts of their life that they no longer find fulfilling. This sense of finiteness may also explain why they are so driven to create meaning in whatever they are doing.

One of my clients, Alain, provides an example of the experience of quantum-like change. Alain was a senior vice president of a large industrial company. At a dinner in a restaurant in an African country he experienced the destruction brought about by a suicide bomber. After this young man detonated his suicide vest, most people in the restaurant died. Alain was "lucky," if that's the appropriate word to use, and survived, but not without many, many months of reparative surgery. After the incident, Alain explained to me, his outlook on life had become quite different. When he was back on his feet and was invited to return to his old position in the company, he refused. He had decided to leave his job. He wanted to devote his life to working with radicalized youth. He told me that he felt that he had been given a second chance in life—and wanted to use it in what was, for him, the most meaningful manner.

From what I know of people who have had such an experience, they suddenly realize the untapped potential at their disposal. Like Alain, this may lead to a shift in values or goals, but it can also mean freedom from unhealthy behaviors, changes that lead to greater inner peace. Alain had a much more upbeat outlook on life after his terrifying experience. He no longer whined about things that had happened in the past. He welcomed the chance to take on new assignments, whereas he would previously have been reluctant to do so. He cherished what the present offered him. He told me, "Why complain about things that I can't or am not willing to change?" *Carpe diem*—seize the day—became a major leitmotiv of Alain's life. It was as if he had discovered a new, meaningful reality, as if an important truth had been revealed to him. As an aside, Alain said that although making big life changes was scary, what he found even scarier was the possibility of not doing something and regretting it later.

I have my own perspective on this. More than a decade ago, I was in the mountains of Kamchatka in Siberia, visiting what's probably one of the wildest places on Earth, and looking for the giant brown bears that live in the region. My snowmobile driver suddenly shouted at me to hurry up and jump on the back seat of his vehicle. He had seen one of these bears climb onto the next ridge and was thoroughly overexcited. He wanted to have a closer look, so we went full throttle after the bear. With his attention fixed on our target, my driver failed to notice a deep crevice in the snow. After the crash, he didn't have a scratch on him but for me the accident turned out to be a life transforming experience. When I regained consciousness—I must have been out for only a short time—the first thing I heard was him telling me, "No problem, antibiotics." But antibiotics were not going to be the answer to what turned out to be a broken spine. Descending the icy slopes on a sledge without the help of painkillers was one of the most grueling experiences of my life. Returning to Paris from the other side of the world was another excruciating affair. Then having to lie immobile in bed for many, many months due to a series of spine operations was yet another endurance test. During that period, like Alain, I was repeatedly told that I had been "lucky," as I was only a few millimeters away from being paralyzed for life. Perhaps the "lucky" part was that this experience gave me a greater appreciation of the preciousness of life—the need to live it to the fullest. It also taught me—lying flat and miserable in a hospital bed—something about the kindness of strangers. It made me aware of how powerful small gestures can be. Ever since, I have actively practiced similar small gestures. To put a positive spin on a horrifying accident, I believe my experience has added to my effectiveness as a helping professional. There is some truth in the saying that changed people change people.

As I said earlier, and despite my personal experience of it, quantum change is rare. Most of us, despite our conscious good intentions, find our unconscious takes a very different look at the dynamics of change. These unconscious resistances explain why we are often so reluctant to undertake a change effort. While we say that we want to change, our unconscious says something very different. Far too often, our fear of the unknown makes us cling to status quo behaviors that might have been highly effective in the past but that have become dysfunctional in the present. We seem to be blocked by hidden forces. In resisting change, we focus more on what we have to give up, instead of what we could gain. Strangely, we might have become too attached to our neuroses. Hardwired as we are to specific patterns of behavior, we are very good at finding excuses for not doing what seems to be in our best interest. This explains both our immunity to change and why the process of change takes a lot of courage.[2]

## Only *You* Can Change Your Life

Whether we like it or not, life is about change. Sometimes we know a change will happen; sometimes change comes suddenly and unexpectedly. All of us will experience transitions in work and relationships, changes in our physical and mental health, and new events in our local communities and the wider world. Some changes are inevitable, the result of physical aging, and part of the natural cycle or order of things. Other changes are more or less under our control, the result of encounters with significant others—family, friends, colleagues, and other intimates. Still other changes—like Alain's experience or my Kamchatkan date with destiny—are the result of accidents. But whatever the situation, it is much wiser to change before we need to.

As I emphasize throughout this book, the process of changing from what you are to what you would like to become can be arduous, but it can also be very rewarding. And while you cannot change your destination instantly, you can do a lot to change the direction you take. What this process of change is going to look like will very much depend on your outlook. One thing is sure, however, spending time and energy on finding excuses for not changing is not the answer, as change is going to catch up with you. And as a matter of fact, fighting the old may become a self-defeating strategy; it's much more constructive to build on the new and decipher the hidden forces that hold you back. In short, the most effective way of dealing with change is to embrace it. Hasn't it been said, if you never change your mind, why bother to have one?

Human nature being what it is, there are times when I wish my work was not so complicated. It is hard work to help people out of their comfort zones. It is difficult to help people who are stuck in vicious circles. It is hard to have to tell people that if they are beating a dead horse, it is high time to dismount. We should remember that we are likely to repeat what we don't repair. On the positive side, however, although bad things happen to everyone—while we cannot change the past—we don't have to perpetuate it. Thus, although it

---

[2] Robert Kegan and Lisa Laskow (2009). *Immunity to Change: How to Overcome It and Unlock the Potential in Yourself and Your Organization*. Boston, MA: Harvard Business Review Press.

may be difficult to forget the past, we can build on it to create a new future. I sometimes remind my clients of the old Texan saying, "If all you ever do is all you've ever done, then all you'll ever get is all you ever got."

If you were my client, I would tell you that the key to creating a new future is that you have to face what has happened to you, accept that certain things can't be changed, and then move on. Instead of worrying about what you cannot control, shift your energy to what you can control. Also, don't be driven by fear—be driven by hope. In many cases, once you're able to move on and close old doors behind you, new doors may open, and better opportunities come your way. We often find our greatest strengths in our darkest moments.

## Where Do You Want to Go?

If you want to change parts of your life, it is important that you clarify what you really want. What do you want to accomplish? This might sound obvious, but there is not much hope you will get what you want unless you have a better idea what that is. It's important to have clarity about your goals—so, why don't you close your eyes and imagine the best possible version of you. Visualize the life you would like to have. And if that's what you really want to be, let go of any part of you that doesn't believe it. Try to hear beyond those negative voices.

I have learned from experience that most people don't take the time out to actually do this kind of thing. They never visualize the kind of life they want for themselves. Given their brain structure, it is something they can do. And, even if they are dissatisfied with their present situation, they never ask themselves why they don't try to work toward a new kind of life. But if only they would clarify what they really want, they could work toward whatever that is with a greater sense of purpose. This is why having clarity about your goals is so important. There is something to be said for living less out of habit and more for intent.

## Endings or Beginnings?

You may want to figure out where you are on your life's journey. Are you at the beginning, the middle, or the end? And perhaps the end is not really the end. More confusingly, what you see as a beginning could also be an end. What's more, a bad beginning doesn't necessarily keep you from having a good ending. Thus, while you can't go back and change the beginning, you can start where you are and change the ending. But one thing is sure, you will never get a new ending if you keep starting with the same tired beginning. Just because the past may not have turned out the way you wanted, doesn't mean your future can't be better than you've ever imagined.

While you are on the journey that's your life, remember that the path is not always going to be smooth or even clearly marked. Sometimes there will be strange detours. But, while taking these off-piste excursions, try to enjoy the journey. Also, it's good to stop every now and then and appreciate the view from right where you are. And realize that it is okay to make mistakes and it's okay to not be good at everything. What will show your true mettle, however, is your ability to get up after a fall. Don't let what you can't do interfere with what you can do. And don't measure your progress by someone else's ruler. Own your own life.

# 12

## The Whisperer's Dance

*Look at the world around you. It may seem like an immovable, implacable place.*
*It is not. With the slightest push—in just the right place—it can be tipped.*
—Malcolm Gladwell

It must be clear by now that I see my major role in life is to guide my clients when they decide to make changes to their lives. Hopefully, these will be changes for the better. I have had the good fortune to be present on many occasions when the people I worked with became unstuck and I helped them to reach a tipping point—the crucial moment in time when they were prepared to change. Perhaps that's the reason why, on occasions, some of my clients have called me a CEO whisperer. I remember laughing the first time one of them gave me this moniker, shortly after the 1998 movie *The Horse Whisperer* came out. Based on the novel of the same title, the movie starred Robert Redford as the eponymous horse whisperer, a man with an in-depth understanding of how to communicate with horses.

The movie tells the story of two teenagers who go out for a winter morning's horseback ride. As they chat away happily, their horses suddenly lose their footing on the icy ground, slide across a road, and are hit by a truck: one of the girls and her horse are killed. The other has her right leg amputated. Her horse, which miraculously survives, is traumatized, seemingly beyond help.

Desperate for help dealing with the calamity of her daughter and horse, the girl's mother hears about a horse whisperer, a cowboy who can communicate with horses. According to these accounts, this person re-educates horses, returning them to normal after accidents or ill-treatment. The mother decides to bring her daughter and the horse to horse whisperer and ask him to deal with their trauma. He turns out to be a man of great patience, who, faced with a mother, child and horse in great need, heals the horse, dissolves the girl's mental trauma, and, to boot, helps the mother become less of a workaholic. (Horse whisperers are a real thing: their deep understanding of horse psychology enables them to interpret a horse's body language and elicit their cooperation.)

After I saw the movie, I understood my client's comment. Instead of whispering to horses, however, I whisper to executives, many of whom (in spite, or because, of all their successes) have acquired dysfunctional behavior patterns. I see my task as helping them overcome dysfunctionalities that range from compulsive, to narcissistic, to bipolar behavior patterns. For my work to be effective, I need to be able to interpret my clients' verbal and non-verbal communication.

## The Working Alliance

When faced with challenging C-suite executives I initiate a whisperer's "dance." To make this "dance" work, I need to take a number of steps. The first is to establish a working or therapeutic alliance.[1] This is an important clinical concept that helps explain the dynamics of change and why change can take time.

What is a working alliance? Basically, it is how I connect, behave, and engage with each of my clients. It pertains to the feelings of trust between me and my client that allow us to work together effectively. A working alliance is also characterized by mutual respect—the confidence that both parties feel genuinely understood and valued—but an effective working alliance will also include an agreement about goals, what my role will be and what my client wants to accomplish. Importantly, a purposeful collaborative relationship between me and my client correlates with positive progress. Therefore, if you are the client, you should always keep in mind that the quality of the working alliance will be a much better predictor of whether the intervention works than whatever your preference is for a particular orientation to therapy or coaching.

When I am building a working alliance, in which trust is the critical factor, I have to pay attention to the peculiarities unique to each of my clients. A

---

[1] Ralph R. Greenson (1967). *The Technique and Practice of Psychoanalysis*. New York: International Universities Press.

further complicating factor is that my whisperer's dance never plays out in a vacuum; it unfolds within a specific context. Predictably, given the variations between individuals' characters, there are going to be situations where the relationship does not click and where the dance grinds to a halt. Occasionally, I will not be the right person for a specific client.

I have found that the secret in building a working alliance with challenging executives depends not only on what I whisper to them, but also, and equally importantly, the way I listen to what they whisper back to me. For CEO whisperers, deep, active listening is an essential requirement to be able to decipher the verbal and non-verbal clues that clients present. I have to listen carefully not only to the things that are being said, but also to the things that are *not* being said. In addition, not knowing, and being prepared to accept not knowing, is part of the challenge as a whisperer. Frustrating though this is, I need to be able to tolerate my ignorance, which is not easy as, like most people, I would prefer some form of closure.

## Countertransference

My ability to be empathic and sensitive is the bedrock of my work as a whisperer. Empathy refers to my capacity to experience what others experience while still being able to attribute these experiences to the other and not to myself. The way I relate emotionally to my client—right brain to right brain or unconscious to unconscious—is essential in creating this kind of attachment bond. I need to be able to recognize the client's early emotional patterns and become conscious of them as separate from myself, so as to be able to use this information effectively.

This is what is meant by countertransference—the redirection of my feelings toward my client—in other words, I need to untangle my personal emotional entanglement with my client, that is, my emotional reaction to my client's statements—how I unconsciously project my feelings onto the client. I need to decipher what my client is trying to enact and how I am tempted to react to the material he or she presents, and then help both of us not to act out our usual scripts but to create a new, healthier outcome. I have described this process as "using myself as an instrument."[2] I should not acquiescence under pressure (in spite of the fact that certain lines in a client's script may reverberate with my own script) and buy into the client's script. What I need to

---

[2] Manfred. F. R. Kets de Vries (2009). *Reflections on Character and Leadership: On the Couch with Manfred Kets de Vries*. San Francisco: Jossey-Bass.

engineer in these situations is a reenactment, but a reenactment with a twist. The outcome must be different.

Countertransference serves as a sensitive interpersonal barometer, a finely tuned instrument in the field of social interaction. But how countertransference is used in the dance between me and my client can make the interface either helpful or problematic. It always remains extraordinary difficult to figure out how the other feels. It means that I have to be extremely cautious of not projecting my own feelings onto the other.

Furthermore, while countertransference is undeniably an important source of data, it is not always a source of hard evidence. The information that can contribute to greater understanding needs to be sorted out carefully in the interchange. Complicating this sorting process is the fact that I need to operate on two alternating levels: I have to be an objective observer of my client's ideas and emotions while also being a subjective receiver. I need to sort out the "me" from the "not-me." And I need to handle these two levels deftly, using my subjective emotional life actively and directly in the dyadic interchange.

As with any dance, the opening steps are critical. I know from long experience that the first encounter with a client will always be the trickiest one. It is the moment of mutual assessment when we determine if we will be able to work together. If my potential client doesn't feel engaged or doesn't feel that he or she can build some kind of relationship with me, there is very little chance that a working alliance will be established.

## Transitional Space

To nudge my clients along in this dance, it is important that I show a modicum of understanding of their predicaments. Making them feel comfortable is the first step in creating this working alliance. To make our relationship work, I also need to generate a transitional space—a safe space within which both of us can explore the kinds of changes we are looking for—a space where we can "play."[3] The transitional space can be described as an intermediate area of experiences between our inner and outer world, where fantasy and reality overlap—a space created by both parties. It can be a strange and confusing place but also be one with great potential, enabling creativity.

But in order to "play," my clients need to feel safe, accepted, respected, and comfortable. They should be able to talk to me without the fear of ridicule or judgment. Many people come into a coaching or consulting session fearful of

---

[3] Donald W. Winnicott. (1951) 'Transitional objects and transitional phenomena', in *Collected Papers: Through Pediatrics to Psycho-analysis* (1984), London: Karnac, pp. 229–242.

"letting their guard down." They may fear being laughed at or ridiculed about the problems they present. It will not take much to switch their defenses into overdrive. If they are unable to open up, they will not get much out of the interface. Good interventions are situations where my clients are willing to push themselves out of their comfort zone and try things that are new, unfamiliar, and may even be scary at first.

I try to be careful while creating a safe space. I have seen how easily the magic between client and coach, or therapist can evaporate. Seemingly innocent comments can be perceived as threatening and may jeopardize the working alliance. Clients who feel judged will start withholding information, which impedes progress. Generating an atmosphere of mutual respect depends very much on my openness, degree of warmth, and earnest desire to see things from my clients' perspective. They want my help in achieving their objectives, whatever their objectives turn out to be. Building a strong working alliance also necessitates giving these people reassurance, showing sympathy, and demonstrating tolerance for possible peculiarities. This requires that I come across as non-judgmental, even about a client's values and beliefs that are very different from my own.

As a CEO whisperer I need to demonstrate not only a degree of objectivity about my client's problems but also understanding. In the opening moves of the dance, I am mainly supportive and offer interpretations sparingly. The last thing clients want is to feel that they are being lectured to and controlled. I have discovered that, when appropriate, humor can be a highly effective tool to create a bond between both parties.

As the dance progresses, my challenge is to remain attuned to the person I am whispering to, to generate curiosity, to be gently challenging, and to create a framework for the future relationship. To be able to do so, I encourage people who want to work with me to tell me about their stressors, frustrations, and dissatisfactions. For my part, I need to match their expectations; I need to formulate the goal component of the relationship.

While keeping all these concerns in mind, I always find it useful to wrap up the interchange by asking how the client feels about working with me. This is a way of getting feedback on the initial impact of the dance: whether the client feels safe, really heard, taken seriously, and cared for. Of course, hope is always hovering in the background, in expectation of a successful outcome.

During the opening interview, I ask the client a number of questions to elicit their thoughts and desires. Examples are: What brought you to see me? What do you feel is presently wrong in your work and personal life? What are the issues you would like to work on? What can you say about yourself? What would you like to be different in your life? I also ask them to imagine that they are looking into a crystal ball and tell me their fantasies about the future. In other words, what would they see as the best outcome from working together? After the initial niceties of the opening steps of the dance, I concentrate on the answers to these questions. Essentially, I invite the client to imagine a desired future, and to create a mindset focused on progress.

To help me better understand a client's inner theater and what makes them "tick," I also ask them to tell me something about their personal history, including their childhood experiences, education, the nature of their relationships (I am thinking of attachment patterns), their current living situation, and their career trajectory. I also like to get some sense of my client's life anchors. I am always very careful, however, about questioning my clients about sensitive areas of their lives. While they might talk openly with some people about their sexual desires, intimate relationships, childhood, and work lives, they should be able to decide when, how, and with whom they want to discuss these things. It can take some time before some of these issues emerge in a coaching or therapeutic relationship.

Generally speaking, I prefer to ask open-ended questions and am in favor of having an open-ended, unstructured dialogue. And while I do this, I always look for recurrent themes in the dialogue that represent the client's experiences. I try to link their feelings and perceptions to their past experiences. I draw attention to feelings that they experience as unacceptable and, if the timing is right, I point out the way they avoid their feelings. I focus on the here-and-now relationship I have with the client, drawing connections between my relationship with the client and comparing this to other past and present relationships the client has. (This is the concept of transference, which I discuss in more detail in Chap. 14.)

During the whispering dance, it is of utmost importance to be aware of and adapt to what does and what doesn't work, what resonates and what doesn't, and to balance spontaneity and self-control. Even the client says something that doesn't make sense, I modulate my reaction. I think twice before I challenge the client's views, in case I inadvertently raise issues that the client isn't ready to face. The dance will not progress if I focus too much on unpleasant things in the beginning. My general aim is "to strike when the iron is cold"— the client needs to be ready to digest specific observations. I need to assess how much truth the client can handle and avoid pushing their defenses into overdrive. This means keeping my mouth shut, if necessary. When I make an interpretation, I better make sure the client is ready to hear what I am whispering. At the same time, I refrain from easy praise or false assurances. It is more important to offer the hope that the client can and will change his or her life for the better.

Once a working alliance has been established, I try to pique the client's curiosity and attention by carefully challenging them to reflect on an issue or by making a trial observation or interpretation to see how they respond. The process of *clarification* and *confrontation* becomes important here, although there will always be some confusion whether my questions can be classified as the first or the second, depending on how the recipient perceives them. I am not a stranger to the occasional "wild analysis," either. I accept that, at times, I could be accused of communicating a conclusion without regard to therapeutic tact, interpreting a client's mental life with claims that might not yet be solidly based on the evidence of the case. Tact or no tact, I maintain that serious leader whispering requires delving into uncomfortable, difficult, and vulnerable aspects of your life. While too quick a judgment risks triggering resistances and defenses, seeing how a client reacts to trial observations or interpretations helps me to assess how well the dance is likely to progress.

It will not come as a surprise that character make-up plays an important role in how the dance evolves. From supervising the work of colleagues, I have seen how their personal attributes can have a negative influence on the working alliance, in instances where the executive coach or therapist is too rigid, uncertain, exploitative, critical, distant, tense, aloof, or distracted. Some types of interventions can also have a negative impact on the working alliance, such as over- or under-structuring the intervention, excessive self-disclosure, and inappropriate transference interpretations (trying to make unconscious behavior patterns conscious at inopportune times).

Creating a working alliance is going to be more difficult with clients who are overly defensive, are extremely guarded or quiet, or do not have any idea what they want to get out of the intervention. The client must be willing to engage in the change effort. When people don't have any curiosity about themselves, it doesn't augur well. The whispering process will also be impeded by clients with specific psychological challenges, such as depression, and bipolar, borderline, paranoid, narcissistic, sociopathic, or psychotic personalities.

The psychologists Mary Smith and Gene Glass carried out research into the effectiveness of different types of psychotherapy.[4] The results of nearly 400 controlled evaluations of psychotherapy and counseling were coded and integrated statistically. Generally speaking, the findings provided convincing evidence of the efficacy of psychotherapy. On average they concluded that the typical therapy client was better off than 75% of untreated individuals. More interestingly, they found that the type of therapy received by the client had a limited bearing on the rate of success. Their conclusions support the idea that

---

[4] https://psycnet.apa.org/record/1978-10341-001.

the relationship between the client and the therapist will be the deciding factor for a successful outcome.

## The Rhythm of Change

There is a rhythm to my interventions with clients. They increasingly learn more about their feelings and patterns of thinking and behaving. Although I cannot engineer dramatic "Aha!" moments, I can create an environment conducive to some kind of transformation. There tends to be a specific pathway to getting where they want to be.

First, the client needs to experience a feeling of concern about their current situation. Setting the process of change in motion usually requires a strong inducement in the form of pain or distress—discomfort that outweighs the pleasure of the secondary gains (like sympathy and attention) that create an immunity to change. The trigger could be family tensions, health problems, negative social sanctions, an accident, feelings of isolation leading to a sense of helplessness and insecurity, problem behavior, distressing incidents happening to someone close, or simply daily hassles and frustrations. When isolated incidents of discontent become a steady pattern of unhappiness it becomes difficult to deny that something is wrong. These emotions signal that there will be serious negative consequences of continuing dysfunctional behavior. They set the stage for a tipping point, the preparedness to finally break the status quo.

The insight that drastic measures are required does not automatically compel someone to take action, but it could set in motion a mental process of visualizing alternative scenarios. Having made the transition from denying to realizing that all is not well, a person might be able to move on to a position where they are ready for a reappraisal process. They may come to the point when they realize that neither the passage of time nor minor changes in behavior will improve their situation—indeed, it is likely to become even worse if nothing substantial is done about it.

For Elise, an owner of a luxury goods company, divorce from her husband of many years became her focal event. The divorce made her relatively comfortable life fall apart and served as a wake-up call for her to re-evaluate her lifestyle. Elise made changes at home, for example, deciding to spend more time with her children, and becoming involved in leisure activities that she really enjoyed. But the divorce triggered changes at work, as well. As various repressed feelings came to the surface, she realized that she had been quite unhappy at work. Consequently, her company had been stagnating. She had been on automatic pilot, suppressing her creativity. The divorce crystallized her discontent and provided the impetus for change, helping her to take her organization in new directions.

The third step of the individual change process is some kind of public declaration of intent, which research suggests is a sound indicator of someone having a high degree of commitment to change. Recognizing the language of change is important. Telling others, in a more or less social context, what they plan to do, indicates that someone has reached a certain degree of acceptance of their problem. It shows that traditional defense mechanisms (such as splitting, repression, denial, projection, and rationalization) have largely run their course. In many of my workshops, I have seen how making a public commitment is crucial, because it doubles momentum: it influences not only the person making the commitment, but also to the people in that person's environment. A dialog is set in motion that will lead to further insights, and others will put pressure on the participant to follow-up on his or her commitments. If someone states the intention to give up alcohol, for example, acquaintances who approve of that decision are less likely to offer them a drink and will probably comment if they take one. A public declaration of intent means the willingness to assume a more vulnerable position and to move the problem from a private to a public stage. Someone making a public declaration is expressing a wish to establish a different way of behaving, and to establish a distance from their former, less desirable self.

Eventually, the client may be prepared to take action. Their resistance to change starts to down. Their habitual immune system stops working. They may have acquired new insights about their situation and see new possibilities. Instead of helplessness and hopelessness, their emotional energy has been transferred from the concerns of the past (which contributed to their dysfunctional behavior patterns) to concerns about the present and future. They may feel as if a heavy burden has been lifted. Mentally, they become ready to work toward a more constructive future. And as they progress through the various phases of successful personal change, they may demonstrate a growing ability to give up their old identities and roles and adopt new ones. They begin to reorganize the world in which they live in a significant way. They re-evaluate their life's goals and meanings, let go of the old and accept the new.

I try to help people leave their comfort zones. I try to align people's actions with their desires. I try to help people recognize that they are worthy of respect and love. I try to help them to eliminate the lies from their lives to live more authentically. I try to get them to accept the insanity that comes with being human. I try to improve their social skills. And I try to stimulate the altruistic motive by having them give to others.

As a coach and psychotherapist, I also try to track patterns in the flow of these interactions, with their uneven phases and shifts, their stabilities and instabilities, their progressions and regressions, their repetition and novelty, and their often substantial uncertainty. Multiple ideas, fantasies, representations, relationship patterns, and feelings all merge, changing and transforming each other over time, and transforming their interrelations as well. I need to be constantly aware of the slightest transformations and calibrate them properly. I need to nudge my clients forward.

As a leader whisperer, I coax my clients to examine their lives in order to release their capabilities and help them function at their true potential. Too many people, however, cruise through their life without much reflection about their destination or purpose. I strongly believe that without reflection, these people are just stumbling in the dark, groping for a black cat in a dark room. It is here that leader whisperers can make a real difference, helping their clients to see things as they are, not as they wish them to be.

# 13

# Creating "Aha!" Experiences

*Perhaps the journey towards epiphany is an unseen, steady process towards understanding. Likened to a combination safe, as you scroll the dial towards the inevitable correct combination you cannot tangibly see your progress.*
—Chris Matakas

*Creativity and insight almost always involve an experience of acute pattern recognition: the Eureka moment in which we perceive the interconnection between disparate concepts or ideas to reveal something new.*
—Jason Silva

Regression is an unconscious, emotional defense mechanism in which we revert to behaving the way we used to an earlier stage of our development. As a coping mechanism, regression is an attempt to return to a time when we felt safer than we do in our current state. We felt safe because we were taken care of. Regression can be harmless and subtle, but it can also become problematic and overt. Higher levels of stress will create more dramatic forms of regression. Typically, we see regressive behavior among children, brought about by any traumatic event, stress, or frustration. This doesn't mean, however, that adults can't also regress in response to situations that prompt worry, fright, irritation, and uncertainty.

# Regression in the Service of the Ego

The psychoanalyst Ernst Kris differentiated between two kinds of regression that can occur during the encounter between client and therapist. The first type—simple regression—is revealed when the client abandons age-appropriate coping strategies in favor of earlier, more childish patterns of behavior. In the second type—what Kris called regression in the service of the ego—regression takes a much more constructive form. In these situations, unconscious material rises to consciousness and is used in the service of personal growth and creativity. According to Kris, artists and other creative people in particular resort to this more creative form of regression but in my work with executives I have observed that this regressive pattern is not just the preserve of creative artists. All of us have the ability to regress in a more constructive way. Using mental images derived from our unconscious, we can arrive at alternative ways of thinking, feeling, and behaving.

Some time ago, Louise, the VP Finance of an energy company, presented me with a dream she had had the previous night. In her dream, she was sitting in a taxi that was driving on a narrow country road running alongside a deep ravine. There was snow at the side of the road, which was also icy. The driver was speeding up, ignoring her pleas to slow down. As he kept on driving faster and faster, she became more and more anxious, afraid that the car would slide off the road and fall into the ravine. She felt helpless but also very angry. Suddenly, the landscape of her dream changed. Louise found herself in a strange but also somewhat familiar house, sitting on a chair. She was rocking a crib, trying to calm down a screaming baby. To her great surprise, she managed to calm the baby down—and woke up.

With a little prompting, Louise began a stream of consciousness narrative about her dream. The themes that gradually emerged centered on losing control and wanting to gain control—represented by her lack of control over the taxi driver, and her success in calming down the crying baby. Interestingly, the images of the taxi driver and the baby made Louise think of her husband. Her husband resembled the taxi driver in her dream—out of control. Even though she felt that she was babying him, she also thought that he was uncontrollable. Some of her close friends had told her that he was having an affair but despite the overwhelming evidence they put to her, Louise didn't want to hear any of it. When I pushed her to say more, she said she was scared to confront her husband, as she was dependent on him for emotional support. But as soon as she made this comment, Louise started to cry, and told me that enough was enough. Who was the baby, she wondered? Her husband, who took advantage of her and liked to be babied, or Louise herself? Whatever, she had had enough. She would no longer tolerate the situation. Scary as it might be, it was high time to take charge. She confessed that she was quite worried what would come of her relationship with her husband if she did so. But she realized that she had a lot of things going for her: she was very successful in her job—much more so than her husband. In fact, she was the real breadwinner in the family. Also, most of their friends were fond of her but couldn't care less about her husband. These reflections made her realize that it was high time that she took greater control over her life. It was time to stop being a baby.

In hindsight, the dream turned out be an "Aha!" moment. Before the dream Louise had been terrified by the idea of leaving her husband, scared that if she divorced him, she would become seriously depressed. The idea of being alone frightened her. She was afraid she would never stop crying. In the dream, however, she had the strength to calm down the baby, which stopped crying. Clearly, the associations she made with the dream clarified that it was high time to make changes in her life. She couldn't continue to live as she had been. She realized that her current situation was not sustainable. The dream imagery gave Louise the courage to end her ostrich-like behavior—not wanting to see how her husband was taking advantage of her. Instead of continuing in her passive-dependent mode, she decided to act. She had a serious talk with her husband, telling him that she wanted a divorce. Her dream, in which the baby played a major role as a regressive object, became a turning point in her life.

## "Aha!" Moments and the Amygdala

Unsurprisingly, neuroscientists have been trying to figure out the neural basis of these transformational moments. What's taking place in the brain when these moments occur? What neural activity is associated with this specific type of rapid learning and insight? Fortunately, functional magnetic resonance imaging (fMRI) research has helped us understand how the brain generates the spontaneous and relatively unconstrained thoughts that are experienced when the mind wanders.[1]

---

[1] E. M. Bowden, M. Jung-Beeman (2003). Aha! Insight experience correlates with solution activation in the right hemisphere. *Psychonomic Bulletin and Review*, 10, 730–737; K. Christoff, A. M. Gordon, J. Smallwood, R. Smith, J. W. Schooler (2009). Experience sampling during fMRI reveals default network and executive system contributions to mind wandering. *Proceedings of the National Academy of Sciences of the United States of America*, 106, 8719–8724; G. Claxton (1997). *Hare Brain, Tortoise Mind: How Intelligence Increases When You Think Less*. New York, NY: Harper Collins; A. Dietrich and R. Kanso (2010). A review of EEG, ERP and neuroimaging studies of creativity and insight. *Psychological Bulletin*, 136, 822–848.

From a neurological point of view, the emotional "Aha!" is in part a right brain phenomenon, the intuitive, spontaneous, emotional, and imagistic aspect of mind that allows us access to our unconscious. When we experience an "Aha!" moment, a process in the brain bypasses our more rational thought processes but accesses other parts of the brain to find answers. Thus, when we suddenly get the answer to a riddle or understand the solution to a problem, we can practically feel the light bulb click on in our head.

Neuroscientists have pointed out that the right hemisphere of the brain is critical for the exploratory processing of novel cognitive situations to which none of the preexisting codes or strategies in our cognitive repertoire readily apply. In contrast, the left hemisphere of the brain is critical for processing based on preexisting representations and routinized cognitive strategies. If we can allow our right hemisphere to solve problems and trust it to function out of awareness—not to rely on our left brain's need to "solve" the problem logically—then we are more likely to arrive at these insights. The amygdala, an almond shaped-like brain structure, famously known as the seat of emotions, modulates all of our reactions to events that are important for our survival. Given its central role in emotional management, the amygdala plays a significant role in "Aha!"" moments. As neuroscientists have found out, during these moments of insight, there is high activity in this particular part of the brain. It signals to different cortical regions that an event of significant neural reorganization has occurred, and by doing so incorporates these moments of insight into our long-term memory. Helped by the amygdala, once we have had an "Aha!" experience and realize that there is another way to solve a problem, or when we understand how to perform a task better and faster, we are unlikely to forget that insight. With the help of the amygdala, a new way of looking at things will have affected our brain, contributing to a reshaping of our internal world. Past patterns of thinking, feeling, and acting will be discarded. A shift in attitude and behavior has culminated in the redefinition, and even reinvention, of the self.

## The Ebb and Flow of Associations

Although psychoanalysts had long known that certain interventions were experienced as especially productive by both clients and analyst, Kris was the first to examine these moments systematically. He pointed out that, in the case of regression in the service of the ego, we do not strain to find new memories. As Louise's experience demonstrates, these memories appear unbidden. They just flow forth. And more importantly, the ability to uncover new memories can coincide with the capacity to understand the significance of what is being uncovered. In such "good interventions," associations appear in context, symbolizing significant events and helping to reorganize psychic structure. In Louise's case, her capacity to uncover new associations coincided with her ability to grasp the significance of what had been uncovered.

In a therapeutic situation, Kris noted that such interventions generally began with the patient recounting a recent incident. While talking about what had happened, the client would show some restlessness, or even behave in a negative way. But at a certain point during the interchange a marked change would occur. What was once a pattern of confusion, increasingly assumed greater clarity. As the encounter progressed, things started to fall into place. Whatever material came to the surface, there was little or no resistance in associating to it. New memories and associations became readably available.

When I worked with Louise, all I needed to do was ask her one or two questions and what followed was an avalanche of associations that led to a variety of interpretations. Suddenly, everything seemed to make sense to her. On other occasions she had been hesitant to present material, but when she recounted this particular dream, she was prepared to associate to it. And as she did so, new insights emerged. She saw her situation with great clarity. And this "Aha!" experience brought her a great sense of relief.

Louise's insights were not suggested by me. The interesting thing about "good interventions"—interactions that create "Aha!" experiences—is that the client owns them, making it much more likely that they will take action. Of course, as a CEO whisperer, I am often the catalyst to make it happen—I allow associations to come to the fore and help create "Aha!" moments. But before such a point is reached, I often encounter an increase in resistance and the client may appear to be stuck. This is the point in the interchange when the work between the client and me starts to feel like very heavy lifting. I can usually see this coming. Knowing how to deal with these resistances to change is essential to being able to overcome them. As a CEO whisperer I need to be able to tolerate and deal with these difficult reactions.

## Doing Nothing?

When a client is resistant and stuck, it sometimes feels as if nothing is happening but of course, that's far from the case.[2] There is no such thing as doing nothing. You are only doing nothing when you are brain dead. A better way

---

[2] Manfred F.R. Kets de Vries (2015). Doing nothing and nothing to do: The hidden value of empty time and boredom, *Organizational Dynamics*, 44, 169–175.

of describing this stasis is as part of the process of regression in the service of the ego. Often something much more profound is happening when you look like you're doing nothing. I strongly believe that many people would be better off if they did less and reflected more. *Niksen* is a Dutch term for making the time to do absolutely nothing. Strange as it may sound, being in a *niksen* mode might be the best way to deal with complex issues.

There is a well-known story about the Renaissance sculptor and painter Michelangelo that illustrates this. In 1466, a sculptor called Agostino di Duccio was commissioned to sculpt a figure of David for the cathedral in Florence. He began work on a large marble block from the famous quarries at Carrara in Tuscany but only managed to mark out the shape of the legs, feet, and drapery before he abandoned the project for reasons that have remained unclear. For the next 25 years, this block of marble was left exposed to the weather in the courtyard of the cathedral workshop, until Michelangelo was asked to revive the abandoned project. Although the marble had deteriorated, Michelangelo accepted the assignment. According to the story, soon after, rumors began to circulate that Michelangelo was making very little progress. It was said that he would stare at the marble for hours on end, doing nothing. When a friend saw him and asked the obvious question—"What are you doing?"—Michelangelo replied, "I'm working." Years later, after the block of marble had become the great statue of David, he said, "I saw the angel in the marble and carved until I set him free."

Another anecdotal account of a creative individual actively doing nothing is that of the French mathematician Henri Poincaré. He recounted:

> [...] I left Caen, where I was living, to go on a geologic excursion under the auspices of the School of Mines. The incidents of the travel made me forget my mathematical work. Having reached Coutances, we entered an omnibus to go some place or other. At the moment when I put my foot on the step, the idea came to me, without anything in my former thoughts seeming to have paved the way for it, that the transformations I had used to define the Fuchsian functions were identical with those of non-Euclidian geometry. I did not verify the idea; I should not have had the time, as, upon taking my seat in the omnibus, I went on with a conversation already commenced, but I felt a perfect certainty. On my return to Caen, for conscience' sake, I verified the result at my leisure.[3]

Unfortunately, too many of us are not doing too little but are trying to do too much. Keeping busy has always been a highly effective defense

---

[3] Jacques Hadamard (1945). *Essay on The Psychology of Invention in the Mathematical Field.* Princeton, NJ: Princeton University Press, p. 13.

mechanism, in many instances deployed to ward off disturbing thoughts and feelings. But while you are trying to be busy, you lose sight of how you're really feeling and what is troubling you. Busyness allows no periods of uninterrupted, free-associative thinking, creativity, and insight. Busy people don't realize that allowing unconscious thought processes to come to the surface can be more productive than plugging away at problem solving.

In many instances, I have found that what looks like doing nothing is, in reality, the mind's way of stimulating unconscious thought processes. I am not making excuses for people whose inner life seems vacuous—those who seem to have no interests, who suffer from mental emptiness, don't care about much, or aren't interested in things. For a variety of reasons, these people are hampered by depression or another form of mental incapacity. But most of us have a rich inner life. The question is whether we use the imagery in our inner world creatively? And if so, can we figure out what this inner imagery is telling us?

As we all know, our unconscious excels at integrating and associating information by carrying out associative searches across our broad database of knowledge. While engaged in this process, we are much less constrained by conventional associations and are more likely to generate novel ideas than when we strain to focus consciously on problem solving. However, the outcome of these search processes might not always enter our consciousness immediately, which can be frustrating. Creative solutions take their time to incubate. In the meantime, we should remember the example of Michelangelo.

In my work, I have always seen their ability to balance activity and solitude, noise and quietness, as a great way to tap into my clients' inner creative resources. This can be invaluable in nurturing whatever creative sparks they possess. It can be extremely beneficial to take a step back and consciously unplug from the compulsion to always keep busy; to get away from the habit of shielding themselves from certain feelings; to turn down the volume of life. This will bring them to regions of the mind they are usually busily avoiding. But this is exactly the place where they are more likely to generate novel ideas. By inducing unconscious thought through reflection—seemingly doing nothing—they can modify the nature of their search for innovative solutions to complex issues. What may appear like doing nothing may turn out to be the best path to solving knotty problems. Of course, this is easier said than done. Many work situations are not exactly conducive to this kind of approach, given the need to look busy.

Another one of my clients—let's call him Michael—the CEO of a consumer goods company, told me that he felt excessively tired, even burned out, and depressed. I assumed that a high degree of stress and anxiety was inevitable, given the fast-paced environment he worked in. The incessant demands of his many direct reports, the endless stream of emails and voice messages, contributed to the question he kept asking himself: why was he doing what he was doing? Wasn't there another way to live his life? As he made his way to work each day, Michael would be overwhelmed by the many responsibilities he had to deal with. He told me that by the time he arrived at work he was often ready to explode (or was it implode?). At the office, he found himself thinking how much he disliked his job. Work gave him little or no pleasure.

I asked Michael if there was anything that made him feel alive? Was there anything that energized him? He couldn't respond to these questions immediately. He was incapable of discerning the themes that were really important to him. His manic behavior put him into too much of a fog. He was unable to see connections. Instead, he compared his life to drowning in quicksand. Keeping himself very busy was his escape mechanism.

As I listened to Michael, my thoughts were that he needed to overcome his sense of being victimized. He needed to stop complaining and instead become the master of his own fate. I decided that as a starter, I needed to make him more aware of why he was behaving the way he did. What were his trigger points? I wanted him to become more intimate with his thoughts, feelings, and emotions.

Initially, my questions only increased Michael's sense of confusion. Whatever I said, nothing sank in. My contributions were water off a duck's back. Eventually, when we had established some kind of a working alliance, an entry point was provided by the results of his Inner Theater Inventory (see Chap. 9 for more about this tool). The results moved Michael away from his defensive mode and out of his comfort zone. I pressed him about some of the issues the inventory raised. What would he like to see for his children? What values did he want them to embrace? Would they like the role model he presented? How did he think his behavior affected them? As he responded, Michael became more willing to address the issues that were really important to him. He made a conscious effort to take time out for himself—time to think. And, as I had expected, he didn't like what he saw. He began to reflect on his relationship with his parents and how they had affected him. He started to recognize repetitive patterns and that he was behaving in a similar way to his parents. This made him afraid that he would transfer these behavior patterns to his children. He realized that he was stuck in a rut. This insight became a turning point in our relationship, an "Aha!" experience.

From that point on, Michael learned to make sense of his associations and watched the emerging imagery with an attitude of curiosity. He became more aware of the triggers that led to his feeling of explosion or implosion. In our subsequent meetings, Michael brought along an increasing amount of material about his work and his private life. It was as if a dam had been broken. Many previously repressed memories came to the surface, making our interactions truly flow. I would make observations about the associations he offered, paying attention to his feelings, his past experiences, and his own theories about life. I made an effort not to become didactic or to lecture him.

My challenge during this period was to help Michael discover the truth about himself, his life, and his feelings and enable him to make the changes needed for him to function more satisfactorily. Not long after this "Aha!" experience, he took a number of creative steps that had a life-changing effect. He went way beyond superficial change. He decided to step out of his comfort zone, stop complaining, and take action.

Michael sold the family business. As he was now financially secure, he decided to go back to university, and restart his aborted studies in archeology. He realized that archeology was what really interested him. He had reached the moment when all the pieces of the puzzle that made up his life were falling into place. He also worked hard on his relationship with his children. As he took these steps, the pendulum of depressive thoughts shifted from despair to hope.

In the field of coaching and therapy, when "Aha!" moments" occur, specific patterns of behavior are illuminated, and at the same time the way to change these patterns becomes clearer. A visible shift occurs in the client. It is as if the brain makes a connection and registers the insight, comparable to flipping a light switch. At these split-second moments in time, I was often able to observe my clients gain new perspectives and understanding of their personal selves, the issues with which they were struggling, and how they were impacting others. "Aha!" moments" are great learning experiences.

Knowledge is power and since most people are not completely aware of the personal challenges they face, awareness needs to take place before behavior change or self-growth can occur. Much preliminary work needs to be done before "Aha!" moments of insight happen. What may seem spontaneous and dramatic is the result of all the work going on behind the scenes. Already more than a century ago, the great scientist Louis Pasteur said, "Chance favors the prepared mind." He realized that sudden flashes of insight don't just happen out of the blue but are the product of lengthy periods of preparation. But when a tipping point has been reached, I have seen, over and over again, how a person's self-limiting beliefs and negative conditioning evaporate. I have witnessed the disappearance of automatic patterns of thinking and behaving that have kept people from living life to its fullest. It is at this point that the person will be willing to consider new hopes and dreams and be prepared to live life with greater authenticity and purpose.

These "light bulb" moments can be compared to an epiphany—a sudden manifestation of the essence or meaning of something that will (or can) contribute to significant change. This intuitive perception of or insight into the reality or essential meaning of something that comes out of the blue, can make deep and lasting healing a real possibility.

Once individual clients understand their problems, they may still need more help to get past former behavior patterns. Insight alone is not enough. They need to learn how to modify their maladaptive behavior into something more constructive. In particular, if they're caught in a cycle of dysfunctional behavior that's causing problems for them, even if they begin to know why they're doing what they are doing, they will be wise to continue to seek help. This is where I, as a whisperer, continue to give assistance—to help them with the steps that lie ahead. And while doing what I am doing, I always keep in mind that whispering is all about the client. It is all about helping clients make choices; to make them realize that they are not passive recipients of whatever life throws at them. Surprisingly enough, the ability to take a proactive stand, to see that they have a choice about their own wellbeing, is an eye opener for many. But when they accept that this is possible, it will have a forceful stress-reducing effect. It's my hope that through subtle guidance, I will continue to induce my clients to engage in these forms of regression in the service of the ego—while they also appreciate the value of doing nothing.

# 14

## Are You a Prisoner of Optical Illusions?

*Transference…dominates the whole of each person's relations to his human environment.*
—Sigmund Freud

*Knowing your own darkness is the best method for dealing with the darkness of other people.*
—Carl Jung, *letter to Kendig B. Cully, 25 September 1931;* Letters *vol. 1 (1973)*

After settling himself in an easy chair in my office, Dirk told me he was puzzled about something that had just happened. He had asked Nancy (a recently hired senior executive), to come to his office to discuss their future working relationship, nothing more. When he mentioned that she might want to deal more proactively with a number of the company's clients, she suddenly became angry, started to cry, to ran out of his office. He wondered what he had done to cause such an explosive reaction. Nancy was a very valuable employee with much expert knowledge. It had taken quite some effort to get her on board. But given her strange, inappropriate behavior, Dirk wondered if they could really build a productive working relationship?

He learned from the HR director, who had lunch with Nancy, that she seemed to be utterly confused after the incident. She kept on repeating during the lunch, why had she reacted the way she did? What had happened? Usually, she was in control of her emotions. This time, however, Dirk's comments about her being able to do better had somehow been a red flag. The way he had talked to her had made something snap inside, and she just could not control herself. Now she was embarrassed about her emotional outbreak—confused about what had made it happen. If only she could understand what had caused this inexplicable reaction.

## Optical Illusions

Think of what went wrong between Dirk and Nancy as an optical illusion. Optical illusions reveal how easy it is to trick our brains into seeing something simply because we expect to see it, even if it isn't actually there. When we see a picture or an object that we have not encountered before, our brain tries to make sense of it by putting shapes and symbols together like pieces of a jigsaw puzzle. And when we do not quite understand the picture or object, our eyes send information to our brains forcing us see something that does not really match reality. This—seeing something that isn't there—is an optical illusion. Our brain takes a shortcut by making assumptions about how the world should be instead of how the world actually is. An interesting example of this is the Ehrenstein illusion, devised by the German psychologist Walter Ehrenstein (see Exhibit 14.1).[1]

The four lines produce an entirely imaginary circle at their center. When you see the picture, your brain tries to make sense of it by spontaneously creating a figure based on similar round figures you have been exposed to in the past. In short, your brain acts as a sort of pattern matching and pattern generating machine, and when things aren't already in the expected patterns, it tries to make sense of what it sees by fitting it into familiar shapes. Like a computer program, your previous experiences are used as a shortcut to understanding and interpreting new information. And this makes a lot of sense: if a

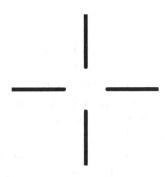

**Exhibit 14.1**   The Ehrenstein illusion

---

[1] Ehrenstein Illusion (http://www.newworldencyclopedia.org/entry/Ehrenstein_illusion).

match can be found between new and old data, then your stored knowledge can be applied to the new situation at much less "cost" (energy) than your brain having to figure it all out once again.

The same kind of sense making process is at play when it comes to your relationships with other people. Drawing on your existing relationship data bank, your brain unconsciously organizes new experiences in such a way that they fit the relationships that you are familiar with. Thus, when you are trying to understand someone you don't know well, but who reminds you of a previous acquaintance, your brain tricks you into assuming that this person will behave similarly to the familiar other. You feel good about a person who reminds you of a loved one and alarm bells will go off in your brain if a person reminds you of someone in your life who caused you pain. In this way, you often attribute to people characteristics that aren't really there, automatically and without thinking. We tend to slot people into boxes: good boxes, bad boxes, and boxes that leave us indifferent.

## Transferential Processes

Looking at in Nancy's experience, we might imagine that she had a rather authoritarian father who often criticized her and with whom she had frequent fights. If she has this kind of history, and if Dirk happens to remind Nancy of her father, Nancy's will respond to Dirk's perceived criticism with a similar emotional outburst to the one she would have had with her father in the past. The same kind of pattern matching that explains why we are tricked by optical illusions is at play here: we perceive and react to people in the present based on our experiences in the past.

This erroneous interpersonal connection was first described by Sigmund Freud in his famous Dora case study. He called it transference.[2] Freud understood that the reason for his unsuccessful therapeutic intervention with Dora lay in his failure to recognize the projection of emotions that pertained to a person from Dora's past onto Freud himself. Subsequently, but belatedly, he understood that a person's transferential reactions revealed a lot more about them than a patient could put into words. Freud realized that transference could be used as an important instrument in therapy. Like many other psychodynamically oriented therapists, coaches, or consultants, I view transference issues as central to my work. Transference reactions, like other fundamental human processes, reveal and illuminate motives and thoughts

---

[2] http://staferla.free.fr/Freud/Freud%20complete%20Works.pdf.

that otherwise would remain hidden, even from the person who is enacting these feelings. But these transferential reactions provide me with a window into what my clients desire and what they want to avoid. They illuminate motives they are often unaware of, or don't want to see. They reveal their secret prejudices and their unfulfilled wishes. But knowing what I do about transference, I always keep in mind that everything that irritates me about others tells me something about myself. As the novelist Hermann Hesse put it, "If you hate a person, you hate something in him that is part of yourself. What isn't part of ourselves doesn't disturb us."

In essence, transference is a psychological phenomenon characterized by the unconscious redirection of feelings from one person to another. It's really an interpretation and an illusion, generated inside the brain when it is trying to make sense of the world. It is a universal, interpersonal phenomenon—a special form of displacement—to be viewed as a kind of repetition. This repetition may be an exact duplication of the past, or it could turn into a modified or distorted version. People caught up in transference, however, are not aware what they are doing (although they can be made aware of it).

As transference reactions concern reliving the past, often (as in the case of Nancy) the reaction can become inappropriate, even bizarre, in the context of the present. Of course, the original sources of transference reactions are the important people in our early years. They usually are our parents and other caregivers, siblings, and other close family members, in short, the dispensers of love, comfort, and punishment. Given the important role they play in our inner theater, it will not come as a surprise that transference reactions tend to be directed toward people who perform similar roles to those originally carried out by our parents. Physicians, teachers, performers, celebrities, and in general, authority figures are particularly prone to activate transference responses. In my role as a helping professional, I am highly conscious that I am an easy subject of transference reactions. Coming back to my expression of "using myself as an instrument," it is one of the most important "tools" in my repertoire. In the various roles I play vis-à-vis clients, my greatest instrument is myself.

It is transference when you fall in love at first sight with a person who reminds you of someone with whom you had once an intense relationship. It is transference when you trust someone immediately, without realizing that this person reminds you of a trusted figure from the past. It is transference if you are enthralled by a politician who resembles an encouraging and supportive grandfather. It is transference when you instantly mistrust someone because that person bears some resemblance to the black sheep of the family in manners, appearance, or demeanor. And you might also have an instant "negative" transference reaction when being introduced to a complete stranger, as this person may remind you of your overbearing mother or a critical father. Thus, in any interpersonal encounter, there are many people present, in reality and in fantasy. There will be the other person, but also looming in the background are memories of significant people from the past, which distorts our perceptions of the other. Actually, from the point of view of perception, in every two-person encounter, there are not two, but six people in the room: what each person is; what each person thinks he or she is; and what each person thinks the other is. This is why interpersonal relations can be so complex.

Transference reactions can be very seductive. In projecting magical qualities on me—being connected to someone bigger and more powerful than they imagine themselves to be—my clients hope they will be transformed. It helps boost their self-esteem and well-being. This is the idealizing transference that I mentioned in Chap. 9. My challenge becomes to bring these people back to reality. If I accept their fantasies, gratifying as they might be to me, my clients will remain diminished. This means I need to pay sharp attention to my own countertransference reactions. I need to hold what my clients transfer toward me, make sense of it, and not be seduced by it. I need to keep my head, in spite of some very powerful projections.

## Recognizing Transference

All of us should be able to recognize transference reactions due to their inappropriateness (they don't fit the current situation), intensity (they are characterized by intense emotional reactions), ambivalence (simultaneous opposing feelings), capriciousness (a inconstant, erratic, whimsical aspect), and tenacity (a rigid holding on to them). The most outstanding characteristic, however, is the complete inappropriateness of the reaction.

Transference reactions happen all the time and in moderation are not worrisome. They can create problems, however, when our reactions become excessive, and when they prevent us from building an appropriate relationship with someone who can have a strong influence on our lives, whether privately or at work. And when we are prone to repetitive, excessive transference reactions, they are a sign that we are troubled by deeper issues or unfinished business from the past.

While your unconscious transference reactions can easily lead you astray, creating awareness of them can make you more appreciative of your hidden motivations and help you to avoid or repeat mistakes and so be more in control of your life. Without this awareness, unchecked transference reactions can easily wreak havoc on important professional relationships. In Nancy's case, Dirk's response was colored by her strong and inappropriate reaction, making it hard for both of them to build a healthy working relationship based on their real-time interactions and personalities.

## Creating Awareness

There are different ways to become more aware of your own transference reactions by trying to make a greater part of your unconscious, conscious. Here are two suggestions that will help you arrive at a better understanding:

- Reflect on patterns of behavior that have gotten you into trouble, and where you feel your judgment has been repeatedly poor. To help you with this self-analysis, ask yourself the following questions: What kinds of people make me feel mad, sad, bad, or glad? What do I like or dislike about these people? Who in your past do these people remind you of? In what way are they similar/different?
- Find a psychologically astute executive coach or therapist who can help you recognize your transference reactions. I am always aware that clients will bring the template for how they deal with relationships into the consulting space and transfer them to me. If I handle these reactions correctly, my transference interpretations allow my clients to re-experience childhood conflicts in the safety of the space in which we are working. Working with emerging relationship patterns will point out that clients might be angry at me because I remind them of their dominating father, or that I'm being idealized because I remind my client of a much-loved grandmother. With the help of these kinds of interpretations, these past conflicts can be worked through to a satisfactory conclusion.

To cut a long story short, recognizing transferential reactions helps me (and everyone dealing with the complexities of interpersonal relationship) to be more effective. Taking the client's perspective, it's also quite helpful for them to separate the past from the present so that the ghosts and imprints of the past no longer interfere with their life in the present. By becoming aware of the reasons why repetitive and inappropriate behavior occurs, they may be encouraged to find new ways to deal with old dangers—a belated mastery of old anxieties. In the words of Sigmund Freud, "Out of your vulnerabilities will come your strength."

# 15

# The Loneliness of Command

*It's only lonely at the top if you forget all the people you met along the way and fail to acknowledge their contributions to your success.*
—Harvey Mackay

*People say it's lonely at the top, but I sure like the view.*
—Charlie Sheen

Recently, Patricia, the CFO of a large industrial enterprise, asked to meet me. I decided to see her for lunch, when she took the opportunity to complain non-stop about her CEO. She explained that while he had held regular meetings with his top team at the start of his tenure, these meetings were now rare. According to Patricia, her boss now spent most of his time brooding in his office. Organizational morale was affected by his erratic behavior during meetings. He frequently lost focus, had bouts of anger, and would harass some of the people present. Not surprisingly, the CEO's mercurial way of dealing with his people didn't augur well for the future of the company. And the figures spoke for themselves. Sales had been dropping sharply. Given the company's dismal financial picture, some subordinates even wondered whether their CEO was falling apart in front of their eyes. Patricia wanted to know from me if there was anything she could do about it.

It's a cliché that it's lonely at the top, but for many top executives it's all too true. Being in a leadership position can be quite isolating. A CEO's responsibility comes with unique challenges: sleepless nights, tight deadlines, and constant worries about having made the right decisions. Often, C-suite executives are under a lot of pressure—the kind of emotional strain that most

© The Author(s), under exclusive license to Springer Nature Switzerland AG 2021
M. F. R. Kets de Vries, *The CEO Whisperer*, The Palgrave Kets de Vries Library,
https://doi.org/10.1007/978-3-030-62601-3_15

employees never experience. This sense of isolation can create an aura of aloofness and distance, which, in turn, makes it even harder to be effective within the organization.

I have observed over and over again that the incessant stress of years of working too hard makes CEO burnout a real threat, especially if there are no support systems to contain the pressure. Often, there is nobody with whom CEOs can share their concerns. Men in particular (in traditional cultural contexts they are more likely to take their family and friends for granted) will let relationships take a back seat to their professional ambitions. If they continue to neglect these relationships, however, they may find themselves with nobody to rely on when times are tough. And tragically, in trying to cope with their loneliness, they may resort to patch-up solutions, such as having affairs, or turn to alcohol and drugs.

Despite the fact that the loneliness of command is such a serious problem, it's an issue that is rarely addressed upfront. Instead of giving it due attention, I have seen many C-suite executives make a heroic effort to keep up the façade of being a superman or superwoman. Of course, there will always be some decisions that need to be taken alone. But how lonely can you be? What is so bad about having confidants? However, too many C-suite executives go to great lengths to maintain an exterior of unflappable confidence, desperately concealing any signs of insecurity or anxiety. And maybe it is the thing to do. Perhaps, they are forced to act in this manner. Who wants a waffling CEO to run the business? Isn't confidence needed to inspire confidence in others? Weren't ancient kings often killed when they showed any signs of weakness?

What these executives don't seem to realize is that this kind of charade puts an extraordinary amount of pressure on them. Needing to be strong all the time can be very exhausting. Sadly enough, many C-suite executives don't recognize the high price they pay for their pursuit of success and power. This façade of being in control—the Lone Ranger approach to leadership—will eventually have a negative effect on individual, team, and organizational performance, as illustrated by the dramatic drop in the average tenure of CEOs.[1]

Concepts taken from the clinical paradigm can help us understand the psychodynamics at play with respect to top executives. To start with, people in these positions should realize that when they become number one, a power distance is created, making it much harder to speak to anyone with vulnerability and true honesty. What was once a complex network of interrelationships—offering     many     possibilities     to     unburden     challenges     and

---

[1] https://www.equilar.com/blogs/351-ceo-tenure-drops-to-five-years.html; https://corpgov.law.harvard.edu/2018/02/12/ceo-tenure-rates/.

frustrations—changes dramatically when an executive reaches a top position. The leader starts bearing the weight of responsibility for others, often having to make many decisions alone.

Not only do newly promoted executives experience a sense of unease at being in the number one position, their former colleagues undergo their own sense of unease in dealing with their new boss. Whatever well-meant efforts CEOs try to make to reduce this power distance, their subordinates will always be cognizant of the power their boss holds—that he or she can make decisions that might dramatically affect their careers, typically promotions and salary increases. Given the discomfort experienced by both parties, distancing becomes a rational response to an unnerving situation. In these circumstances, I have observed how many CEOs become engaged in a delicate dance: they have to be close enough to relate to their subordinates but far enough away to motivate them. Getting too close might lead to accusations of favoritism. On the other hand, if they are too distant, they might be judged as cold and aloof. Whatever they do, they are to some extent damned.

Given the complex psychological forces at play, CEOs would be wise to pay attention to a number of things when assuming a top management position.

## Being the Target of Hostile, Envious Feelings

One of the things that contributes to the loneliness of command is the way these executives handle "containment"—how they absorb a host of negative feelings that others transfer to them. Envy is common. Clearly, C-suite executives have many privileges that others long to possess. Envy is deeply ingrained in the human psyche; in fact, envy has played an important part in our evolution as a species. It sets the foundation for our competitive edge; it motivates us to strive to attain what someone else possesses, or even to surpass it.

Given its omnipresence, people at the top had better pay attention to how envy influences the way subordinates relate to authority figures. They should accept that superior-subordinate comparisons make some people feel insecure. Feelings of insecurity vis-à-vis the person in charge not only creates envious competitiveness but can also give rise to the wish to put the other person down. This destructive interpersonal dynamic is one of the reasons why people in higher leadership positions are often resented, and why they are prone to be the target of hostility and unrealistic judgments.

Being the target of envious, hostile feelings puts a lot of pressure on whoever is at the top. I have encountered several C-suite executives who try to downplay their capabilities as a way of managing these feelings, to the point of becoming paralyzed and incapable of making decisions. They may have been effective as a number two but being at the top is too much to handle. They have an unconscious fear that standing out from others has put them at the risk of rejection, criticism, and even ostracism. The difficulty they have in containing these subliminal pressures contributes to their sense of isolation.

## Living in an Echo Chamber

Another phenomenon that leaders at the top face is the danger that they become shielded from organizational information. I have been privy to many situations where CEOs are given limited and filtered information about their operations, employees, and customers. Unfortunately, this kind of filtering is an insidious process that's difficult to detect. It arises from subordinates' ambivalent feelings about power and authority. I have cautioned many C-suite executives that they should realize that the people who report to them will tend to agree with them even when they are completely off the mark. In many instances, they will do anything to please. And I have also seen that, in spite of heroic attempts by many CEOs to make themselves approachable, to relate to their subordinates, and to ask for honest feedback, many of their reports remain very uncomfortable and apprehensive about doing so. They do not really feel safe; they fear saying the wrong thing; and they are afraid of the potential consequences and retribution that might follow.

Sadly, C-suite executives need to realize that their subordinates are likely to tell them what they want to hear. It has become a truism that the moment you are a top executive, there is a good chance you will be surrounded by liars. The result of being in this kind of echo chamber is that many top executives find themselves increasingly isolated from reality, with nobody to test their perceptions. Without frank feedback, they will not know how well they are doing.

## Paranoid Thinking

When the person in charge can't be sure what is the truth and who can be trusted, paranoia understandably makes an easy entrance, with some justification—CEOs face many genuine threats, both obvious and hidden. In any organization, there are always going to be people who feel stepped upon and dream of (or try to enact) retaliation. There will always people who envy the power of the person in charge and plot to get it for themselves.

Like it or not, if you have a top position in an organization, you have to make hard, unpopular decisions. At times, you have to say no to people you like. You will rub people up the wrong way. I have said repeatedly, if you really want to be loved, sell ice cream—but as a leader, there will be times and situations when you have no choice but to play dentist and inflict pain. Thus, for many C-suite executives, feelings of persecution are a rational response to a world populated by both real and imagined enemies. Vigilance in the presence of perceived or likely danger is simply an extension of the drive to survive. But there is an ever-present danger that healthy suspicion (moderated by a sense of reality) could turn into fully-fledged paranoia.

## What to Do?

With all these pressures on C-suite executives, what can be done to mitigate the loneliness at the top? What can be done to prevent a leader's derailment? And how can we help top executives to contain the "garbage" that comes their way?

To start with, C-suite executives need to realize that playing the Lone Ranger can be detrimental to their health. As a top executive, being the general "garbage can," or emotional "container" for everything and everyone, can be very stressful. They may not be physically alone, but mentally there is nobody in sight. In reality, however much organization members might wish it, no CEO is a superman or superwoman. All of them need someone to talk to and to unburden the stress associated with their position. All of them need people who can provide some kind of "holding environment" to experience empathy and advice.

Some top executives are fortunate in having a significant other who can take on the role of confidant. But far too many CEOs are reluctant to confide to people close to them for fear of burning out a relationship with persistent talk about work, or because their loved ones simply don't have the experience to relate to their challenges. Other C-suite executives may conclude that their significant others are too self-involved or have enough on their plate dealing with their own problems.

Whatever the situation, I strongly believe that, as a leader, you owe it to yourself—and to your organization—to make sure the loneliness of command doesn't interfere with your effectiveness. Being at the top of the leadership pyramid doesn't mean you will suddenly have all the answers and it's unreasonable of others to expect you to. Everyone needs help. Even the most talented leaders have blind spots. Thus, it's imperative that C-suite executives develop a support group that can relate to their challenges and offer advice in a sympathetic, confidential way. There are a number of actions they can take:

1. Many prospective CEOs need greater preparation before taking on the top executive position. I have seen far too many executives who are unprepared for the loneliness that comes with the job. They don't realize the intensive psychological labor that goes with the new position. Knowing that they are accountable to all stakeholders—investors, financial advisers, the public, the press, politicians, and regulators—is a very daunting proposition. They need on-boarding preparations before stepping into post. Asking for advice from people who have been in the same situation is an obvious and sensible first step.

2. To avoid becoming insular, I strongly recommend that C-suite executives should go out of their way to solicit different points of view. This is essential, for both strategic but also for emotional reasons. If you have taken on this position, consciously and mindfully, you need to build a support system of trusted advisors and peers. Otherwise, you risk finding yourself in an echo chamber, hearing only what people think you want to hear.

There are various ways to break the loneliness of command. For example, one of the reasons for the success of the CEO seminar that I run every year at INSEAD (see Chap. 1) is that it is a great opportunity for many leaders to deal with the loneliness of command. Realizing that they are not alone helps create an extremely powerful social support network. During the time they spend together, they establish deep relationships with a cohort of people outside their chain of command with whom they can share their concerns. And they continue to use each other as an enduring support network. Organizations like the Young Presidents' Organization (YPO) also offer the opportunity to take advantage of mutual support networks.

Another way to create a support network is to find a consultant or executive coach who will provide a safe space to discuss a leader's challenges in order to reduce stress levels and maintain mental health. Of course, the key question is whether the leader is ready for this kind of help.

A considerable amount of my work as an executive coach or therapist (apart from giving occasional advice on strategic and human capital decisions) seems to amount to an executive lonely-hearts service—my clients are looking for someone who can be a good sounding board. In my case, the advantage of being outside the system is that it allows me to give frank feedback—helping my clients to get out of their echo chamber. I can also play the fool, in the sense of the wise fool who speaks truth to power—think of the Fool in

Shakespeare's *King Lear*. I have often played this role to prompt clients to take a close look in the mirror. At times, I have to make it clear to the executives I deal with that on occasions the worst place they can be is in their own head. This is a real risk for those who keep too many things to themselves, finding it difficult to talk to people who will understand their predicaments.

I have also developed a number of 360-degree leadership assessment instruments that provide C-suite executives with the opportunity to receive feedback about the leadership challenges they face.[2] Discussing the findings from these questionnaires with other executives is another way of counteracting isolation. It makes difficult issues more discussable, as well as being an antidote to the loneliness of command.

Making friends outside the organization, people with whom you can engage in non-work activities, is a no-brainer when it comes to preventing social isolation. If life consists is all work and no play, executives are at risk of losing their sense of balance. Too much of a work ethic can make you a bore and invites burnout.

1. A very generative way of slowing down the process of isolation is to express gratitude to the people with whom you are interact, quite simply, thanking them for work well done. Expressing gratitude for work that really made a difference can be an extremely powerful tool for increased well-being in all sorts of settings. Recognition—feeling valued—has an enormous impact on people's life because it engages their brain in a virtuous cycle. It helps release the oxytocin that fosters prosocial behaviors such as trust, generosity, and affection. Used authentically, expressing gratitude can be a transformative organizational practice. Generous leaders develop the gift of making all their people feel a part of that connection and create a sense of belonging. By acknowledging and celebrating how every role contributes to a company's purpose, they can help prevent their subordinates feeling left out or on the edge. Making this a general practice will create a culture where it is more likely that employees will have a "healthy disrespect" for their leaders, and have the courage to disagree, when appropriate—the antidote to living in an echo chamber.

It has been said that we are born alone, we live alone, and we die alone. But should we make this our credo? Is that what life is all about? All of us may have experienced how being alone can be very stressful, making loneliness not only our biggest fear, but also our ultimate deprivation. Very few people can

---

[2] https://www.kdvi.com/tools.

handle being alone. If you have the feeling of being alone, however, you should it as a flashing sign that something needs to change. After all, one of our major existential needs is human connectedness. C-suite executives, in particular, had better pay heed to this warning sign and wise up to the knowledge that the antidote to loneliness is community.

# 16

## The Icarus Syndrome

*Like Achilles, the hero who forgot his heel, or like Icarus who, flying close to the sun, forgot that his wings were made of wax, we should be wary when triumphant ideas seem unassailable, for then there is all the more reason to predict their downfall.*
—Dwight Longenecker

*Never regret thy fall,*
*O Icarus of the fearless flight*
*For the greatest tragedy of them all*
*Is never to feel the burning light.*
—Oscar Wilde

Let me tell you about David. For a long time, he had been on quite a high. Everything in his behavior indicated that he liked the smell of success, and in particular, he liked to be the center of attention. I remember him telling me how pleased he was to be named businessman of the year. But what had really put him in the public eye was when his picture appeared on the front cover of the country's major business magazine. His reputation was also boosted by his role as a regular commentator on a general interest TV program. David liked the admiration; he liked to be recognized. Recognition had always been a major theme in his inner theater. Everyone knew he was no stranger to narcissism. And the press intensified his feeling of being special. Many articles portrayed him as the person who had "reframed the industry." His numerous

© The Author(s), under exclusive license to Springer Nature Switzerland AG 2021
M. F. R. Kets de Vries, *The CEO Whisperer*, The Palgrave Kets de Vries Library,
https://doi.org/10.1007/978-3-030-62601-3_16

successes encouraged him to make his boldest move: the takeover of his largest competitor.

But then the wheel of fortune changed direction. The trouble started when one industry analyst commented that he had paid far too much money for the newly acquired company. Once the golden boy, David was increasingly criticized and attacked. His difficulties were aggravated by the banks' demands, as they became nervous about his credit line. David would work himself up over the stupidity of these bankers, saying, "They should know a good deal when they see one." But what really got his goat was when the newspapers joined the fray, writing that "it had been painful to watch his degree of self-sabotage, after his many truly remarkable successes." According to David, these comments were blatantly unfair, as was another biting remark: "not only has his latest takeover been a mistake, but his endless side ventures, like buying an upscale star restaurant in London and a linked catering business, the sponsoring of a football club, and the financing of a private clinic, seem to have become too great a drain on the company's resources."

According to David, the media were distorting the facts. Right or wrong, however, the damage was done. After so many magazines had fêted him as a poster boy for entrepreneurship, he was once again front-page news, but this time as an example of someone who had flown too high. I remember reading the commentary of one business analyst, who wrote that David's "air of superiority, his dismissiveness of the opinions of others, and his endless pursuit of new acquisitions, had made his fall to earth inevitable." The article added that "his fall from grace was an extremely expensive one, costing the jobs of thousands of people."

## Wax and Wings

In Greek mythology, Icarus and his father, Daedalus, were imprisoned on the island of Crete by King Minos. To escape, Daedalus created two sets of wings made from wax and feathers for himself and his son. Daedalus warned Icarus not to fly too close to the sun, as the wax would melt, and not too low, as the feathers would get wet with sea water. But Icarus, overcome with the excitement of flying, ignored his father's advice. Intoxicated by the experience, he flew higher and higher, and closer and closer to the sun. And when he was too close, the wax in his wings melted. He tumbled out of the sky, fell into the sea, and drowned. Icarus and his fate became bywords for recklessness and overestimation of human strengths and abilities.

I have seen many manifestations of the Icarus Syndrome. It's what occurs when leaders, seduced by success, embark on overly ambitious projects that come to nothing, and in doing so cause harm to themselves and others. Fueled by the excitement of their ambitions, these people fail to rein in their misguided enthusiasm until it is too late to avoid disaster. This syndrome afflicts leaders who have an insatiable desire for recognition and applause. Narcissism, not uncommon among executives, goes to their head. They become too full of themselves. Their grandiose sense of self-importance and their feelings of entitlement are ultimately self-damaging.[1] They may fly for a while, but eventually reality strikes, and they find themselves crashing to earth. Unfortunately, in many instances, this crash involves significant collateral damage for everyone in their sphere.

Many of us associate successful leadership with charisma, charm, the ability to inspire, persuasiveness, breadth of vision, willingness to take risks, grandiose aspirations, and bold self-confidence. However, there is a flip side to this profile. Excessive confidence in their own judgment and the associated feelings of omnipotence may lead to reckless and restless behavior; contempt for the advice and criticism of others; and make such leaders ignore the practicality, cost, or damaging consequences of their actions. The arrogance associated with this syndrome can be blinding. The Icarus Syndrome has felled many executives who planned too grandly but failed miserably by overestimating their knowledge, foresight, and ability.

Folktales, Biblical stories, and the world's literature are full of descriptions of people falling victim to the Icarus Syndrome—think of Captain Ahab in Herman Melville's *Moby Dick*, and Satan in John Milton's *Paradise Lost*. In all these tales, the dark themes of pride, vanity, ambition, power, insolence, disdain, defiance, rage, and retribution are ubiquitous.

All of us can cite many contemporary political and business leaders who have flown or are flying too close to the sun. Prime examples are Mohammed bin Salman (MbS), the Crown Prince of Saudi Arabia; Carlos Ghosn (the former chairman of the Renault-Nissan-Mitsubishi Alliance); and Mark Zuckerberg, the chairman and CEO of Facebook. The case of MbS speaks for itself. Actions like the terrible war in Yemen, picking a fight with Canada, and his alleged complicity in the murder of the journalist Jamal Khashoggi, have seriously endangered his quest to reshape the Middle East. In the case of Ghosn, Nissan (the Japanese carmaker he once helped to rescue) abruptly accused him of significant acts of financial misconduct, including the

---

[1] Manfred F. R. Kets de Vries (2016). *You Will Meet a Tall, Dark Stranger: Executive Coaching Challenges.* New York: Palgrave Macmillan.

personal use of corporate assets and the understatement of his compensation. His daring escape to Lebanon may be his swan song. As for Mark Zuckerberg, the jury is still out, but his case illustrates that there are clear limits to feeling omnipotent. Many media outlets have described him not only as a member of the arrogant corporate elite but also as a coward, who has been reluctant to face up to the many data privacy problems his company has created.

A positive self-image is psychologically healthy, and self-confidence, proper ambition, and authentic pride are necessary qualities for any successful leader. Unfortunately, as these various examples show, these qualities can become excessive, turning into contempt for others. The ancient Greeks called this hubris, the dangerous cocktail of overconfidence, overambition, arrogance, and pride that led heroes to defy the gods and bring disaster down upon them. Hubristic leaders have an inflated view of their capabilities and they expose themselves to terrible danger by overlooking the evident risks they take for themselves and others.

Colorful details aside, the trajectory of these leaders suggest that all of us should be on guard against the Icarus Syndrome. But many leaders, who have floated too long in a gilded bubble, untethered from reality, are unable to do so.

## Preventive Measures

The million-dollar question is how to prevent the Icarus Syndrome and the damage it can create from coming to the fore. Is preventive maintenance possible? Sadly enough, from my own observations, the Icarus Syndrome remains an occupational hazard for many business leaders and top politicians. But is it an inevitable aspect of those who crave power, or simply the extreme manifestation of normal behavior along a spectrum of narcissism?

For reasons of mental health, we all need a healthy dose of self-confidence. When this self-confidence becomes too inflated, however, it can turn into unrestrained narcissism. In light of this risk factor and given the very negative repercussions of the Icarus Syndrome, every executive would do well to recognize the signs that trouble is on its way. For example, as I have often discovered the hard way in my work with executives, one indicator of the Icarus Syndrome is an executive's excessive confidence in his or her own judgment. Another indicator is an executive's exaggerated or unrealistic self-belief in what he or she can achieve. Leaders who make all of their own decisions without consulting others are also asking for trouble. Solo performances can lead to poor decisions and put their organizations at risk. Another danger sign is when subordinates hesitantly agree with the leader's excesses, indicating that leaders have created a no-bad-news culture. Their subordinates have learned to fear the leader's response to disagreement. By behaving in this way, leaders demoralize and disempower their teams, which may contribute to psychological disengagement. One of the consequences of such behavior is that their most capable employees will leave. People who are subject to the Icarus Syndrome, seem unwilling to accept that candor can be cleansing, in that it clears out the haze of smoke and mirrors that they create.

An effective countermeasure to the Icarus Syndrome is to aim for diversity. On many occasions, I have seen how diversity in a leadership team can turn into a highly effective way to prevent groupthink[2]—to help in boundary setting if a member of a team has Icarus tendencies. Although it may be true that management teams with common backgrounds and perspectives make faster decisions, this doesn't mean that they make quality decisions. On the contrary, quick decisions made by teams that are too uniform increases the likelihood that data that do not fit their preconceived ideas will be filtered, meaning alternatives worthy of consideration are overlooked. Too much groupthink may occur. This pattern of decision making is less likely to occur in diverse teams.[3] Preventing the Icarus Syndrome ultimately demands a culture where people are prepared to tell the leader uncomfortable truths—an environment where people can disagree without the fear of reprisal. It requires a culture where people feel safe and where there is a minimum of fear.

Non-executive members of Boards of Directors can exert power here. When faced with early signs of the Icarus Syndrome, independent directors have the power to address the issue and suggest some form of intervention. But corporate governance notwithstanding, we should not be overoptimistic that they will act. Generally speaking, some great drama is needed before these watchdogs take any countervailing actions, and usually do so only when things have already gone too far. More often, both the victims of the Icarus Syndrome and the people around them fail to see that matters are getting out of hand, mesmerized as they are by their leaders' seductive behavior.

Here's a cautionary folk tale for these executive Icaruses:

Once upon a time, there was a bird that was told that it had to fly south for the winter. But the bird thought it knew better and in spite of the warnings from all the other birds, it decided that there was no hurry. When the other birds left, it

---

[2] Irving L. Janis (1982). *Groupthink: Psychological Studies of Policy Decisions and Fiascoes.* Boston: Cengage Learning.

[3] Manfred F. R. Kets de Vries (2011). *The Hedgehog Effect: The Secret of building High Performance Teams.* San Francisco: Jossey-Bass.

stayed put. Then, as they had warned, the weather turned icy. Assailed by the cold wind, the little bird froze and fell to earth. As it lay on the ground, a cow came by and dropped some dung on the bird. The warm dung thawed the bird out, making it feel warm and happy, and it began to sing for joy. A passing fox heard the bird's song and came to investigate. Clearing away the manure, the fox discovered the little bird and gobbled it up.

Unfortunately, this ending is typical of people prone to the Icarus Syndrome. Many suffer an ignominious downfall due to overconfidence, self-importance, boasting, or generally speaking, hubris. All C-suite executives should remember that the sweet smell of success can easily turn toxic. For those in a top position, excessive narcissism will always be an occupational hazard, and arrogance a sign that they need to do some sharp work on their mental health.

# 17

## How Greedy Are You?

*Greed is a bottomless pit which exhausts the person in an endless effort to satisfy the need without ever reaching satisfaction.*
—Erich Fromm

Humankind's history is full of stories about the disastrous consequences of greed. But in spite of these cautionary tales, when it comes to greedy behavior, it appears we never learn. We aren't always good at controlling the greediness that lurks inside us. Why do we behave like this? Can we break the vicious cycle of greediness? Most importantly, what impact do greedy people have on themselves, others, and society at large?

## The Basic Fault

Is it possible to look at greed as nothing more than a coping mechanism? Is it a way, dysfunctional though it may be, to resolve mental health problems? What's the matter with greedy people? Why do they behave so outrageously? Is there anything they can talk about besides money? When I nudge clients who fit this profile to explain themselves, I don't get much of a response. Perhaps their greed has something to do with their unresolved feelings of inner emptiness—the feeling that there's something missing. But if that's the case, where does this feeling come from?

Ineffective role modelling when a person is growing up seems to be a significant factor in the development of greediness, as it is in so many instances

© The Author(s), under exclusive license to Springer Nature Switzerland AG 2021
M. F. R. Kets de Vries, *The CEO Whisperer*, The Palgrave Kets de Vries Library,
https://doi.org/10.1007/978-3-030-62601-3_17

of psychological dysfunctionality. A lot of the stories I'm told by greedy people feature early negative parental experiences that set the stage for feelings of low self-esteem, creating a kind of "basic fault"—a life-long search for "something that's missing" that would give them some form of satisfaction.[1]

The psychoanalyst Michael Balint introduced the idea of the basic fault and viewed its emergence as the result of a skewed relationship between the child and its caretakers, a trauma that leads to unsatisfactory relationships with others, contributes to intense and overwhelming anxiety, and creates regressive behavior when under stress. Consequently, during children's early stages of development, they will adopt behavior patterns—that later turn into compulsions—to cope with a considerable discrepancy between their psychobiological needs and the care provided by a faulty environment. In short, Balint's notion of a basic fault referred to very early and fundamental psychological damage due to inadequate caretaker responses to the infant's needs. This failure contributes to a split, creating a differentiation between a true self and a false self.

The idea of true self versus false self was introduced by the pediatrician and psychoanalyst Donald Winnicott.[2] According to Winnicott, all of us wear masks that enable us to survive and interact appropriately in a wide variety of interpersonal contexts, where, by necessity, we show different sides of ourselves. These different social masks help us to manage our lives in a balanced and integrated way, making it possible to develop a cohesive integrated identity. But when our emotional needs are either unmet, or met unreliably, we learn not to trust the environment, or who we are. Our natural infant spontaneity will be in danger of being encroached on by the need for compliance with our parents' wishes and expectations. Adaptive as this way of interacting may be, it could lead to the development of a false self in the form of a defensive façade that is tiresome to maintain. Keeping up a façade toward others can result in our feeling depleted, drained, or emotionally numb. In contrast, being able to spontaneously project our true self will make us feel more truly alive. But if there is a split within the self, if we are unable to integrate its various parts, we will have the subjective experience that something essential is missing inside. This is the kind of feeling that contributes to the sense of a basic fault.

---

[1] Michael Balint (1992). *The Basic Fault: Therapeutic Aspects of Regression.* Evanston, IL: Northwestern University Press.

[2] Donald W. Winnicott (1960). "Ego Distortion in Terms of True and False Self," in *The Maturational Process and the Facilitating Environment: Studies in the Theory of Emotional Development.* New York: International UP Inc., 1965, pp. 140–152.

## A Leaking Bucket

From what I have seen, many greedy people obsessively pursue wealth as a substitute for what they feel is lacking inside. One person described this feeling to me vividly, explaining that "deep inside, I feel like a leaking bucket that can never be filled." This man seemed to be compelled to keep at his greedy pursuits to create the illusion of completeness. Through the acquisition of wealth, he hoped to feel at least temporarily better within himself, and better than his peers. But he forgot the high price that greed exacts. He forgot that it can contribute to a stunted life, to feeling inauthentic, and worsen his own dysfunctionality.

Narcissistic disorders and greed are close cousins: profound self-doubt forms the base of both. In both instances, people doubt their importance, significance, or value. But in differentiating these two dysfunctional ways of dealing with life, I suggest that narcissistic disorders have more to do with emotional self-aggrandizement, while greed is a form of materialistic self-aggrandizement. In whatever way we differentiate them, both are poor choices when it comes to leading a fulfilling life.[3]

Greedy people use their materialistic pursuits to find some form of relief for their emotional discomfort. Their behavior can be compared to people who suffer from substance abuse. However, like with these addicts, any relief they find will only be temporary. Their attempts to fill their inner void with material things will only aggravate the problem: there won't ever be enough. Like drug addicts, they will soon need another fix. Without even being aware of it, the greedier they are, the more self-destructive they will become, and the worse they will feel. Their endless acquisitiveness will not ameliorate the underlying feeling that deep down they aren't good enough. It is mission impossible.

Greedy people, consciously and unconsciously, link their self-worth to their financial worth. It has become their main way of keeping score. Yet greed is not really a financial issue; it is all about having a troubled mind. Not only do greedy people damage themselves, they will cause considerable damage to others. Overly competitive and aggressive, they will take ruthless advantage of every opportunity to turn a profit—at any price.

---

[3] Manfred F. R. Kets de Vries (2007). *The Happiness Equation: Meditations on Happiness and Success.* IUniverse.

# Evolutionary and Societal Considerations

But to play devil's advocate for a while, is greed really so bad? Why should we be so negative about the accumulation of wealth? If evolutionary theory is to be believed, competition for scarce resources is a basic human characteristic. From an evolutionary perspective, greed may be essential for our survival. As greed encourages us to accumulate things, and wealth is an important signifier of status, having many possessions shouldn't be such a bad thing. It is a very effective strategy if you want to attract a mate. After all, having a mate helps us to perpetuate our genetic code. Doesn't that make greed nothing more than a purely biological imperative? Perhaps Gordon Gekko is right to suggest that greed is programmed into our genes.

This evolutionary, selfish gene argument about the benefits of greed is accompanied by societal and existential considerations. Some believe that without a dose of greed, an individual, community, or society might lack the motivation to move forward. Without greed, would we accomplish anything? Would we be able to defend ourselves against the greediness of others? Without having a modicum of greed, wouldn't we become too vulnerable?

Some people have suggested that greed is also Homo sapiens' way of dealing with existential anxiety, a way of transcending death. The acquisition of stuff creates the illusion of eternal life. We may die, but our acquisitions will live on. Greed is simply a fact of life and we should embrace it, not fight it. Since the dawn of time, greed has been the driving spirit of civilization.

True enough, greed is a major driver of many successful societies, the fuel that drives the economy. Some argue that political systems designed to check or eliminate greedy behavior have invariably ended in abject failure. Without greed built into their fabric, societies would quickly descend into poverty and chaos. I think, however, as is the case with most things in life, that it's all a question of balance. We can all see how the unrestrained pursuit of our own interests creates problems for ourselves and others. Also, some of us have learned the hard way that other people resent it when we take more than our fair share. Greed, like all potentially destructive human drives, needs to be tempered by social norms. When greed becomes perverted, it leads to social unrest.

Thus, although greed plays a role in economic progress, uncontrolled greed contributes to economic decline. Like a great cancer, the lust for possession and greed will destroy the soul of humanity, metastasizing throughout society. And we don't need to look very far to see how our consumer culture—our tendency toward conspicuous consumption—can inflict severe damage. We have also seen the damage financial engineers can do to society, the banking crisis of 2008 being a prime example. Excessive greed also contributes to corruption. Even the lack of foresight with respect to the coronavirus pandemic—as there has been a lack of needed investments—may be attributed to greed. I would go as far as to say that the victory of greed over compassion could be the downfall of our civilization.

## A Faustian Pact

Greed addicts can do great harm. In their obsessive pursuit of wealth, they are often grossly insensitive to the needs and feelings of others. And as excessive narcissism is part of the greed equation, empathy will be in extremely short supply. These people care about money, but that's all they care about. As they are never happy with what they have, their desire only increases with their possessions. Greedy people leave reason, compassion, and love by the wayside. To them, the richness and complexity of life is reduced to little more than a quest to accumulate and hoard as much as possible of whatever they desire.

What these greed obsessed individuals don't realize, however, is that they may have made a pact with the devil, which takes us back to the concept of the basic fault, being troubled by feelings of emptiness and meaninglessness that aren't going away. No wonder that greed becomes tied in with negative emotional states like stress, exhaustion, anxiety, depression, and despair and maladaptive and unethical behavior patterns, such as gambling, scavenging, hoarding, fraud, and theft. In the pursuit of greed, family and community ties will fall by the wayside. Greed can undermine the values on which society and civilization are founded, when people are unable to distinguish need from greed.

## Is There Hope?

From a professional point of view, I must admit that I don't find it easy dealing with greedy people. And I am not alone in this. Many of my colleagues in the helping professions are also wary of dealing with them, and for good reason. Given (or perhaps because) greedy people have everything they think they want and more, many are unable to adapt and reformulate what they really want. They find it difficult to explain why they feel incomplete and why they are so obsessed with money.

Another complication when working with these clients is that in their pursuit of wealth there never seems to be an endpoint in sight. They have no concept of "enough." Making money seems to be the only thing that gives them any satisfaction, the only salve they know that brings temporary relief. The process whereby they accumulate their riches has become an end in itself. But surely life should be about more than getting a chemical "high" (or dopamine release) every time they make a deal, turn a profit, or make a "killing?" But like any other form of addiction, as their system develops a greater tolerance for the dosage, they need to increase it continually, as previous highs no longer give them same degree of satisfaction? Greedy people need to make bigger and bigger killings to feel good about themselves—at least temporarily. But unfortunately, the subterranean doubts they have about themselves will not go away.

What makes the treatment of greedy people so difficult is that a substantial number of people view greed and its related traits as desirable rather than as potential mental health problems. Understandably, they find some of the derivatives of greed, like ambition and success, attractive. Given society's ambivalence toward the issue, many greedy people don't even recognize the difficulties they are in. They are not ready to acknowledge that their behavior is harmful to themselves and to others.

The challenge is how to make clear to them the greater value of generosity above material wealth, how to explain that helping others will make them feel more fulfilled, and to convince them that generous people have greater satisfaction with life. They need to understand that greed is a compulsion and to decide whether they are willing to work on it. Are they willing to choose who will be in charge of their life: will it be the demons inside them, or themselves?

I remember one very successful investment banker, I'll call him Arnault, who came to me for help, prompted by his impending divorce. His wife had told him that she had had enough of living with him; she wanted to "have a life." She was fed-up with catering to his self-centered pursuits and serving merely as a cheerleader. She had had enough of him being so cheap and controlling how much money she was allowed to spend. Arnault also said his grown-up children weren't happy with him. He confessed that he had never paid much attention to them, as he had always been too busy making money. Now, as adults, they only visited him at Christmas. Their relationship was quite distant. When I asked Arnault what he did apart from making deals, I didn't get an immediate response. Eventually, he admitted that deal-making had always been all that mattered to him. It was the only activity that made him feel alive. It wasn't difficult to figure out what his major Life Anchor was. When I asked him if he had any other interests, I was faced with a stony and lengthy silence. Finally, Arnault responded that he had always felt compelled to work. He needed to earn money—and now he had to make even more, given the substantial alimony he would have to pay his wife. When I prompted Arnault to give me some reasons why he was so concerned about making money, he told me that when he was growing up, his entrepreneurial father had gone bankrupt a number of times. He remembered how embarrassed he had been when the family turned off the house lights and hid to avoid creditors. He also recalled how the neighbor's children used to make fun of him, knowing the family's dire financial situation. He added that his parents didn't provide much emotional support when he needed them, recalling a number of incidents when they had led him down. It made him decide to rely only on himself (it wasn't difficult to figure out his attachment pattern, either).

I remarked that Arnault should be pleased with what he had accomplished. As he had no longer any financial worries—being independently wealthy—he could now do whatever he wanted to do. Now he had a wide range of choices. Because of his wealth, he had many more options than just making deals. But Arnault's instant response was that he still wasn't financially secure enough. This led to a litany of reasons why he could still get into financial difficulties. As I tried to go beyond his defensive rationalizations, I asked Arnault again, "Do you really have no other choices?" I tried to point out to him that he was allowing the intensity of his needs and his underlying fears to hijack his mind, overriding his ability to step back, and to do other things. I was trying to help him make sense of how the cycle of greed was operating within his mind. However, his confused reactions made me wonder how aware he was of his options. Did he understand the underlying craving that kept him looking for yet another deal?

I remember how hard it was to convince Arnault that his compulsive striving to keep on making money was not rational, despite his numerous rationalizations. I tried to point out that he was spending so long trying to get what everyone else had that he didn't even realize that he already had it all. I told him that he seemed to have unlimited quantities of various things—and tried to accumulate more—but like everyone else, he had only a limited quantity of other things, such as health, and time with the family. Why risk the things he had limited amounts of to increase the quantities of things he had unlimited amounts of? What would he rather look after, his money, his health, or his family? I added that if money was his only measure of success, he shouldn't be surprised when it turned out to be all he would ever have. His relentless pursuit of money, combined with his avoidant attachment behavior, would make him end up a very lonely man, like Charles Dickens' Ebenezer Scrooge. I also pointed out that money is a very cold currency compared to intimate relationships. His greediness meant he would always be dissatisfied because he would never be able to get everything he desired. I pointed out that greed never allows you to think that you have enough. Greed will eventually destroy you by making you strive ever harder for more.

At one point I asked Arnault how much money would be enough. Could he give me a figure? Could he tell me the level of income he needed? It was this question that started Arnault's process of realization that there would never be such thing as enough. Not immediately, but slowly, it began to dawn on him how illogical and destructive his behavior had always been; that he should pay more attention to things he did have. I suggested that perhaps he should learn how to enjoy those things. I explained that life isn't just about ticking the boxes for his acquisitions, then moving on to the next item on the list. There is more to life than making lists.

I spend quite some time with Arnault, dealing with what was under the surface of his greed. I helped him identify the "lack," or whatever it was that he was so afraid of—the complex interpersonal dynamics that had created this "basic fault." Together, we explored his associations between these anxieties and his greed-based actions. Discussing his background, I made him more conscious of why he was doing what he was doing. I think these explorations of his family history helped liberate him from the chains of his psychological enslavement. Gradually, Arnault came to understand—to his great surprise— that his real obsession was not with wealth at all. What he really needed was greater emotional intimacy. Behind this obsessive pursuit of wealth lay his need for rich, satisfying relationships. I helped him understand that he didn't need to be a prisoner of his compulsions—that he did have choices.

One of the most difficult tasks for greedy people is learning to be selfish in a different way. They need to become more attentive to their inner self. As the case of Arnault exemplifies, this isn't easy to do. It requires persistence, patience, humility, courage, and commitment. But this long-term investment in the self—as a counterweight to feelings of deprivation—can be a powerful antidote to greed, gluttony, avarice, and other forms of addiction. Arnault had never realized that the less you want, the happier you are. Perhaps it is a truism to say that you truly succeed in life when all you really want is only what you really need. In contrast, the more you desire, the greedier you will be. In the words of the Buddha, "Let your diet be spare, your wants moderate, your needs few. So, living modestly, with no distracting desires, you will find content."

# 18

## Don't Regret Regrets

*My one regret in life is that I am not someone else.*
—Woody Allen

As a helping professional, I often have to deal with the topic of regret. I recognize there will always be situations where we will not get closure but nevertheless, it is better to move on. It is better to look forward with hope than to look back with regret. For some people, however, their only regrets are the opportunities they didn't take. What should we regret, the things we have done or the things we haven't done? My hope is that people don't regret the past but learn from it. But can you regret the life you didn't lead? Some people will regret the endings, but they very much enjoyed the journey. Why have regrets if what you were doing at the time was exactly what you wanted to do?

One of the best-known songs of Edith Piaf, the famous French singer, songwriter, and cabaret performer was "Non, je ne regrette rien" ("No regrets"). She did not write the song herself, but she recognized instantly it was played to her that it would be her greatest hit. It is tempting to wonder whether the song's success was boosted by the public wish that it might be true of the singer—and whether Piaf herself shared its message. After all, she had had a difficult and unhappy childhood and adolescence and many challenges and tragedies in her later life and career. Did this song evoke some kind of resolution, embracing all the things that had happened to her, recognizing that they made her who she was? Is that why it appealed to her so much? We will never be certain whether Piaf's promotion of this song and its sentiments

© The Author(s), under exclusive license to Springer Nature Switzerland AG 2021
M. F. R. Kets de Vries, *The CEO Whisperer*, The Palgrave Kets de Vries Library,
https://doi.org/10.1007/978-3-030-62601-3_18

was life-affirming or delusional. Her last words were, allegedly, "Every damn fool thing you do in this life, you pay for."

Many of my clients raise the issue of regret. Clearly, dealing with regret is a universal human experience. Many of us remember situations we found ourselves in and ask ourselves "What was I thinking?" or play with alternative scenarios ("I should have done so-and-so"). Many of us experience disappointment and sorrow about what might have been and make wrong or foolish choices that we regret later. Regret not only reminds us that we made some unfortunate decisions, it also tells us that we could have done so much better. However, our major regrets are usually about not having done something.

I have learned from my clients that our greatest regrets seem to revolve around pivotal life choices, such as education, career, romance (including regrets about affairs), marriage, parenting, and work. This is not surprising: decisions in these areas tend to have long-term and sometimes irrevocable consequences. Other regrets that I often hear while listening to my clients relate to finance, health, friendship, charity, loneliness, travel, worry (too much), and even about having led too conventional a life.

However, quite a few people, when asked about their regrets, have a kind of knee-jerk reaction and insist they don't have any. More than that, they resist the discomfort of reflecting on their past life, actions, and decisions. At times, I wonder whether their avoidance of regret arises from an existential fear of confronting their darker side. At the same time, it may be a telling indication of their current state of mind.

I think what makes it so difficult to talk about regret is that it often brings up negative experiences and emotions, such as sadness, shame, embarrassment, depression, grief, annoyance, anger, and/or guilt. For some people, past actions or behaviors subconsciously affect the quality of their life and reflecting on them is a rude awakening. What's more, when reflecting on regret, we may realize that we've hurt ourselves and others—damaging our careers, relationships, and reputations, thus limiting our options.

Unfortunately, I have found that when you subject yourself to repetitive, negative, self-focused ruminative thinking about regret, it becomes maladaptive, contributing to self-blame and even depressive reactions. It can become a self-fulfilling prophecy. Strong feelings of regret can have a serious emotional, cognitive, and even neurophysiological impact. Being tormented by regret will stymie your personal growth and development and may even cause mental health problems.

How intensely you experience regret depends very much on your narcissistic equilibrium. I have observed that if you have self-esteem issues, you tend to be more susceptible to regret, which can further impede your sense of self-worth. And although your willingness to face regret may be commendable, how you work it through is another matter altogether. Too much rumination could even make you risk-averse, fearful of making yet another bad decision. Being stuck between regret for the past and fear of the future is not a very good position to be in.

Not only do I think that there is a connection between someone's self-esteem and regret, I also believe that aging affects how you deal with regretful feelings. I know from personal experience that when you grow older and realize that your time is running out, you are more likely to reflect upon the past, review your life, and try to sort out the mistakes you have made during your life's journey. This is a time in your life when you will be more open to making a realistic assessment of the things you have done, realizing that the opportunities for making changes are rapidly evaporating. It makes you more aware that the lessons you have learned from life may be used to prevent future regrets: most of us strive for a life well lived.

For some of us, these life reviews bring resignation vis-à-vis our limitations, which will temper feelings of regret. Others will mourn their losses, try to deal with unfulfilled dreams and ambitions, and reconcile themselves with what cannot be changed, regretting wrong choices. The acceptance of the expected vicissitudes of life will rescue their present and future from the wasteland of unbearable remorse and generate a new intensity for life. However, there will be some for whom wallowing in regret will lead to a depressive crisis of despair and feelings of bitterness.

## The Power of Retrospection

Having said this, I should add that, from an evolutionary point of view, regret might also have a survival function. From this perspective, the experience of regret can be considered as a psychological construct related to decision-making, coping, and learning. Regret forces you to engage in a retrospective analysis in order to understand the reason why you thought or acted in the way you did. This kind of review might help you to identify specific patterns or behaviors that have made you who you are, and that continue to influence you unconsciously—behaviors that keep you from stepping out of your comfort zone or leading a better life. By analyzing regrets, and getting past the past, you might be able to understand why you do the things you do, discover dysfunctional behavior patterns, and take remedial action. Regret can become a positive impetus for repairing, rebuilding, and finding new constructive resolutions and moving forward in life. Thus, in more than one way, dealing with regret could be your brain's way of telling you to take another look at your choices; to signal that some of your actions had very negative consequences; and to try to do things differently in the future.

Unfortunately, from what I can see, despite the importance of regret as a guiding mechanism, most of us pay insufficient attention to it. Generally, we make an effort to manage our level of stress, we try to articulate our career goals, we control our diet, we deal with our finances, and try to manage pretty much everything else, but we are reluctant to manage our regrets. However, if we can do it, managing regrets will help each of us to make sense of our world, provide us with greater insight about ourselves, help us avoid future dysfunctional scenarios, and improve our decision-making skills.

We would do well to keep in mind that, in dealing with regrets, the challenge is not to try to change the past but to shed light on the present. You cannot change what has happened to you, but you can change how you react and how you are going to live in the future. Self-assessment and healthy introspection could help you to analyze your own shortcomings and prevent you from repetitive dysfunctional behavior. Learning from your mistakes, you will be able to incorporate these learning experiences into your subsequent decisions and actions. You will be less likely to get stuck in "if only" thinking. Having the freedom to choose and wondering whether you have made the right choices will always be an existential dilemma.

However, paying attention to your regrets will help you to consider alternative future opportunities more clearly. It will help you take advantage of opportunities that would otherwise have slipped by. You might even engage in forms of reparative action, like making amends to people whom you have hurt. It will also make it easier for you to come to terms with the realization that some instances or events were completely out of your control.

My message is that instead of avoiding regrets, it's much wiser to deal with these feelings up front. Edith Piaf's famous song suggests regretting nothing; to forget about the past. Of course, you shouldn't let past regrets set the tone for the rest of your life, but you would be wise to use your regrets constructively, not just sweep them away. You need to find ways to forgive yourself for what you have done and, if possible, make amends and determine to do things differently next time. When all is said and done, it's best not to live life regretting yesterday but to live your life so that you don't regret how you live it today. In the words of another famous singer: "Regrets, I've had a few, but then again, too few to mention."

# 19

# Managing Disappointment

*That which does not kill us, makes us stronger.*
—Friedrich Nietzsche

*Inside every cynical person is a disappointed idealist.*
—George Carlin

When I asked Robert how he was doing, his immediate response was that he was upset. He didn't know what to think about his current situation. He was still trying to get a grip on his disappointment. How could this have happened to him? How could he have misjudged the situation so badly? He felt angry, sad, and betrayed. Mostly, he was deeply disappointed in the people who had let him down.

From what I understood, disappointing experiences were not new to Robert. Over the years, there had been a number of occasions when he felt let down. One had been a skunk work he had initiated a number of years ago. From a very small beginning, this innovative high-tech project had become an extremely profitable venture. His successor, however, managed to turn gold into lead. She had been incapable of transitioning the project to the next phase. The most capable people in the team left soon after her arrival, and the project started to flounder. Their common complaint was that she was too abrasive.

Now the same thing was happening again, with his current project. How was it possible that he found himself in such a predicament once more? He

M. F. R. Kets de Vries, *The CEO Whisperer*, The Palgrave Kets de Vries Library, https://doi.org/10.1007/978-3-030-62601-3_19

had put everything he had into making this new project a success, and now he was watching it fall apart.

Robert told me that because he was coming up to retirement, he had carefully groomed a successor to continue the venture. The company's main decision-makers had assured him that they agreed with his choice. But when push came to shove, they vetoed his candidate. Instead, they appointed someone else to take the lead, in spite of his telling them that this person didn't have what it would take to bring the project to successful completion. It was at this point that Robert realized how much he had underestimated office politics. But whatever reasons he could give for this unexpected decision, he had only himself to blame. He had been too naïve. His expectations of people had always been far too high. Unfortunately, this incident left him with a sense of futility about what to do next. He felt totally bewildered, demotivated, unable to concentrate at work, and, although he was reluctant to admit it, depressed.

Many people succeed in working through their disappointments. Somehow, they have the strength to take stock of what has happened to them, learn from the incident, and move on. They emerge from such disappointments stronger. As a matter of fact, dealing constructively with disappointment can be a self-curative process that contributes to personal growth and greater resilience. These people show their real worth after having overcome the disappointments that are inevitable in life.

Winston Churchill provides an example of such developmental progression. Churchill was a political leader who managed to transcend the various disappointments that came his way. After the disastrous military campaign at Gallipoli during World War I, which Churchill directed, it must have been extremely difficult for this very ambitious man to have to resign from his position as First Lord of the Admiralty and put his career on hold. However, this setback may have made Churchill much more resilient. After the calamity of Gallipoli and his subsequent humiliation, Churchill refocused his attention and energy on himself. He took time to explore what had happened to him and what it had taught him. His soul-searching provided him with new information about himself, the world, and others, and became a lesson on how to deal with future challenges. As a result, during World War II, Churchill emerged as a transformational leader, a person who really made a difference. To Churchill, working through disappointment seems to have been a catalytic event. To the best of my understanding, strengthened by a process of self-examination, he turned his negative experiences into positive ones, determined to continue playing an important role on the world stage. A glimmer of how he was able to reinvent himself shines through the speech he made on

October 29, 1941 at Harrow, his old school: "Never give in. Never give in. Never, never, never, never—in nothing, great or small, large or petty—never give in, except to convictions of honor and good sense." This remarkably short speech must have been the result of deeply felt personal experiences.

## Managing Expectations

Disappointment is the feeling caused by the non-fulfillment of our hopes or expectations. All of us, at one time or another, have experienced disappointment. We should see it as part of our journey through life. You may have been passed over for a promotion; you may not have gotten the job offer you really wanted (thinking of my disappointing experience at the Harvard Business School); a superior, a coworker, or a subordinate might have let you down; or you may even have had a romantic disappointment. Some of these disappointments will not make much difference to your life, but there are others that can change its course.

William Shakespeare wrote that "Oft expectation fails, and most oft there/ Where most it promises." He recognized that we experience disappointment when our thoughts and expectations are out of line with reality. Disappointment comes with a sense of finality. It forces you to admit that you did not get what you wished for; that reality is very different from what you expected. What makes disappointment such a complex and confusing feeling is that many of our desires are unconscious, sublimated, and frequently contradictory.

Paradoxically, you may also be disappointed when you get what you want. For example, in his 1916 essay "Some Character-Types Met within Psycho-Analytic Work,"[1] Sigmund's Freud explored the paradox of people who are "wrecked by success," who become depressed not as a result of failure but due to success. Freud observed that "people occasionally fall ill precisely when a deeply-rooted and long-cherished wish has come to fulfillment." He concluded that the "forces of conscience"—our sense of guilt in general—induce illness as a consequence of success. Unconsciously, these people believe that success was unjustified. They think they are impostors. Thus, even when you do get what you want, you may discover that what you wanted so badly doesn't bring the expected bliss and happiness. As such, you better learn to accept that no experiences will be entirely free from disappointment.

---

[1] Freud, S. (1916). Some Character-Types Met with in Psycho-Analytic Work. *The Standard Edition of the Complete Psychological Works of Sigmund Freud*, Volume XIV. London: The Hogarth Press and the Institute of Psychoanalysis.

## Developmental Trajectories

As we know, the way we look at things is very much influenced by our developmental trajectory. Early childhood is a critical period in which much imprinting takes place. Growing up, some of us may have been exposed to parental overstimulation or under-stimulation, or subjected to inconsistent, unpredictable childhood experiences. Each of these different developmental tracks can contribute to the development of a fragile sense of self and cause a different form of narcissistic injury.[2] Sometimes, our reaction to parental stimuli is to accept the image offered to us—even if the message is one of disappointment. In such cases, disappointment becomes a self-fulfilling prophecy. In other situations, our life task could be to do everything to prove our parents or early caregivers wrong. How secure or tenuous your self-esteem is, will determine the kinds of defensive action you take when faced with disappointment.

Depending on your developmental experiences, you may also become an underachiever. If you have disturbing memories associated with experiences of disappointment, you may unconsciously go to great lengths to set the bar low and avoid taking risks, in order to prevent yourself or others from being disappointed. Unconsciously, you may decide that the best strategy is not to have high expectations about anything. If you don't expect anything, it's hard to be disappointed. Such behavior turns into a form of self-preservation. However, it can also lead to mediocrity and an unfulfilled life. You may disappointment everyone, including yourself.

I have seen others, following a very different narcissistic trajectory, who seek to avoid disappointment by being over-achievers. Although they may tell themselves that their expectations to perfection are appropriate and realistic, these presumptions turn out not to be false. The bar is set far too high to make whatever they want to achieve attainable. They forget that perfectionism rarely begets perfection, or satisfaction—instead, it often leads to disappointment.

## Being Good Enough

The concept of "good enough" parenting was first used by the pediatrician and psychoanalyst Donald Winnicott[3] "Good enough" refers to the kind of

---

[2] Heinz Kohut (2009). *The Analysis of the Self: A Systematic Approach to the Psychoanalytic Treatment of Narcissistic Personality Disorders*. Chicago: University of Chicago Press.

[3] Donald W. Winnicott (1973). *The Child, the Family, and the Outside World*. London: Penguin.

parents who adequately meet the child's needs, keeping in mind that it is highly unrealistic to try to be perfect. Perfection is not within the grasp of ordinary mortals. Imperfection is part of the human condition. You better recognize that you will not always succeed as fully with your children as you would like to. This being the case, you should be able to forgive your own imperfections.

We should not expect our children to become perfect individuals. The best we can do as parents is to provide the conditions required for a satisfying childhood; to give them a secure environment. Good enough parents allow their children to make mistakes; they allow them to fail, knowing that mistakes and failures are inevitable components of learning. They create a secure base for their children, who feel supported rather than controlled, and who are able to play, explore, learn, and acquire the inner strength to cope constructively with the inevitable setbacks that will come their way in their journey through life.

## Styles of Coping

The question of how we cope when faced with disappointment is a defining moment for many of us. Returning to Robert, I noted how he was caught in an emotional rollercoaster. I saw how he wallowed in his disappointment, feelings of self-doubt, apathy, irritability, discouragement, a sense of abandonment, and demonstrated depressive reactions.

I have encountered far too many people who, when faced with disappointment, tend to attribute negative life events to their own personal failings. They resort to obsessional self-blaming, as they feel ashamed or humiliated of not measuring up to the image of their ideal self. As a result, they direct their anger inward toward themselves, causing depressive reactions. They may say "I deserved what was coming to me"; or "I was just not good enough." Others, however, turn their anger outward toward others who didn't fulfill their expectations. But doing this only leads to feelings of spite, vindictiveness, and bitterness. Unfortunately, both emotional reactions will keep people stuck in a web of disappointment.

People who remain disappointed are at greater risk of emotional or physical difficulties, or both. They are prone to a range of affective reactions: frustration, embarrassment, worry, anger, jealousy, guilt, confusion, rejection, hopelessness, and helplessness. Also, in many instances, disappointment can turn into a lingering sadness—a feeling of loss, a sense of being let down, or even feeling betrayed. This is especially the case when disappointment has been inflicted by people whom they trusted deeply. Furthermore, from a neuro-physiological perspective, feelings of disappointment can interfere with the normal levels of serotonin in the brain. When serotonin levels become disrupted as a reaction to stress, we begin to feel sad, anxious, and depressed. These chemical/neurological imbalances contribute to gastrointestinal problems, sleep disorders, and disturbances of other bodily functions.

## Overcoming Disappointment

Unpleasant as disappointment may be, we can always learn something from it. Whatever our developmental history may be, disappointment can provide us with valuable information about our beliefs about ourselves, other people, and what makes us happy.

So how could I help Robert? First, I told him that in order to deal constructively with disappointment, he needed to understand what had happened. His reality testing needed to be more effective. Were his expectations reasonable? If his expectations were unrealistic, could he readjust them? As he had revealed that disappointment was a theme throughout his life, I suggested it would be a positive step for him to reevaluate the source of this perception: was it the result of dysfunctional or irrational thinking? I encouraged him to be honest with himself about what underlay his perceptions and behavior in various situations.

If you belong to that group of people that sets their expectations too high, working constructively through disappointments may help you to modify your expectations. You may learn to move away from perfectionistic standards; you may start to be satisfied with "good enough." Others, who have set the bar too low due to disappointing experiences, should stop hanging on to false beliefs like "There's no hope," or "Nothing ever works for me." You may have to learn that avoiding disappointment is not a very constructive way of dealing with life's challenges.

To become more effective at coping, you may need to ask yourself whether you are aiming too high or setting your goals too low. Whatever your mental trajectory, are you inviting disappointment? Should you have been clearer in communicating what you expected from others? Do you really know what you expect from yourself? Are you listening to what others are saying to you? Could you have done something different to arrive at a different outcome? Also, given what you know about yourself, how can you adjust your expectations to be more effective from now on? What support and resources do you have at your disposal to help you manage your feelings of disappointment?

You also need to acknowledge that while some disappointments are predictable and preventable, there will be situations that are unavoidable and beyond your control. For example, none of us has control over political calamities, the economy, the job market, or other matters of this kind. Nobody could foresee the lockdown following the global covid-19 pandemic. Therefore, in managing disappointment, you need to differentiate between situations that are within your control, and factors that are beyond it. Being able to recognize the difference will help you to deal with your frustrations more appropriately.

The secret to dealing constructively with disappointment manner is to not let it deteriorate into apathy and depression. Sustained negative thoughts are no prescription for change. When you become preoccupied with bad news, you lose sight of what is right in your life and in the world around you. You internalize feelings of sadness and anger. Hanging on to these feelings can result in your unconsciously making them part of your identity.

I encouraged Robert to catch himself thinking negatively, and to try to redirect his energy and focus toward positive solutions. Hanging on to a disappointing experience would be detrimental in the long run. Dwelling on disappointing situations, like the failure of his early venture, was creating unnecessary stress. It would be much more constructive to reframe his disappointments as learning experiences to be able to cope better in the future, and to use disappointment as a catalyst for personal growth.

Remember that disappointment is not meant to destroy you. If taken in your stride, it can strengthen you and make you even better. In spite of its devastating emotional impact, you may even consider encounters with disappointment as journeys toward greater insight and wisdom. But to be able to make these journeys of self-reflection and re-evaluation meaningful, you need to look beneath the surface. Many of the psychological dynamics that contribute to disappointment are unconscious. Only by paying attention to these hidden mental processes can you mourn and transcend your losses. Only by working through painful associations will you be free from them. In spite of the disappointing experiences that will come your way, your challenge will be to stop bitterness taking root. Tell yourself that although disappointment is inevitable, feeling discouraged is a matter of choice.

# 20

## A-Players or B-Players?

*First-rate people hire first-rate people; second-rate people hire third-rate people.*
—Leo Rosten

*If each of us hires people who are smaller than we are, we shall become a company of dwarves. But if each of us hires people who are bigger than we are, we shall become a company of giants.*
—David Ogilvy

## B Trumps A

The following story was told by an executive who had come to me for advice. The XYZ Company had a vacancy for a new sales director. In due course, facilitated by a headhunting firm, the number of candidates was narrowed down to two. Given the company's ambitious expansion program, most people who had met the two final candidates were convinced that candidate A was the much better choice. In light of this candidate's extensive sales experience (she had worked for one of XYZ's major competitors), most of the executives who had interviewed her were convinced that she would be able to introduce the innovative sales management techniques needed to attain the projected growth targets. But to everybody's surprise, the VP Sales & Marketing decided to select candidate B. Given candidate B's more conventional sales background, all those in the know strongly believed that he was not the right person to serve the company's future needs. They thought his skill set was too similar to that of the person he was replacing. The VP's choice came as a surprise to everyone.

© The Author(s), under exclusive license to Springer Nature Switzerland AG 2021
M. F. R. Kets de Vries, *The CEO Whisperer*, The Palgrave Kets de Vries Library,
https://doi.org/10.1007/978-3-030-62601-3_20

# Personal or Company Agenda?

The opening quote at the start of this chapter says that A-grade people hire A-grade people, and B-grade people hire C-grade people. Of course, it goes without saying that individuals are much more complex than this suggests. They don't slot neatly into A, B, or C grades. But these kinds of rankings can be basic differentiators, to simplify our assessment of people.

## The Deadly Sin of Envy

It is certainly a common phenomenon in organizational life that some B-players—who may not be confident about their own level of competence—end up failing to hire the best people. Their feelings of personal insecurity, and the idea that someone might out-perform or even replace them, are too threatening. These people may be subject to the "deadly sin" of envy, a ubiquitous behavior pattern that colors all human relationships, and which I already wrote about in Chap. 15. Envy explains why so many people are capable of spiteful, vindictive actions. Because they covet something another person possesses or feel threatened by another person's abilities, feelings of envy can become very destructive.[1] It is a feature of the kind of social comparisons that accompany it, that threaten the envier's self-image, leading to feelings of deficiency, inadequacy, and inferiority. In turn, these induce feelings of resentment toward others who are perceived to be more successful, whether in terms of money, power, status, beauty, luck, or simply happiness. When this happens, the envier not only succumbs to unhappiness, but also becomes spiteful, wanting to hurt the envied person in various ways. Enviers can become withholding, and generally unhelpful. Consciously or unconsciously, these B-players feel they have been treated unfairly—and that the perceived wrongs they have experienced justify their behavior.

## A, B, or C?

It is not surprising that some B-players, tormented by envy, do not hire people as competent as them and end up hiring C-players. Interestingly, they often get away with it. After all, nobody wears an obvious sign labeling them A, B,

---

[1] Peter Salovey (1991) *The Psychology of Jealousy and Envy*. New York: Guilford Press; Joseph Epstein (2003). *Envy: The Seven Deadly Sins*. New York: Oxford University Press.

or C. But although these decisions might fit their personal agenda, they are not going to be in the best interests of the organization.

The case I began with signifies that in every hiring decision, the people doing the hiring are faced with the question whether they should hire someone perceived to be above their level, in the organization's interest, or hire a less competent person who would make them look better and make them feel more secure in their position, notwithstanding the cost to the organization. In most instances, the way the hiring process evolves will depend on the hirer's level of emotional security—the fragility of their self-esteem. If a person has a secure sense of self-esteem, faulty hiring decisions are less likely.

From what I have seen, given the various psychodynamic processes at play, insecure B-players tend to be intimidated by A-players. They worry that high-flyers will make them look bad, and fear, consciously or unconsciously, that they are out to replace them. No wonder that so many insecure B-players prefer to surround themselves with people who, in comparison, make them look good. Some are even inclined (again, not necessarily a conscious decision) to use office politics to stifle the ambitions of other B-players and try to turn them into C-players by, for example, withholding important information or insisting on following pointless hierarchical procedures—all tactics aimed at holding others back. Unfortunately, this behavior either gives B-players a false sense of security or fails to give them the security they crave for. Both outcomes are unsatisfactory. Seeing organizational life as a zero-sum-game—a place with only winners or losers—stops an organization moving forward and sets the stage for organizational decline. When such attitudes prevail, nobody wins, and everyone loses. The most likely scenario, when there are too many mediocre people in an organization, is that the climate in the workplace deteriorates, productivity slips, the work environment becomes less professional, and the company goes into the red. As a result, the best people will feel marginalized and even leave, lending truth to the saying, "Good enough is the enemy of great."

Another, less Machiavellian, explanation of why B-players are selected is that some B-players fail to recognize A-players. They tend not to be very good at talent assessment. Another factor that can influence selection procedures is that some A-players may come across as arrogant. By behaving like know-it-alls, they rub B-players up the wrong way, exacerbating emerging feelings of envy, and ending up not being hired.

Returning to the case of XYZ Company, and its surprise choice of a new sales director, the fears of many turned out to be valid. According to my client, it didn't take very long to discover that the chosen candidate wasn't up to par. Given his limited knowledge of new sales techniques, he was unable to respond to the challenges posed by the competition. Sometimes later, not only was he blamed for the resulting decline in sales, but his mediocre performance also negatively affected the reputation of the VP who had hired him, who was ultimately held responsible. Although the VP tried to attribute the lack of success to external factors beyond his control, his lame excuses did not fool anyone. I found it ironic, knowing that if he had realized that the smart decision would have been to have the courage to hire someone more capable than himself, his position within the organization might have been more secure.

To finish this depressing tale, as the company's market position deteriorated, the CEO told the VP to fire his chosen candidate, and soon after, given the sales fiasco, the VP was also asked to leave. Apparently, the CEO felt he had no choice but to step in and do some damage control. He had learned from hard experience that hiring the wrong people was the quickest way to destroy a company. Following this incident, the CEO decided to become much more involved in the hiring of senior people and make talent management, rather than damage limitation, a priority.

## Different Scenarios

Returning to the question of A-players versus B-players, I have seen how many A-players do indeed recognize the benefits of working with other A-players. They are not afraid of talented people—in fact, concern for their own careers can motivate them to develop the people who work for them. They understand that the people they work with will determine the success of the organization and support their own personal success. They recognize that organizations full of talented people will offer them more space for growth and development. All of this means that they are prepared to hire people better than themselves. This is a very different mindset from those B-players who prefer to keep their subordinates' skill levels well below their own. Such people do not prioritize leadership development and the career progression of others.

From a more political perspective, there will always be some A-players with a hyper-competitive outlook who prefer to work in companies full of Bs and Cs, seeing this as an opportunity for a rapid rise to the top. Consequently, they may sabotage the hiring process in their favor. A less cold-blooded scenario is one where A-players realize too late that the company that they have joined is full of B or even C performers. Not having seen this coming, they become disenchanted, and worry that these Bs and Cs will drag them down to their level. It will not be good for their further development. Their situation will be worsened if B-players perceive them as a threat and sabotage whatever they are doing. Some high performers could even become the target of convoluted psychological games to get them out of the organization. More optimistically, some A-players—with a more constructive outlook—will rise to the challenge that such organizations offer and try to change the place for the better. Realistically, however, the greater likelihood is that such people get tired of fighting uphill battles and decide to leave.

It is, of course, possible to have too many A-players in an organization. After the alternative scenarios I've presented here, organizations full of A-players may sound like best places to work. Unfortunately, managing and retaining so many high-flyers can become very hard work. Too many A-players can shake things up too much and their restlessness means they are always on the lookout for better positions elsewhere. Also, with too many ambitious A-players, organizational culture can become over-competitive, raising the possibility of an uncomfortably Darwinian scenario, having become an environment based on the survival of the fittest.

Of course, it is also true that not everyone aspires to be the king or the queen of the castle, and not everyone has the same motivations. Some people will be very achievement-oriented, while others prefer a more balanced lifestyle. Some kind of mix between As and Bs would be ideal but for each this always begs the question of how many is too many?

A company's long-term performance—even its survival—is often the result of the unsung commitment and contributions from its B-players, at least those who have a solid dose of inner security. These people are often the workhorses that bring stability to the organization, counterbalancing the A-players who may be inclined to engage in risky destabilizing behaviors. These more secure B-players—less interested in organizational gamesmanship—just get on with their work.

Another frequent scenario that I have encountered is the presence of a significant number of Bs in A-dominated organizations. Some of these Bs may be delighted about the potential learning opportunities this scenario offers; for others, the experience may be less positive, as the As might not make life easy for them. Dazzled by the capabilities of this elite group, many insecure Bs may find it hard to stand up to them. For their part, some As may find it difficult to deal with the B team, whom they might have labeled "dumb," or incompetent. They might find it tiresome having to communicate ideas that, to them, seem quite obvious. Obviously, these frictions will not make for a great working environment.

There will also be situations where the loyalty of A-players is questionable. Because they are in high demand, with ample opportunities in other organizations, some of them are inclined to believe that the grass is greener on the other side of the fence. Some A-players may even look at their current organization as a temporary holding station—a great place to learn and then move on, part of a well-thought-through career strategy. In comparison, B-players tend to be more loyal, recognizing that they do not have so many opportunities elsewhere—another reason why it is wise to have a mix of street-smart, pragmatic Bs and more conceptual A-thinkers. That combination can take an organization a long way.

What I consider the worst scenario, from a talent and cultural perspective, is when a company gradually goes down the drain due to the presence of too many B- or C-players.[2] As the top performers leave, the Bs and Cs start to look good but that is nothing more than another kind of optical illusion: they only look better because the quality of the talent pool in the organization has been diminished. When that happens, in relative terms, the Cs begin to look like Bs and the Bs more like As. This downward slide is an insidious but relentless process until mediocrity becomes the norm. In many instances, alarm bells only start ringing when there is a steep slide in profitability and the competition starts outperforming the organization. Unfortunately, from this point on, it becomes increasingly difficult to bring good people back into the company.

I don't have a simple formula for what makes people and an organization successful. Just as there is no baby without a mother, there are no A-, B-, or C-players without a context. It is everyone's challenge to create a context where people can operate at their best. I don't think that anyone has to be stuck for life with a B or C label. Given the right learning opportunities, I have seen many people going through a remarkable transformation. If senior management put real effort into leadership development, many B-players have a good chance to transform into A-players. Also, some people may be ranked as B-players simply because they are less attention-seeking than A-players, and are overlooked when it comes to promotions, or because they don't disguise their preference for a more balanced lifestyle over a high-pressure job. Or again, some B- or C-players are just in the wrong job, or the wrong company, which can be very demotivating. They will probably be much happier—and ranked differently—in a different position or different organization.

[2] Manfred F. R. Kets de Vries & Danny Miller (1984), *The Neurotic Organization*. San Francisco: Jossey-Bass.

# The Psychodynamics of Hiring

As I suggested, the majority of the workforce in most organizations is made up of competent, stabilizing B-players. The question remains, however, whether they can be trusted to be unbiased when making hiring decisions. Are they capable of hiring people better than themselves? Will they be tempted to go for Cs rather than As or other Bs? Typically—given the psychological effects of insecurity and envy—downward hiring is not made at a conscious level, but the effect is no less real because, even at their best, C-players are only marginally competent.

Unfortunately, C-players are not always easy to spot. Like most of us, they try to present their best selves during interviews. The references they provide are often not much help, either. As a general rule, references should always be read with caution.

As we can see from the XYZ Company case, C-players are usually recognized for what they really are after a relatively short period of time on the job, even though they may attribute their lack of success to factors beyond their control. But being found out as C-players doesn't necessarily mean they will disappear. As the case indicates, some B-players may fear that recruiting, then removing, a poorer performer will be taken as a sign of their ineffective leadership, and so they tend to hold on to C-players for as long as possible, which can turn out to be very costly for the organization.

A major take-away from the scenarios that I have outlined here is that you should pay considerable attention to unconscious psychodynamic processes when making hiring decisions—rather as you do when you are dating. Hiring and dating actually have a lot in common. Both are complex psychological processes during which either party can make huge errors. When hiring or dating, you do well to acknowledge that unconscious biases exist; if you don't take these into consideration, they can have an insidious effect on the whole process of finding the right fit. It's not enough to base hiring decisions on gut feelings. Much more is needed to be able to identify and hire talented people.

A-players are a scarce commodity, and it takes time and effort to develop the discipline necessary to put A-level hiring standards in place. Getting the right mix of A- and B-players requires much sensitivity and skill. No organization sets out to deliberately hire only B- or C-players but the people doing the hiring need to recognize that ineffective hiring practices will rapidly degrade the talent management pool, drive out potential A-players, and prevent the company from attracting new ones.

I recommend that all executives should keep in mind that hiring should always be part of a long-term strategy, not a quick fix for an immediate problem. I believe that the tougher the hiring process, the easier it will be to manage the people that are hired later on; so, from a procedural point of view, it is useful to have organizational discussions about (unconscious) biases, and the steps that need to be taken to minimize their negative effects. Although it is not always easy to admit to our personal insecurities, and how these might affect hiring decisions, these discussions will never be wasted. If the organization's leadership is prepared to deal with "undiscussables" when embarking on hiring, much harm will be avoided.

Selection processes are never going to be perfect but giving more people voice when hiring decisions are made is a highly effective way to minimize the effects of unconscious biases. As a general rule, it is advisable to involve people with very different outlooks in the selection process. The greater the diversity (in age, race, gender, experience, education), the more likely it is that biases will be minimized, groupthink will be avoided, and more thoughtful decisions will be taken.

From what I have learned from having been involved in many of these activities, the hiring process should always start with well-crafted job specifications that clearly define the skills, capabilities, and level of experience required for the position. But as well as verifying these essential qualifications, decision-makers need to assess a candidate's ability to fit in with the existing organizational culture. Generally speaking, very unstructured interviews aren't always helpful here. Standardizing the hiring process as far as possible, so that each candidate follows the same steps, will facilitate this assessment. When the people doing the hiring commit themselves to high standards for recruitment, and take a long-term view of expectations, the organization can only benefit.

Another important consideration is that the people involved in hiring should always be prepared to push back against calls to fill a position quickly. This sort of pressure only compromises hiring standards. It is better to delay a hire and resume searching rather than accept a lower-quality candidate who will take a long time to come up to par or, worse still, self-destruct. If several people involved in the hiring decision are ambivalent about a specific candidate, it would be wiser not to go ahead.

Finally, once hiring has taken place, the people who have made the hiring decision need to be able to explain clearly why they have chosen a particular candidate. Undertaking this kind of review will help identify whether certain types of candidates are being deselected or whether an opportunity to hire suitable candidates has been affected by unconscious biases in the selection process. Always remember that time spent on hiring is never wasted. A rush to recruit, with the risk of taking on the wrong person, is so much costlier.

The redoubtable business leader Lee Iacocca once said, "I hire people brighter than me and I get out of their way." This could be taken as a mantra for the hiring process. However, this involves successfully transcending our inner demons of insecurity and envy. In short, you better remind yourself that people who lack inner security are more likely to make self-interested decisions that are not in the best interests of the organization.

# 21

## How Close-Minded Are You?

*I am not arguing. I am simply explaining why I am right.*
—Anon

*Perseverance is stubbornness with a purpose.*
—Josh Shipp

In my experience, there is a fine line between stubbornness and persistence. I have learned from personal experience that, at times, being stubborn was the only way that I could turn what I thought was a good idea into reality. It was stubbornness that made me persevere. It was stubbornness that helped me to stand my ground when everyone else was trying to tell me I was wrong. So, I believe that stubbornness can be a great leadership quality—with the substantial condition, that is, that you are right in what you are stubborn about. In some circumstances, stubbornness can turn into a major determinant of success.

Stubborn people know what they want, and often tend to be more decisive and determined than others. They have a greater focus. Furthermore, they get things done. Qualities like vision, action orientation, grit, resilience, and persistence are derivatives of stubbornness. We might even argue that perseverance is stubbornness with a purpose.

To me, a great example of stubbornness is the French President Charles de Gaulle (1890–1970). De Gaulle was stubborn about his goals, but flexible about his methods. He refused to admit defeat after France was overrun by Germany in World War II. Determined as he was about this mission—in spite of being up against overwhelming odds—he knew how to persuade the

French that they would ultimately prevail. Having an unwavering belief in the greatness of his country helped him to turn his vision into reality. Again, after the war, through his determination, he managed to secure a permanent seat for France at the United Nations, authorized an independent nuclear deterrent for the country, and made sure that France played a major role in post-war Europe, turning it into a highly respected, global player.

In the case of Charles de Gaulle, stubbornness became a blessing. Unfortunately, there are not many stubborn great men of his ilk. This is because there is a fine line between constructive stubbornness and obstinacy. There is also a very narrow gap between stubbornness and stupidity. Some people have a tendency to get stuck on early evidence and refuse to budge. They are impervious to subsequent, relevant information. But this way of looking at things can have a very detrimental impact on interpersonal, group, and inter-group relationships. People will stand their ground for the wrong reasons.

When there is overwhelming evidence that you are wrong, but you still insist on doing things your way, it is questionable whether you are doing the right thing. In such situations, it's high time to ask yourself what motivates you to dig your heels in. What is happening in your inner world that makes you persist in acting apparently irrationally and detrimentally?

When we have to deal with stubborn people, we shouldn't be fooled by outside appearances. These people may seem invincible but there is a great difference between a strong person and a stubborn person. I have seen over and over again that although stubborn people may give the impression of strength and power, it is only a façade. Often, stubbornness appears to be the strength of the weak. If you dig a little bit deeper, you may discover that behind the façade, these people turn out to be insecure. Despite their external bluster, their inner world is haunted by unexpected demons. Contrary to appearances, they are making a heroic effort to hold on to very fragile mental equilibrium. Often, the least secure people will behave in the most dogmatic ways. Truly strong people know how to compromise, when necessary.

Every new situation is a threat to stubborn people. They are often fearful of change, which explains the rigidity that characterizes much of their behavior. At an unconscious level, given their delicate mental equilibrium, attempts to change their mind are equated with personal attacks on the self. This is why they are always on their guard, lashing out at anyone who tries to question their ideas. Admitting they could be wrong is non-negotiable. Instead of accepting new information, or that someone else could be right, they prefer to argue in defense of their original point of view. And once these stubborn people have made up their mind, they are unlikely to budge, even when faced with overwhelming evidence that they are wrong. They put psychological mechanisms in place to preserve their particular *Weltanschauung* and keep things the way they want them to be. The poet John Milton gave Satan this stubbornness in *Paradise Lost*. His Satan delights in having "A mind not to be chang'd by Place or Time," and determines that it is "Better to reign in Hell, than serve in Heav'n!"

## Confirmation Biases

In persisting in their faulty beliefs, stubborn people become prisoners of their own assumptions. Their insecurities make them ideal candidates for confirmation biases[1]—the tendency to process information only in ways consistent with their existing belief system. In such situations, pre-existing beliefs will interfere in the way they think, make decisions, and take actions. Due to their inflexible, fixed patterns of thought, their ability to form a more objective and nuanced picture of what's going on around them is limited. Apparently, the eye sees only what the mind is prepared to see.

But as I suggested before, beneath this pattern of stubbornness you often find deeply vulnerable people. Their oppositional behavior should be looked at as a form of compensation for feelings of inadequacy. Because they are so insecure, it is hard for them to back down and admit they were wrong or made a mistake. Backing down is interpreted as losing, being humiliated, and being diminished as a person. Conversely, insisting that they are right helps protect their fragile sense of self and protects them from feeling inferior.

## Power Games

Stubbornness also touches on the dynamics of power. When stubborn people perceive a threat to what they stand for—whether it is their dignity, honor, or pride—they may resort to power games in which there are only winners and losers. These emotionally charged matters become intertwined with stubbornness, making them even more likely to hang on to mistaken decisions. The novelist Somerset Maugham captured this exactly in his description of one of his characters: "Like all weak men he laid an exaggerated stress on not

---

[1] Raymond S. Nickerson (1998). Confirmation Bias: A Ubiquitous Phenomenon in Many Guises, *Review of General Psychology*, 2 (2), 175–220.

changing one's mind." Often, the theme that guides stubborn people is, "If I weaken, people will walk all over me." But trying not to appear weak only worsens the situation. Stubbornness becomes a self-defeating exercise.

## Transforming Stubbornness into Dogma and Ideology

Given their desire for closure, stubborn people cling to simplified ideas to make sense of what happens around them, even if the ideas they hang on to are inaccurate or incomplete. They don't understand cognitive complexity; they are poor at perceiving subtle nuances and differences. Other people are quickly categorized as "good" or "bad," depending on whether or not they agree with their ideas. They prefer simplistic, absolutist, all-or-nothing thinking, with no gray areas of uncertainty or disagreement. They are often prejudiced and resort to stereotyping.

Given stubborn people's close-mindedness, this behavior pattern comes to full fruition when it involves religions, ideologies, political philosophies, economics, and wellness issues. Embedded opinions in these areas are the hardest to change, as they are more subject to personal judgment and idiosyncratic interpretation. Often, these people will clung to miraculous outcomes, defying rational thought, even though there may have been a psychological rationale behind their way of thinking.

People's stubbornness can lead to the endurance of enormous opposition and numerous setbacks in the quest to remain faithful to a set of principles bound up with feelings of self-worth. They willfully ignore any fact that does not support their particular ideological principle, as their belief system has become the primary source of their self-validation. Bending these core principles is seen as a betrayal of what they are all about.

### Being Oppositional as a Survival Strategy

Some of you may be a mystified why people turn out to be so stubborn. But like most behavioral problems, it helps to look at the origins of stubbornness, which is usually a reaction to underlying emotional issues. Prevailing parenting practices can have a deep and sustained influence on a child's personality, and a great deal of what makes people stubborn is learned behavior.

I have seen many times that the way parents act vis-à-vis the developing child can either minimize stubborn behavior patterns or contribute to more adaptive ways of behaving. "Good enough" family and parenting interventions create the foundation of a healthy personality with positive self-esteem, a high level of self-acceptance, and self-confidence.[2] In contrast, imperfect parental skills can contribute to dysfunctional behavior patterns and create the foundations of stubbornness.

Generally speaking, the leitmotif of stubborn people is to resist any situation in which they feel forced to do something against their will. They are responding to a deeply rooted need to be individuals in their own right and have control over their lives. However, as the example of Charles de Gaulle reminds us, oppositional behavior shouldn't always be considered negative. For some people, stubbornness evolves into perseverance, not to mention other successful leadership qualities.

We can look at oppositional behavior as a defining pattern at a certain stage in child development and part of the natural process of individuation, the period when children try to differentiate themselves from their parents, recognizing that they are not merely an extension of their parents but separate entities. This mind-opening experience makes them want to exert more control over their world and to feel more independent.

We should also realize, however, that most people keep this oppositional behavior within reasonable bounds. Their childish stubbornness transforms into constructive behavior patterns such as perseverance, the determination not to give up easily. But in situations of family instability and high levels of stress—which contribute to insecure parent–child attachment patterns—oppositional behavior can become a child's customary way of attracting attention. It becomes part of its identity.

In short, we should keep in mind that for stubborn people, oppositional behavior is their way of rebelling against anyone in a position of authority and preventing them from telling them what to do. It becomes their way to exert more authority, to be in command, to play a winning hand. It becomes a major thread running through their lives: "If I don't win, others will find out how weak and vulnerable I am."

If this character trait is assigned to children by their parents, this specific behavior pattern becomes even more intensified. They internalize statements like, "You're as stubborn as mule, just like your uncle"; or "You remind me of your grandmother, she was stubborn, too." From a learning perspective, regular attribution contributes to internalization. It becomes part of their identity—a negative one at that. No wonder that the dominant mantra for many of these people is "I won't, therefore I am."

---

[2] Donald W. Winnicott (1973). *The Child, the Family, and the Outside World*. London: Penguin.

## Dealing with Stubborn People

You may have learned from this discussion that stubborn people have adopted a maladaptive strategy to maintain their sense of self-worth. Troubled by a host of insecurities, they have misconceptions about how to value themselves, others, and life in general. This makes them very difficult people to deal with. It is hard to interact with people who always need to be right, for whom to be proven wrong is interpreted as an attack on the essence of who they are.

But because stubbornness contributes to conflict, some of these people might want to change. In most instances, however, trying to change by themselves is going to be hard. And it should be said that in spite of their manifest willingness to change, it is difficult to help people who do not really listen and constantly push back. They are really in two minds about changing. Thus, to be effective, any potential helper—whether a significant other, family member, friend, colleague, or professional advisor—had better possess a solid dose of empathy.

Because stubborn people think poorly of themselves, helpers need to understand the story behind their stubbornness. Understanding where they come from will be the first step in helping them change. Digging deeper may help them discover some of the experiences that led to their stubbornness, to recognize that stubbornness is a survival mechanism to cover up vulnerability and maintain their psychological equilibrium.

As stubbornness has been their major strategy when dealing with others, stubborn people will not give it up easily. It is a game they have been playing all their life and they have become quite good at it. Thus, even when stubborn people realize how self-defeating their behavior is—how they have gotten stuck in these private rituals—they will be reluctant to accept that the game is over.

I've had considerable experience of dealing with stubborn people and I can say with certainty that if you want to help them, you need to be very careful how you go about it, not least because of their aversion to control. Stubborn people should never feel that others are trying to control them or force ideas on them (even in their best interests). I usually resort to a form of emotional judo. You need to go with the flow and control the impulse to oppose them; you should never move directly against their defenses.[3] Whatever resistances stubborn people put up—and however irritating they may be—you should try to remain empathic. Arguing with stubborn people will not pay off. They

---

[3] Stephen Rollnick and William R. Miller (1995). What is Motivational Interviewing? *Behavioral and Cognitive Psychotherapy*, 23 (4): 325–334.

are virtuosos at constructing arguments. Telling them directly that they are wrong is a very bad idea. But if you keep your cool—and listen carefully to what is being said—it is possible that stubborn people will become less argumentative.

Given stubborn people's vulnerable mental equilibrium, you have to be extremely careful not only about *what* to say but also *when* to say it. And when the time is right to present a different opinion, it should be done very respectfully. If this exercise in emotional judo is done correctly, stubborn people may give your point of view some thought, even though they initially reject it. Most importantly, you need to understand that the only way stubborn people will change is if they believe that the change is their own idea.

In many instances, given the many unconscious dynamics at play, professional help is recommended. But to be helped, to start with, stubborn people need to want to be helped. People can change but only if they are prepared to explore why they do what they do and discover different ways to deal with life. But stubborn as they are, getting them decide to do something about their way of thinking will never be a walk in the park.

However, stubborn people will profit from becoming more aware of the underlying issues behind their compulsion to hang on to specific ideas and persist in self-destructive behavior patterns. If they achieve a modicum of understanding about why they do what they do, there is a possibility that they will decide to let go of some of their rigid attitudes. Through psychotherapy or executive coaching, they may come to recognize that being argumentative or aggressive has become their chosen defensive strategy to compensate for feelings of inadequacy. And they may also come to realize how it has complicated their lives.

If I am able to establish a working alliance and find ways to support their sense of self-worth, I can help diminish a stubborn person's need for argumentation. I may help them learn to appreciate the value of looking at issues from different perspectives; they may even start to appreciate ambiguity. Also, they may discover that a defensive strategy that was quite effective at one point in their life has become outmoded and ineffectual. They may learn to unlearn old defense mechanisms, and to replace them with new, more constructive ones.

However, developing a more stable sense of self-worth is never a quick fix. It takes a lot of time and patience to open a closed mind. It takes a great deal of effort to persuade people that there are other ways to deal with the vicissitudes of life. The hope is, however, that stubborn people will realize that although the world is full of individuals who think they are right, the secret of a person's strength and pathway to greatness is the ability to admit when they have made the wrong decision. Also, they would be wise to recognize that ideology always drives out creativity. Furthermore, they should ask themselves what the sources of their seemingly irrational behavior patterns are. Stubborn people need to move beyond their fixed beliefs, ignorance, and pride. They need to be prepared to take a journey into themselves to explore the origins of their behavior. They need to recognize that stubbornness without reflection is nothing more than plain stupidity.

# 22

## Whatever It Is, I'm Against It

*I don't know what they have to say*
*It makes no difference anyway*
*Whatever it is, I'm against it.*
—"I'm Against It" *(Horse Feathers) (https://www.youtube.com/*
*watch?v=e7cry-4pyy8)*

I have always been intrigued by this song, performed by Groucho Marx in the film *Horse Feathers*. The film seems a bit dated nowadays, but the lyrics capture the spirit of our times. I live in the center of Paris, and I only had to go around the corner from my apartment to witness the *Gilets jaunes* (Yellow Jersey) protests in France every Saturday for several weeks in 2019. The behavior of the *Gilets jaunes* made me wonder whether some people only feel alive when they oppose something. Being against something, irrespective of what it is, seems to be a part of their chosen identity. It is the kind of behavior pattern we sometimes find among children and it has many similar developmental origins as stubbornness. However, in this instance, elements of what makes for stubbornness are transformed into a social movement.

Keeping in mind what I have said about stubborn behavior patterns in Chapter 21, defiant behavior patterns also remind me of the work on the human life cycle of Erik Erikson, the renowned psychologist and teacher, whose work I followed closely during my studies at Harvard University. In his scheme of life stages, Erikson presented the second stage of human development in the form of the polarity of autonomy versus shame and doubt.[1] At an

---

[1] Erik Erikson (1993). *Childhood and Society.* New York: W. W Norton.

© The Author(s), under exclusive license to Springer Nature Switzerland AG 2021
M. F. R. Kets de Vries, *The CEO Whisperer*, The Palgrave Kets de Vries Library,
https://doi.org/10.1007/978-3-030-62601-3_22

early age, young children experience conflicts around control that originate in basic bodily functions. Most children find ways to come to grips with this conflict and move on. But some are not so fortunate and continue to have issues with control. They continue to engage in oppositional behavior, mirroring some of the patterns I described in Chap. 22. For example, the *Diagnostic and Statistical Manual of the Mental Disorders (DSM V)*, lists a category called Oppositional Defiant Disorder (ODD), a disruptive behavioral pattern found amongst children and teenagers.[2] Children with ODD tend to exhibit uncooperative, defiant, and hostile behavior toward their peers, parents, teachers, and other authority figures. Youngsters that are prone to this disorder display a pattern of argumentative, rebellious behavior, and anger and vindictiveness toward authority figures over an extended period of time. They refuse to follow the rules, misbehave, throw tantrums, blame others for their mistakes, seek revenge, or intentionally create disturbance. Their extremely hostile attitude disrupts their home, school, and social life.

To account for the emergence of ODD, imagine situations where children are forced to follow rules that have not been explained or are experienced as unfair and unreasonable. In such instances, children will attempt to break these rules or push back against them. Other situations in which ODD may develop are those where parents impose very strict discipline on the developing child for no good reason. When parents are too controlling, too possessive, and want to make all the decisions about their children themselves, it is not surprising that their offspring will think their freedom is threatened. To resist intrusive parental behavior, children who do not just give up resort to stubbornness as a defensive strategy to avoid the distress of feeling constantly controlled. You may be able to imagine other situations where children exposed to inconsistent parenting (unclear rules and inconsistent enforcement of rules) try to test the limits in the hope of breaking them down. In such cases, rule-breaking could become a dominant behavior pattern.

Although commonly observed in young adults, we can see how, under certain conditions, this pattern can manifest itself among adults, especially during periods of high stress and uncertainty.

To find out if you, or anyone you know, are exhibiting signs of ODD, answer the following questions:

- Do you/they have difficulties in dealing with authority figures?
- Do you/they always need to win whatever argument you/they get into?
- Do you/they always question the rules, or refuse to follow the rules?

---

[2] American Psychiatric Association (2013). *Diagnostic and Statistical Manual of Mental Disorders, DSM V*, Washington, DC: American Psychiatric Publishing.

- Are you/they often angry?
- If a person crosses you/them, will you/they fight that person relentlessly?
- Do you/they sometimes deliberately try to annoy others?
- Do small things easily set you/them off?
- Have you/they been accused of blaming others for your/their mistakes?
- Do you/they believe that when someone double-crosses you/them, revenge is the only possible response?
- Do you/they have the habit of saying nasty things when you/they are upset?

If the answers to most of these questions are affirmative, you might as well start singing along with Groucho.

Adults with ODD-like behaviors defend themselves endlessly when someone points out that they've done something wrong. They feel misunderstood and disliked, hemmed in, and pushed around. Given their *Weltanschauung*, some of these people may even see themselves as mavericks or rebels. Unfortunately, their constant opposition to authority figures makes it difficult for them to maintain jobs, relationships, and marriages

This oppositional behavior pattern is often rooted in one dimension of our identity, bearing in mind that our identity is multi-faceted and contains both positive and negative aspects. (See Chap. 17, where I comment on the dynamics of the true and the false self—the need to wear various masks.) Constructive and nurturing events help us develop a positive self-concept, while negative, hurtful experiences often lead to the reverse. But throughout life, our darker and negative sides will remain a part of our total identity, even if they remain hidden. However, certain adverse conditions, especially those that undermine our sense of control and security, can trigger the emergence and expression of our shadow side.

Thus, depending on what's currently happening in your life, you might feel confident or unsure; optimistic or pessimistic about the future; think you have some control over your life or very little control. Your outlook—depending on your circumstances—will determine which aspect of your identity will manifest itself. Will you have a constructive or destructive outlook? Will you seek positive changes to make things better, or will you be against everything that comes your way?

# The Psychological Dynamics of Being Against It

Applying this to populist movements like the *Gilets jaunes*, most are characterized by being against something, whatever it is. Many of them seem nihilistic, compelled to *be defiant*. Their position is to be at odds with the existing values and expectations of traditional society, rather than proposing and pushing forward a more positive alternative identity—the kind that enables us to move forward in life with purpose and direction. Their attitude is negative, aimed at destroying things (due to feelings of envy, spite, and vindictiveness), and based on the feeling that they have gotten a bad deal in life. These fringe movements have been helped in the context of our information-heavy environment; catchy slogans and inflammatory rhetoric on social media are far more likely to grab our attention than official press releases and formal speeches. The influence of social media is further amplified by the fact that populist-leaning people distrust or don't value traditional media. The rhetoric of these demagogue leaders, perfected online, tends to pit the masses against the elite, immigrants against citizens, never taking any responsibility for policy errors themselves.

That being said, I believe that taking a position of stubborn defiance is the choice of the vulnerable and disempowered, those who believe that socio-economic and political forces are stacked against them. What makes this an attractive choice, however, is that it is much easier to organize around what we're against than what we're for. And unfortunately—given the surge in popularity of fringe movements—it looks like the politics around our world is increasingly defined by what we are against—an opposition to the status quo, perceived as a threat to people's quality of life.

Major socio-economic and political forces have now become extremely disruptive, spreading fear and anxiety throughout large segments of the population. Many people are angry at the dramatic gaps in income levels—where wealth is concentrated amongst the top 1% of income earners. The middle class can no longer take the upward mobility of their children for granted. What adds to their fears is the pace of technological advances, the rise of artificial intelligence, and automation, which threaten many blue-collar jobs. Many are asking themselves, "If I am what I have, and if I lose what I have, who am I?" Their basic sense of self is at risk.

In addition to these concerns, many people are threatened by demographic changes in the form of migration, which has led to a surge in identity politics. Anxiety is also fueled by jihadist attacks and iconic terrorist organizations, such as Al-Qaida and ISIS. Every day, our news describes new atrocities that undermine our sense of security and safety. Since the end of World War 2, we have lived with the threat of a nuclear holocaust. The present coronavirus crisis has only exacerbated this situation, demonstrating fundamental weaknesses in our global economic systems. And, of course, the mother of all fears is climate change—and how we could bring about our own destruction—a fear so great that many people resort to mass denial.

It is clear that all these forces create a sense of helplessness and vulnerability. They also fuel resentment—a feeling of betrayal by the traditional institutions and leadership that, in the past, used to provide stability and a safety net. Consequently, many people no longer believe in the fairness and legitimacy of existing social systems.

It shouldn't come as a surprise that, in response, politics has become increasingly polemic, with voters organizing around opposing institutions and its leaders. Populist parties stoke fears about lost national identity, asserting that the establishment has sold them out, that they have been economically, politically, and socially, left behind. Many demagogue-like leaders of these populist parties pour oil on the fire of an already vulnerable electorate. Working off the fears of the helpless and disgruntled, they package over-simplified ideas: take back control from corrupt elites who are giving away their national heritage (financially and culturally) to dangerous immigrants.

What these people fail to realize is that following these demagogue-type leaders will only provide a temporary outlet for their situation. In the long run, the slogans of these demagogues create more division and only increase instability. Most of the people attracted to extremism seem to have forgotten the terrible atrocities of fascism, Nazism, communism, totalitarianism, and genocide. Instead, they consume an incessant supply of fake news in a sort of theater of the absurd. We no longer rely on the moderation, policy stability, and informal checks imposed by an establishment (notwithstanding all its imperfections) that, before the rise of the social media, would have been able to neutralize extreme populist views.

In the United States, President Donald Trump has been a prime example of this kind of modus operandi. A master of hyperbole, hysteria, slander, and destructive partisan polarization, he is the spirit of "whatever it is, I'm against it," whether "it" is the Paris Climate Accord, NATO, the European Community, NAFTA, or the WHO. Trump's divisive rhetoric and disturbing tweets have created a rise in hate-filled politics, with a cult-like following, in spite of being an example of incredible dysfunctional leadership—his management of the coronavirus crisis a prime example. But his behavior has had a ripple effect, emboldening other demagogues around the globe. Many of these strongmen—like those in Russia, the Philippines, Brazil, Hungary,

China, Turkey, Saudi Arabia and North Korea—are now acting out with impunity because they see a kindred spirit in their illiberal counterpart in Washington.

In Britain, Brexit has been animated by opposition to the European Union rather than any clear alternative to its membership of it. But France's *Gilets jaunes* offer a glimpse of post-establishment politics at its purest, as they can agree only on their anger at the status quo and their great distrust of institutions. Notwithstanding their impressive power to mobilize, their tear-it-all-down philosophy has left them with very little to show for, once more illustrating the danger that the politics of destruction only contributes to social breakdown.

Therefore, a major challenge in today's society is how to deal with this phenomenon of "whatever it is, I'm against it.". What can we do to prevent regressive, ODD-like feelings from becoming mainstream? How can we prevent the shadow side of our identity from becoming to the fore?

A stable positive identity includes the ability to maintain a sense of self (the true self) that stays the course and remains steadfast even under great stress. The ability to fight feelings of helplessness very much depends on how well we retain an optimistic outlook on life. The degree to which we can do this will give us the courage to imagine that we can make a difference, whatever the circumstances.

To create a better society, all of us need to make an effort to prevent our shadow side from gaining the upper hand. All of us should be aware that the language of the negative identity only results in self-limiting and self-destructive behavior. I realize that standing up to "whatever it is, I'm against it" movements will be a daunting task. It is a real challenge to take a stand against destructive leaders like Donald Trump, who aggressively assault justice, humanity, and the environment. We can only stand up against these people if we have a compelling story to tell. We have to present more constructive alternatives.

Populist movements have a point, in that a number of societal changes are highly overdue. Being against something can be a useful agent for much-needed change. Many societies have become deeply unequal, starkly divided into the haves and the have-nots. It is true that the hallmarks of postwar middle-class life—a steady job, a paycheck adequate to support a family, the prospect of a pension—have disappeared. It's also true that finance capitalism, the successor to industrial capitalism, has created immense fortunes without even pretending to distribute the benefits equitably.

As an alternative scenario to divisive everything-or-nothing politics, more than ever, given the coronavirus crisis, we need to create communities of care within our societies that are prepared to take the kinds of action that will overcome the inequities that characterize our world. Instead of breaking and burning, denying and excluding, why not try to find common ground to create bridges that will span our differences.

Our challenge is to create societies governed by shared responsibility and reciprocity—so that people can feel secure in their communities. To acquire this kind of security, however, means rebuilding trust through collective, cooperative action. Therefore, we need to take the kinds of measures whereby the idea of the common good takes on a central place. This implies living in a world less dominated by materialism and selfishness; a world that goes beyond the special interests of the few; a world where it is common sense to be concerned about the common good. As the philosopher-doctor Albert Schweitzer poignantly put it, "To work for the common good is the greatest creed."

We need to create societies where the present generation takes on a greater responsibility for the next, societies where the future of our children and grandchildren takes pride of place. This might sound idealistic, but when people work together in strong communities with shared goals and a common purpose, they can make the impossible, possible—something that will not happen, I believe, if the "whatever it is, I'm against it," movement, has its say.

# 23

## Living in the "I" world

*I wonder if the course of narcissism through the ages would have been any different
had Narcissus first peered into a cesspool. He probably did.*
—Frank O'Hara

*Remember that sometimes not getting what you want is a wonderful stroke
of luck.*
—Dalai Lama

In this chapter, I'd like to build on my comment (in Chap. 22) that our greatest challenge today is to create societies governed by shared responsibility and
reciprocity. In 1887, the sociologist and philosopher Ferdinand Tönnies published *Gemeinschaft und Gesellschaft* (*Community and Society*), in which he
drew a distinction between the two societal forms.[1] In *Gemeinschaft*—
community—social ties are defined on the basis of personalized social relationships, and the roles, values, and beliefs associated with these interactions.
*Gesellschaft*—society—is more impersonal and rational, characterized by indi-
rect interactions, formal roles, and generalized values and beliefs. *Gemeinschaft*
is applied to peasant communities (families, tribes, or villages) within which
human relationships are prized, the welfare of the group takes precedence over
the individual, traditional bonds of family, kinship and religion prevail, and
personal relationships are defined by traditional social rules. In contrast,
*Gesellschaft* is representative of a more urban, cosmopolitan society with an

---

[1] Ferdinand Tönnies (1887). *Gemeinschaft und Gesellschaft*, 8th edition, reprint 2005, Darmstadt:
Wissenschaftliche Buchgesellschaft.

individualistic outlook, where social ties are more instrumental and superficial. In short, self-interest prevails, and efficiency and other economic and political considerations have pride of place.

It is my opinion, reflecting on Tönnies' ideas, that in the best of all worlds, a society should embody both qualities. The challenge is to create a balance, however, between *Gemeinschaft* and *Gesellschaft*—to ensure that both individual and societal needs are accommodated.

## Collectivism Versus Individualism

People who live in a *Gemeinschaft* tend to have a more collective orientation, have solid bonds with the people they interact with, and define themselves in terms of their interdependency—the group has priority over the individual. The collective "good" plays a central role, as opposed to the good of the single person. As people have common goals and values, the aims of the individual will be aligned with those of the group to which they belong. People are willing to sacrifice their own values and goals for the "greater good"—as used to happen in agricultural communities where personal relationships, discipline, and solidarity are vital for survival.

In contrast, individual interests have pride of place if a society has *Gesellschaft* characteristics. People will put their own ambitions before those of the group, pursue their personal values, act on their own judgment, and give preference to their own aspirations and desires over the interests of others. Predictably, these societies lack deep, meaningful connections.

## The Transition Toward *Gesellschaft*

During the last century, a transition from *Gemeinschaft* toward *Gesellschaft* has taken place, a process that has accelerated in recent decades. This implies that the focus on what's best for the community and the family has changed to "what's best for me." In a post-industrial, digital world, there has been a switch toward *Gesellschaft* and the kind of individualistic behavior patterns found in more complex, technologically advanced societies, where a "survival of the fittest" mindset prevails.

There a darker side to this transition from *Gemeinschaft* to *Gesellschaft*. It has transformed the "we" society to an "I" society, social entities where self-promotion and individuality have taken pride of place, and where self-realization is pursued at all costs. The "I" society is oriented toward personal success—as defined by wealth, power, and status. This kind of society is less interested in making meaningful contributions to the greater good. The transformation from *Gemeinschaft* to *Gesellschaft* is reflected in a shift in values from collectivism to individualism, and from civic responsibility to self-gratification. With the rise of individualism and decline of social norms and structures, I fear that the family and community no longer provide the same level of support as they did in the past.

It is paradoxical—and counter-intuitive—that in our hyper-connected digital age, collectivism appears to be on the wane. Strange as it seems, social networking and collectivism diverge. Despite social media mantras about making the world more interconnected, we should not mistake connectivity for collectivism. Social media connectivity tends to be very superficial. Frequently, it simply accentuates feelings of detachment—it makes people aware of their lack of real connections.

The transition to *Gesellschaft* has been detrimental for many people. The breakdown of social ties leaves many of us with feelings of emptiness, a paucity of social meaning, and a sense of disconnection. Moreover, it accentuates a number of potentially dysfunctional personality traits. A high achievement orientation often goes hand-in-hand with personal arrogance and self-involvement. My fear is that this focus on individualism has created the building blocks of a culture of narcissism—and the indifference, egotism, disrespect, and lack of consideration of others that come with it.[2] Social media (as I mentioned before) sow discord through identity politics, populism, paranoia, fake news, hatred of the press, and xenophobia. I view the increasingly polarized and vitriolic tone of the current body politic as a manifestation of this development. I can make the same observation about the increase in hate crimes. What's more, unethical corporate behavior has fanned these flames. In the "I" society, qualities that make for social connection—respect, compassion, empathy, tolerance, humility, and selflessness—seem to have fled.

---

[2] Christopher Lasch (1991). *The Culture of Narcissism*. New York: W. W. Norton.

# The Self-esteem Movement

Changes in parenting styles are driving this transition. In a *Gesellschaft* society, parents put greater value on their youngsters' individual achievements than their civic duties. This particular *Weltanschauung* is driven by studies suggesting a correlation between high self-esteem and being successful in life.[3]

Advocates of the self-esteem movement have a point: we all have an innate need for self-assurance. We want a secure sense of self because it affects the mental, spiritual, social, and physical aspects of our lives. Helping children acquire a solid sense of self-esteem is essential for their development. It becomes a problem, however, when parents go too far, when it leads to extreme individualism. We need to realize that there is a fine line between being a "good enough" and a dysfunctional parent.

Some parents have gone overboard trying to build self-confidence into their children, telling them how special and unique they are, showering them with praise, and even creating situations where it is impossible for children to fail or be exposed to criticism or adverse consequences. These "helicopter" parents fight their children's battles, not realizing that by over-protecting them, nobody wins. They simply insulate them from the difficult experiences needed to facilitate their growth and resilience—and also, at the same time, send them the subliminal message that they will not be able to cope on their own.

Advocates of the self-esteem movement fail to realize that self-esteem is neither conferred nor a gift—it is acquired, through hard work, by overcoming adversity, and by taking risks. Self-esteem cannot be built on a shallow foundation of physical beauty, imagined superiority, feelings of entitlement, and unearned rewards. Confidence comes from competence. When we give our children the opportunity to stretch themselves, they expand their sense of their own capabilities, which makes them feel confident to tackle the next challenge. Authentic life experiences promote independent thinking, enterprise, resilience, and adaptability, enabling a growth mindset. Only when our children are praised for real accomplishments are the foundations for genuine self-esteem laid.

---

[3] Nathaniel Branden (2001). *The Psychology of Self-Esteem: A Revolutionary Approach to Self-Understanding that Launched a New Era in Modern Psychology.* San Francisco: Jossey-Bass.

# The Culture of Narcissism

I believe that these two converging societal shifts—*Gemeinschaft* to *Gesellschaft* and the self-esteem movement—have had a dramatic impact. As both movements encourage a stronger focus on the self, narcissistic behavior and the incidence of narcissistic personality disorders have increased dramatically.[4]

The handbook for psychiatrists, the *Diagnostic and Statistical Manual of Mental Disorders* (DSM V), describes narcissistic personality disorder as "a pervasive pattern of grandiosity (in fantasy or behavior), need for admiration, and lack of empathy that begins by early adulthood and is present in a variety of contexts."[5] Some of the patterns of this personality type are a grandiose sense of self-importance, a preoccupation with fantasies of unlimited success, power, brilliance, beauty, or ideal love. Narcissists believe that they are special, have a need for excessive admiration, possess a sense of entitlement, are interpersonally exploitative, lack empathy, and are envious of others. They are arrogant, believing themselves exceptionally talented, remarkable, and successful. They are highly skilled at exhibiting or "posturing" high self-esteem. But behind the bravado, they are in fact insecure. Indeed, it is likely that their feelings of insecurity are what drive these people to constantly prove themselves in the first place.

This "cult" of the self is quite worrisome. Not only does it exemplify all the characteristics of the narcissistic personality, like grandiosity and self-importance, but it also has touches of psychopathy. These include the use of superficial charm, a need for constant stimulation, a penchant for lying, deception, and manipulation, and the incapacity to feel guilt and remorse.

# Social Media

Social networking sites are an ideal breeding ground for narcissistic behavior patterns, helping to expand the "I" society. As narcissists prefer superficial connections with other people, social networks are a godsend—the ideal medium to validate a person's existence. Digital platforms enhance self-expression, providing tools for budding narcissists to show the world how

---

[4] J. M. Twenge, S. Konrath, J. F. Foster, K. Campbell, and B. J. Bushman (2008). Egos Inflating Over Time: A Cross-Temporal Meta-Analysis of the Narcissistic Personality Inventory, *Journal of Personality*, 76:4, 875–901; http://time.com/247/millennials-the-me-me-me-generation/.

[5] American Psychiatric Association (2013), *Diagnostic and Statistical Manual of Mental Disorders, DSM V*, Washington, DC: American Psychiatric Publishing.

great they are. Social media have become a crutch to help people deal with personal insecurities. And like a drug, they can become addictive.

The Millennials and beyond (Generation Z)—the "Generation Me"— seem to be especially talented in using social media. However, their attachment to these social platforms makes them vulnerable, as it can create a very insular existence. Constantly on their cells and tablets, they spend hours on Facebook, YouTube, Instagram, Snapchat, WhatsApp, or Twitter to advertise their "brand" and to boost their sense of self-esteem. Given the addictive nature of these activities, it is not surprising that many spend more time on social media than "normal" social endeavors, such as eating, drinking, and socializing. I would go so far as to say that social networking sites provide the same kinds of highs as gambling, drinking, drugs, or sex.

The trouble with social networking is that nearly everyone presents an unrealistic picture of themselves—I see this for myself in the messages I receive from my children and grandchildren. All these glorious pictures, enjoyable as they may be, do not exactly reflect the real world. They are a way of showing us at our best. The downside of this kind of exhibitionism is that the recipients of these images and messages often compare themselves negatively to others—overestimating the fun others have and underestimating their own experiences. As a result, they constantly think they are missing out on something. They don't realize that what they are getting is a sanitized version of a generally "messy" human experience. So, rather than feeling good, they start to feel bad about themselves. No wonder that many social network users feel lonely, frustrated, or angry after spending much time on the web—they feel inadequate compared to their "friends."

In terms of developing self-esteem, it doesn't help that Millennials (and beyond) are constantly influenced and pressured by their peers. This is very different from past patterns of learning, where much education and information was transmitted by the older generation. In the socially networked world, people form superficial connections with others, rather than forming rich, community-based, or family interactions. Since they spend so much time looking at screens—as opposed to engaging in face-to-face interactions—they don't develop the communication and empathic skills to understand and connect with others.

# Looking Ahead

What steps need to be taken from an individual, organizational, and societal perspective to create a better balance between *Gemeinschaft* and *Gesellschaft*? How can societies further economic and political development whilst preserving the qualities that make for a livable, cohesive, self-critical community? Does the rise in individualism (the move to *Gesellschaft*) mean that the community and family no longer provide as much social support as they did in the past, and has this created fertile ground for narcissism? Are social media turning into incubators for the creation of self-absorbed, insecure narcissists?

A priority should be to neutralize some of the premises of the self-esteem movement. True enough, as parents we need to instill in our children a solid dose of self-esteem, but praise needs to be tied directly to appropriate, identifiable behaviors and successes—preferably offline. Given the perils of becoming a social media addict, taking a break and having more face-to-face encounters will be beneficial. Parents and educators should make a strenuous effort to increase the amount of actual human (i.e., face-to-face) interaction that children have, to provide the experiences needed to develop essential social skills such as empathy, compassion, and consideration for others. If these are successfully internalized, it will make them more civic-minded and more politically committed than is currently the case.

In organizational life, the challenge is how to make business "a force for good," given the duplicity that's all too frequently taking place. Again, ways need to be found to prevent the "I" society gaining the upper hand, for example, not allowing overly narcissistic individuals to become CEOs or to occupy senior roles within the management team. Too often, under narcissistic leadership, subordinates simply tell these leaders what they want to hear—so that leaders live in an echo chamber, making for behavior patterns and decisions that can have dire organizational consequences, including fraudulent activities. When dealing with such people, we should keep in mind that they may profess company loyalty but, deep down, are committed only to their own agenda; most decisions are determined by self-interest rather than the interests of the organization, its various stakeholders, or society.

To me, the real challenge as an organizational designer and leadership educator, is to create humane organizations—places where people have voice, learning opportunities to express their creative capabilities, and enjoy a coaching culture where leadership is a "team sport," not the bailiwick of the few—and not "Darwinian soups" (i.e., places of work where everyone is out for themselves). These kinds of organizations do not have "shareholder value"—an invitation to long-term disaster—as their exclusive rallying cry. They realize that they have many stakeholders; they take a long-term perspective, focus on sustainability, and seek to be part of a sustainable world.

Although all of us need a dose of narcissism for reasons of wholesome self-esteem, being at the high end of the narcissistic spectrum is a different matter. In more than one way, excessive narcissism is the dark side of individualism. It advocates freedom without responsibility, relationships without personal sacrifice, and a positive self-view that is far from grounded in reality. When it permeates a society, we create an "I" world, characterized by vanity, materialism, entitlement, and fame-seeking. It becomes a society without values or empathy, where superficial, exploitative behavior, greed, materialism, and an excessive consumer culture reign.

The pursuit of unrestrained self-interest—the belief that acting in our own self-interest will create better outcomes for all—is illusionary. "I" societies can bring out the worst in people. They make for a toxic social, economic, and political environment. Indeed, the most recent global financial crises were created in part by the overly narcissistic behavior of investment bankers— rather unscrupulous financial engineers. Many of these "masters of the universe" were driven by narcissistic overconfidence, with dire consequences for society. The same comment can be made about the way many countries have dealt with coronavirus pandemic, largely everyone for themselves with very little cooperation when it was direly needed.

Ironically, when you look at the history of Homo sapiens, the way we survived the harsh savannas of Africa—the way we were able to overcome the much stronger predators—was through cooperation. Given our evolutionary history, we are hardwired for cooperation and prepared to engage in altruistic acts. But although Homo sapiens has a history of altruism, ironically, the leaders we often choose—in light of our dependency needs—seem to suffer from narcissistic or even psychopathic personality disorders. It appears that, as Homo sapiens, there is constant tension on the cooperation-coercion axis. In many instances, these highly seductive people—who offer miraculous cures for whatever ills trouble society—"trump" cooperative processes.

With this kind of leadership, it shouldn't come as a great surprise that the racial and ideological tensions and extreme political partisanship present in many countries today have come about due to a culture of narcissism. Too many policymakers, even though they may make high-minded propositions, are deep down self-focused, interested in short-term gain, and lack the empathy to reassess the world from other perspectives. But these "I" oriented people don't seem to realize that a society driven by selfishness is a lonely place and does significant damage to the people living in it. It is a potential powder keg that can have catastrophic consequences, with the potential to destroy our planet. The coronavirus pandemic has illustrated the extent to which the world we live in is highly interrelated. Just pursuing narrow self-interests is not going to be the answer. And the pandemic has shown that many of our leaders did not have what it takes to deal with this crisis effectively.

I believe that it is high time to restore the balance between *Gemeinschaft* and *Gesellschaft*, so that we are able to live within communities in which social ties and interactions are guided by a sense of responsibility and civic duty, while simultaneously navigating a complex post-industrial and increasingly virtual society. The language of community needs to be restored but there will be no sense of community without a sense of caring. As individuals, our ambitions must be broad enough to include the needs of others, for their sake and our own. At the same time, we should not be seduced by those who seem high-minded but in reality, have only their own interests at heart. We should be cognizant that behind their lofty statements, what they are really trying to do is to transform *Gemeinschaft* into cult-like movements.

# 24

## Are You Attracted to a Cult?

*One person's religion is another person's cult.*
—Philip Seymour Hoffman

*[The behavior of] people under the influence of cults is similar to that we observe in addicts. Typical behavior for both includes draining bank accounts, neglecting children, destroying relations with family, and losing interest in anything except the drug or cult.*
—Keith Henson

Why anyone would be attracted to a cult has always puzzled me. To me, cults only evoke uncomfortable associations—for example, the Manson family, Heaven's Gate, or Jonestown. Cults also remind me of the Hare Krishna movement, and other esoteric eastern religious groups. Beyond these religious groups, there is a lot of cult-like behavior within political and lifestyle groups, and even business associations. Certain political regimes are forms of cults, North Korea being a prime example. I wonder whether the proliferation of cult-like movements is symptomatic of the general social discordance that has plagued post-World War II Western society. And as I suggested in Chap. 23, it may even be a reaction against the movement from *Gemeinschaft* to *Gesellschaft*.

The question that stays with me, however, is why do people join cults? What motivates them to do so? One major reason for taking this step is clearly the search for meaning. Cults promise answers to problems or questions that simply aren't provided in mainstream society. They appear to satisfy basic human desires for absolute answers to questions such as good versus evil, the

M. F. R. Kets de Vries, *The CEO Whisperer*, The Palgrave Kets de Vries Library, https://doi.org/10.1007/978-3-030-62601-3_24

role of religion, the meaning of life, the impact of politics, and the thing disliked in the status quo. The deep human need to belong to a group adds more to a cult's attractiveness. We all have dependency needs. Some people join cults simply out of a desire to be a part of a community.

People are attracted to the promises of power and salvation made by a cult's leadership. Many cult leaders radiate charisma. Charming, engaging, and very persuasive, they have an uncanny ability to seduce followers. Behind all this charm, however, many cult leaders have narcissistic, anti-social, and even psychopathic personality disorder traits.

Quite early in my career I met the leader of some kind of commune, let's call him Ken. I contacted him at the request of the parents of one of his disciples, who had been a student at my university. The parents asked me if I would be willing to visit the commune and tell them what I observed. Curious as I was about different kinds of organizational designs, I agreed. At the time, I was a professor in the faculty of management at McGill University, where I was interested in different forms of organizations, due to the influence of my old friend, Henry Mintzberg.[1]

I have to admit that when I first met Ken, I was taken in by his charm. He had a remarkable ability to beguile and seduce. Actually, meeting him was quite a piece of theater. He was dressed flamboyantly and had an overdramatic way of speaking. One anomaly that struck me was his arrival in a sports car. Apparently, Ken was not only preaching spiritual enlightenment, he also had a penchant for fast cars. When I asked him a few questions about his background, he responded with a number of unclear statements about the supposedly aristocratic milieu in which he had grown up. As an aside, he also mentioned that he had been a disciple of a number of famous gurus before he started to preach his own creed. Later on, I learned that much of what he told me was untrue, made up to conceal his quite plain and ordinary background.

Ken made quite an effort to convince me of the value of what he was doing. He was an extremely smooth talker. As I listened to him, I was struck by the frequency with which he was using the word "I." Interestingly, he was totally oblivious to the frequency with which he referred to himself and was clearly unaware of his overly narcissistic behavior. What was also quite noticeable was his habit of using the primitive defense mechanism called "splitting," by which I mean that his world was very stark, divided into two camps: the people who were with him and those who were against him. He regularly referred to non-members or non-believers as "the enemy." I noticed that anyone who criticized or questioned him was quickly put in the latter category. The way he

---

[1] Henry Mintzberg (1979). *The Structuring of Organizations*. London: Pearson.

interacted with his disciples made it clear that he demanded complete loyalty from them.

Ken believed that he was special, that he alone had the answers to people's problems. He had also a tendency to overvalue himself and devalue those around them. In all situations, he needed to be the center of attention. When I asked him to explain some of his more dogmatic statements, I saw his face hardening: he was obviously unaccustomed to being questioned or challenged and hypersensitive to my comments about him. It appeared that he also had a paranoid disposition. Listening to him, I gathered that he was highly suspicious, imagining that some people—including the parents who had asked me to visit his commune—were conspiring against him. And it is true that there was some reality behind that assumption.

Notwithstanding these less than charming characteristics, Ken seemed to have no trouble attracting followers—people willing to overlook his negative qualities. However, it still puzzled me how, in spite of all the nasty things he did to them, his followers remained perfectly loyal toward him. According to the parents of my student, to mold his followers to his will, he would hurt them emotionally, psychologically, physically, spiritually, and financially. I was also told that he took sexual advantage of a number of his disciples, as some kind of initiation ritual.

It seemed to me that a large number of the cult's members had resorted to the process of "identifying with the aggressor" as part of a personal survival strategy. This condition was first noted by the psychoanalyst Anna Freud among World War II concentration-camp survivors.[2] According to Freud, identification with the aggressor causes the affected individual to "team up" with the "aggressor"—in this case, the cult leader—in order to survive, and in the process take on some of the aggressor's personality characteristics.

As Ken seemed to be interested in enlisting me in his cause, I managed to see him a few more times. During these visits, I was quite impressed by his ability to read people. In particular, he was very skilled in pressing their hot buttons. Also, he seemed to thrive on chaos. When it suited him, he would enact great drama, and create a crisis situation. Generally speaking, his behavior was unpredictable. When he walked into the main building, I don't think any of his followers ever knew what was likely to happen. Would he be pleasant and kind-hearted, or would he be mean? Would he call someone out to embarrass him or her in public, or let it be?

When I asked Ken about the student who was my reason for coming to his commune—a young woman who, to me, seemed in terrible shape—there was

[2] Anna Freud (1946), *The Ego and the Mechanisms of Defense*. New York: International Universities Press.

no indication on his part of his having done anything wrong. Clearly, he was not taking any responsibility for her depressed state of mind—let alone feeling any guilt. His only reaction was to devalue her, saying that she was some kind of misfit, not really suitable to be part of the group.

The more I saw of Ken, the more irritated I was by his "antisocial," manipulative, self-centered behavior. There was no focused, sustained effort to build a real community. The place was a mess. There was a total absence of any form of organizational process. Given his lack of prosocial behavior, it came as no surprise to me that Ken's cult fell apart, shortly after my last visit. One of the main reasons was that Ken was facing a number of lawsuits concerning financial malfeasance. As for the student who was my original reason for visiting the commune, it took a lot of therapy before she recovered from her cult experience.

## Cultish Psychodynamics

As "charming predators"—masters of mind control—cult leaders like Ken know how to address people's anxieties. They are able to make their followers believe in all kinds of outlandish things. But while charming their followers, they also make unattainable promises, such as complete financial security, total health, constant peace of mind, and even eternal life—things that many people may desire, secretly or otherwise. Furthermore, many of their propositions are made so ambiguously that whatever they come up with can never be wrong. Such cult leaders present themselves as the ultimate source of truth— but a truth that cannot be verified. They convince their disciples to "buy" into (sometimes quite literally) whatever they are promoting. Their stories are particularly convincing because they promote simple messages that make sense, the exact opposite of what we often encounter within our typical, humdrum, everyday life.

As Ken's case illustrates, several psychological dynamics are at play in the creation of a cult. For example, cults prey upon the human tendency to indulge in magical thinking—the belief that a person's thoughts or actions, including the spoken word and the use of symbols, can alter the course of events in the physical world without a causal link. Unfortunately, our willingness to engage in this form of thinking reinforces the tendency to endow a cult's leader with omnipotent and magical powers, very similar to the way young children imagine that their parents can read their mind. Similarly— due to the power of regression—members of a cult easily believe that its leader has the same kinds of powers. I have seen how the leaders of these cults also resort to the power of suggestion. The effect of their masterly brainwashing is that their followers find it hard to distinguish between reality and the distorted way of life within the cult. Many of these cult leaders—Ken being a good example—take up techniques from the human-potential, encounter, sensitivity training, and humanistic-psychology movements, and combine them with cult ideology and persuasive sales methods. And as we can see all around us, many political leaders have followed their example.

The pattern of manipulated cult conversions may not appear especially radical to outsiders, since rarely is someone beaten or otherwise physically harmed. But from what I have observed, cult leaders like Ken employ techniques of mind and behavior control that center on severing followers' connections to the outside world. These methods deepen the existing emotional insecurities of the cult's members, encouraging them to become completely reliant on the cult for all their physical and emotional needs.

## Brainwashing

The main purpose of many of these cultish movements is to advance the goal of the cult's leaders, which is to have total control over their members. Whatever their doctrine, it will be the master program for all thoughts, feelings, and actions. They use manipulative mind control and conversion techniques to exploit the vulnerabilities of potential converts and get them to buy into the master program. (I touched upon this when discussing the mental health gurus of instant change in Chap. 9.) To quote the brainwashing expert Ed Schein, they follow a process of "unfreezing" (breaking the person down), changing (the indoctrination process), and "refreezing" (reinforcing the new identity).[3] By creating a psychological imbalance in highly suggestible people, they succeed in having them develop a new type of identity. A fundamental aspect of cult psychology is this process of getting newcomers to let go of their previous, somewhat shaky identity. Subsequently, in any given situation, the cult's master program tells these newcomers how they should act, think, or feel. For members of a cult, not only is critical thinking forbidden, thinking in general seems to be frowned upon. Any form of questioning, doubt, and dissent is strongly discouraged. Personal feelings are suppressed, and members must appear contented and enthusiastic at all times. Much pressure or social punishment is given when there is disagreement with the cult leader.

---

[3] Edgar H. Schein with Inge Schneier and Curtis H. Barker (1961), *Coercive Persuasion: A Socio-psychological Analysis of the "Brainwashing" of American Civilian Prisoners by the Chinese Communists*, New York: W.W. Norton.

*Fear and guilt are central* to any thought reform/mind control program. In most situations, a fearful person can't think critically and has reduced ability to make decisions. Cult tactics also include *inducing fears and phobias* (strong, irrational fears) in group members to allow the leadership to maintain control. Members begin to believe that all sorts of horrible things will happen if they don't follow the rules, if they leave the group, or even think of leaving the group. When fear and guilt are added to this toxic mix, it creates highly dependent people. Eventually, members will come to depend on the leader to know who they are, how they are, and how they're doing.

## Paranoid Thinking

Paranoia is a distinguishing feature of many cults, as Ken's behavior revealed. A cult's leadership maintains its power by promoting an "us versus them" mentality. People outside the cult have it in for them, trying to destroy the "good things" that they have. By throwing oil on this fire, the cult leader generates "a polarized" mentality within members. Creating this kind of mindset is a powerful way of dealing with the outside world because it enables the cult's leadership to successfully isolate members from their former, pre-cult lives. Cult leaders convince their victims that a group, their families, and/or the government is out to get them, and that only the cult can provide safety. This "us versus them" mentality ultimately leads to cult members isolating themselves socially from friends and family. They replace those relationships with new ones inside the cult.

## Targeting the Disenfranchised

Cults are particularly attractive to people with low self-esteem—my student was a good example of this. One of the most common types of people who join a cult are the disenfranchised, people who feel as though they're being denied something, that others don't understand them, or that they're powerless. These are all very strong emotions that might make them feel angry, wanting to lash out at others. In that respect, cults that offer power and the opportunity for revenge are very attractive to the disenfranchised. Terrorist groups often recruit these types of people. They are easier to convince of the many miracles offered by joining the cult. They are easier to break down then build back up in an effort to teach them that the cult is the supportive environment they're looking for. Consciously and manipulatively, cult leaders and their trainers exert a systematic social influence that can produce great behavioral changes.

One technique to convert these people is by "love bombing" the new recruits. People with low self-esteem are flattered, complimented, and seduced in order to train their brains to associate the cult with love and acceptance. Subsequently, cult leaders retain control through mechanisms like public humiliation and self-incrimination through a cult of confession. Ken was especially masterly at pulling these strings. At some point during this process, the potential convert is manipulated into a panicked, disoriented state, and an emotional crisis is manufactured by the recruiters. They assault and overwhelm their converts' senses with techniques that induce a dissociated state, an altered state of consciousness, a trance state, in which mind and body are disconnected from each other. These include sleep and food deprivation, drumming, chanting, lecturing for hours on end, flashing lights, spinning around in circles—all techniques that assault the senses and break down a person's ability to think. Another form of control is "thought stopping" techniques. This can take many forms: chanting, meditating, singing, humming, concentrated praying, etc. The use of these techniques short-circuits the person's ability to test reality. The recruit is encouraged to think only positive thoughts about the group. It amounts to a "cult-conversion syndrome," representing an overload of the brain's ability to process information.

## A Closed System

In a cultic system, the boundaries of knowledge are shut tight and reinforced through resocialization processes, the use of ideology, and the institutionalization of social controls. As I stated before, the goal of this profound shift in worldview is the reconstruction of personality. The ultimate aim is to get the devotee to identify with the "socializing agent"—the cult leader. And the only "friends" will be others in the cult, a barrier to leaving, as leaving will mean losing all your friends.

A favorite tactic of many cult leaders is self-incrimination, a process whereby cult members provide their leader with written statements detailing their individual fears and mistakes. People like Ken then use these statements to shame their disciples publicly. As a consequence of successful indoctrination and resocialization, the relationship between the cult leader and his or her disciples turns into a self-sealing system. Eventually, the truly devoted adherent cannot imagine life outside the group. The desired outcome is a new identity (the cult-shaped persona) whose actions will be dictated by the "imagined will" of the authority figure. In other words, neither the charismatic leader nor others in the group need be present to tell followers what to do; having internalized the lessons and adapted their outlook, loyal and true believers know precisely what they need to do to stay in the good grace of the all-knowing and all-powerful leader. This social-psychological predicament, this bounded choice, explains why it is so difficult to leave a cult or an abusive cultic relationship.

Because they believe they are doing very important things—God's work, saving the Earth, rescuing mankind, or similar—members also believe that *lying, cheating, and deceiving outsiders to get them to part with money or to join to the group are justified.* It is an easy step to take, given the psychopathic tendencies of many cult leaders and their lack of empathy, guilt, or remorse. When you add to this their inflated sense of self-worth, grandiosity and sense of entitlement, and the belief that they can do whatever they like, take what they want, abuse whoever they please, without any consideration for others, you have a very toxic mix. Generally speaking, for these people, the end always justifies the means.

I find it interesting that cult members often have no idea they're in a cult. Although it can be obvious to those around them, people in cults often don't realize what they have become a part of. Most people enter a cult willingly, without realizing the power it is bound to have over them. They seem to be more willing to see the perceived benefits than the potential dangers.

But cult life can have a dangerous and lasting effect. I have seen how cult victims often spend years overcoming the emotional damage they incur during their time spent in a cult. Common negative characteristics exhibited by former cult members include guilt, fear, paranoia, slow speech, rigidity of facial expression and body posture, indifference to physical appearance, passivity, and memory impairment. Major depressive disorders, dissociative identity disorders, and others can be attributed to the agonizing process of joining a cult. The psychoanalyst, Leonard Shengold even labels cults as a form of "soul murder," viewing them as intentional attempts to stamp out or compromise the separate identity of another person.[4]

---

[4]Leonard Shengold (1991), *Soul Murder: The Effects of Childhood Abuse and Deprivation.* New York: Ballantine Books.

# The Cults Around Us

Cult-like behavior is not restricted to far-removed, aberrant incidents like Jonestown, or ideological movements like Al Qaeda. It is everywhere. Many social organizations require strict adherence to a set of beliefs and, in turn, provide a sense of meaning and purpose to their followers. I suggested earlier that this might be a reaction to the movement away from *Gemeinschaft* toward *Gesellschaft*. Sadly enough, we can see an especially disturbing example of cult-like behavior in the United States—an example that finds resonance among the leaders of other countries. Donald Trump seems to have created a cult-like movement, exerting a remarkable degree of mind-control though his tweets and morale-boosting rallies. For many Trumpists, there is no reality apart from what Trump defines, validates, or establishes. As I write, observing the dismal ending of his presidency, many of his followers seem to live in an almost parallel world. According to Trump, the press is "truly the enemy of the people"—disconcertingly, Joseph Stalin said the same. Immigrants represent "an invasion of our country"—another way to keep cult members on the defensive and in the fold. "The European Union is a foe"—instead of learning about other societies, shun them. It's disturbing to see is how Trumpists have become increasingly cut off from our interconnected world, in all the meanings of the word: their human, social, political, and even their own inner worlds. From a psychological point of view, Trumpists aren't just failing to think critically, they are not really allowed any freedom of thought at all. Just as in any cult, they have become each other's thought police. The primary job of cult members seems to be to police themselves, and then one another, and if anyone fails to support or transmit the leader's thoughts, the remedy is rapid, certain, and fierce punishment. Cult members become clones or extensions of the leader—and so are Trumpists. It is frightening to see how behavior similar to that which occurs in extreme cults can occur in all of us.

Generally speaking, I don't think it takes much for any social movement to turn into a cult. Many parts of our society are cultish, and we only need a reasonably charismatic leader with some catchy slogans to take charge—and before we know it, we are in cult-like territory. Eventually, people under the influence of cults display the kind of behavior that can be observed in addicts. Classical patterns are emptying bank accounts, failing to take care of their children, breaking off relationships with family and old friends, and being solely interested in the drug or cult. Therefore, you would be wise, when you meet charismatic-like individuals who say things that don't make any sense, to listen to yourself, not to them. Always welcome the power of common sense, which I have found to be a great antidote to regressive cult-like forces. There is a spectrum of cult-like behavior, from the true cults described in this chapter, to phenomena with cultish characteristics. Due to our dependency needs, we are always looking for some kind of messiah. Given this very human characteristic, you should always be wary of the cult of personality, one of the curses of our communication age.

# 25

# Do You Have a Corporate Culture—
# or a Corporate Cult?

*The only thing of real importance that leaders do is to create and manage culture.
If you do not manage culture, it manages you, and you may not even aware of the
extent this is happening.*
—Edgar Schein

*There is no magic formula for a great company culture. The key is just to treat your
staff how you'd like to be treated.*
—Richard Branson

Each company has its own "culture," by which I mean the way the company
is run, the values and ethics that will define the company, what is and what
isn't appropriate and/or acceptable behavior at work. Basically, organizational
culture defines how you work together in your organization. A healthy culture
comes from a combination of lived core values and unity around a common
goal, purpose, or cause. Another sign that your organization has an attractive
corporate culture is its ability to attract and retain highly motivated employees. If such a corporate culture is in place, it is more likely that the people in
the company know how to manage for sustainability. These kinds of companies can be what's sometimes described as a force for good.

There's no doubt that companies that are able to articulate a clear and compelling vision for the future will be very attractive to their employees. These
organizations provide their people with meaning—and creating meaning
makes a great difference. As I have stated elsewhere, most people are looking
for something greater than themselves to believe in. It gives them a sense of
purpose. Another binding factor that creates an attractive corporate culture is

© The Author(s), under exclusive license to Springer Nature Switzerland AG 2021
M. F. R. Kets de Vries, *The CEO Whisperer*, The Palgrave Kets de Vries Library,
https://doi.org/10.1007/978-3-030-62601-3_25

whether an organization serves its employees' needs for order and structure, while providing a sense of belonging.

That being said, there is a fine line between a strong corporate culture and fully fledged, cult-like, organizational practices. Although I believe that a strong organizational culture is essential for corporate success, there is a likelihood that truly successful organizations will take on cult-like characteristics. The word "culture" cannot be spelled without the word "cult." One organizing form can easily slide into the other, begging the question of what turns a great corporate culture into a cult.

In my opinion, the major differences between a high-performance organization and a cult depend on how qualities such as transparency, accountability, and dialogue are dealt with. Cult-like organizations deal with these qualities in a very different manner from more traditional organizations. The fine line between culture and cult will be crossed when mind control has too prominent a role, when a company seeks to influence too much of its members' thinking and behavior. When this happens, many corporate cultures turn into thinly veiled fronts for cults, due to their indoctrination, motivational, and recruitment practices. It could be argued, however, that using the terms "cult" or "cult-like" is simply a way of describing the far end of a spectrum that ranges from low levels of internal cultural controls by a group of people that work together, to extremely high levels of commitment. From what I have seen, several highly successful companies—like Apple, Tesla, Zappos, Southwest Airlines, Nike, Nordstrom, and Harley Davidson—have managed to build a cult-like following among their employees and customers. To be frank, "cultish" behavior is a fact of life in many corporations. Many of the very best companies like to develop a cult-like commitment from their employees. It becomes a problem, however, when there is such a fanatical devotion to "culture" that it becomes overly embedded in every aspect of the company's operations—processes, policies, the way people speak to each other, patterns of decision-making, evaluations, hiring, and termination practices. As a result, these companies become too inward-looking.

Although there is always the danger of this downward slide toward rigid controls, some companies have intentionally adopted a cult-like approach to dealing with their employees. They try to reposition the workplace as a replacement for family and community. Consciously or unconsciously (and in that respect behaving very much like a cult), they aim to isolate their employees from their families, communities and, most importantly, from having a more open-minded perspective toward their work. The goal of leadership in these organizations seems to be to make the lives of their employees centered entirely around their jobs. They want their employees to become completely emotionally bound to the organization. If they are successful, work becomes more important for their employees than their family or community. The result is that many of the employees in these organizations—in a misplaced quest for emotional support and self-esteem—pledge their deep commitment to the organization, a commitment that is not necessarily reciprocal.

Many of these cult-like organizations excel in behavior and thought control. They often use the same manipulation and control techniques that I described being used by cults (see Chap. 24). Like cults, they try to recruit or attract the vulnerable by targeting their sense of alienation, offering them some form of structure and a sense of belonging. A number of these cult-like organizations even go so far as to regulate their employees' physical reality, including where they should live, what they should wear, and how much time they should spend at work. Unfortunately, as their employees invest increasing amounts of time and energy in the corporation, they do so at the expense of their families and communities. Consequently, they have little time for leisure, entertainment, or vacations. When that is the case, the company starts to replace the family.

The employees in these cult-like organizations are expected to accept whatever organizational doctrine prevails, a doctrine reinforced through indoctrination sessions and group rituals. Individualism is discouraged, while group think prevails. What's more, these organizations are often heavily dependent on the messianic charisma of the leader to whom the employees pledge unconditional obedience. Also, from a more characterological perspective, the organizations' leadership emphasizes people being "good culture fits" when discussing the recruitment of prospective employees. Frequently, various types of personality tests are used to put employees in "boxes," and decisions are made based on each employee's personality type.

Another give-away that an organization is entering cult-like territory is the kind of language used. Like many cults, many of these organizations have their own unique lingo and bizarre euphemistic terminology for internal communications. For example, Disney created an internal language to reinforce its company's ideology. Employees are referred to as "cast members" and customers are called "guests." As an employee, when you are inside the park, you are "on stage." When an attraction is broken down, the code "101" is used.

Nowadays, in most Western companies, it is no longer in vogue to hold mass singsongs to encourage a sense of community at work. These practices are not such distant memories, however. Many years ago, an executive at IBM gave me a remarkable book of songs devoted to its "prophet," Thomas Watson

Sr., the charismatic builder of the company. America's Walmart has a company culture (described by many as "soul-crushing") that still features a compulsory company cheer. It also retains the Walmart pledge: "I solemnly promise and declare that every customer that comes within 10 feet of me, I will smile, look them in the eye, greet them, and ask if I can help them, so help me Sam."

Generally speaking, I suggest that red flags should go up when you are exposed to too many pep talks, slogans, special lingo, podcasts, YouTube clips, motivational team building activities, singsongs, and charismatic CEOs. When a company's culture has a mind-control quality with respect to the thinking and behavior of its members—when some people feel excluded because of how they think or feel—the organization has entered cult territory.

Some might wonder whether there is really anything wrong about these cultural practices. Why object to a company's sports facilities, laundry services, company bars, or restaurants? Why not have a special lingo? What's wrong about having a company-constructed purpose in life? Why object to inclusive company social activities? Wouldn't all of us be happy to work in a place that's so attractive that you love working overtime, on weekends, or giving up on your vacations? Don't both parties would benefit from that?

Some skeptics would suggest that these "perks" are not just altruistic gestures on the part of the organization. On the contrary: they're deliberately designed to brainwash employees to devote more and more time, talent, and emotional allegiance to the corporation, at the expense of their private life, family, and community. Isn't it true that many of the employees in these companies are vulnerable? Is it possible that top management is taking advantage of them, preying on their vulnerabilities?

In situations where employees don't have much of a personal support structure, an all-encompassing corporate environment is a way to fill this void. Like it or not, cult-like work organizations—like cults—have always recruited or attracted the vulnerable. By targeting their sense of alienation, they offer them a sense of belonging. Again, like true cults, they use various indoctrination methods to make their employees emotionally bound to their firms, to the point that their work becomes more important than family and community.

I have learned from experience that when the organizational culture controls every aspect of its people's lives, it stifles innovation, endangering the company as a whole. Excessive cultural indoctrination is not the way to manage for sustainability. In other words, cults are not good for business.

If you're a senior executive, you need to recognize this very real danger and ask yourself if aspects of your organizational culture have become psychologically coercive. Have you created a place of work where employees genuinely believe in the corporate vision, or are they merely parroting the party line? Are your people encouraged to have a personal life? Or are they expected to sell their soul to the corporation? Do they stay because they want to, or because they're afraid of what would happen if they left? If they left, would they feel completely lost?

## Cult-like Experiences

Let me share a recent experience I had with a leading US tech company, where I was invited by the CEO to a rather unusual weekly "get-together." I must admit that, after meeting this CEO, I was initially charmed by him. After a polite conversation about mutual acquaintances, he gave me a rave review of the success of his company. At the end of our discussion, as it was late Friday afternoon, he suggested that I accompany him to the company's auditorium. He told me that the company's employees had a get-together every week.

On entering the auditorium, I was rather surprised to find it packed with a seemingly upbeat crowd. After the introductory "cheer"—during which the crowd screamed out the company name, letter by letter, three times—the CEO handed out the weekly service awards. All the recipients received deafening applause. As each of the candidates walked onto the podium, they were also welcomed with cheers about the company being number one. The ritualistic element reminded me of an evangelical revival meeting. Subsequently, I found much of the commentary about each recipient hard to understand. I figured that for many organizational practices the company had developed its own vernacular. Looking at the audience, I was struck by their rather monotonous dress code. Like the CEO, most people were dressed in black and gray. I also found it interesting, how after the session, all the employees gathered in the company's dining room for a barbecue of sausages, chicken, and beer. All in all, the whole experience felt like a creepy organized fun exercise.

Still, I have to say that I was impressed by the enthusiasm of all the people present. I was also quite taken by the charismatic company CEO. The following week, however, when I spoke to a number of executives, I became less enthusiastic. I understood that many of the company's employees didn't seem to have much of a private life. The company appeared to be the sole provider of purpose and community. Although to all appearances, the company made a valiant effort to create a super-friendly work environment, many of its employees had no time for significant relationships outside work. And if such relationships had once existed, they had been broken off. Family and community seemed to be expendable. Many of the people I dealt with were separated or divorced. Time spent in the company was increased by the unwritten rule that people would work after office hours several times a week. One person even joked to me that he went home only to change clothes—he could stay just as well at work using the facilities in the wellness center. As far as outside activities were concerned, there were occasional company outings, but that was it.

From what I could understand, most of the company's employees were highly dependent on the whims of the CEO. From their comments, I gathered that many looked at him as some kind of "deity." Their main task seemed to be to cater to his wishes. Given the dominant role he played in the organization, I could discern very little independent thinking, which I could see— given the high-tech industry they operated in—was going to cause trouble in the future. Their competitors were not exactly sitting on their hands.

In contrast to this particular organization, companies with great corporate cultures have thoughtful leaders who encourage critical thinking, prize sound judgment, value individuality, and radiate authenticity. They know how to tap into their employees' strengths and knowledge. They don't use a cookie-cutter approach toward how their employees should think and behave. A great workplace culture has transparency and encourages dialogue and give-and-take relationships of mutual respect. In these organizations people have voice and know that they can make a unique contribution. In contrast, in cult-like organizations, too many of the goings-on are about the ego of its leadership.

Executives looking for long-term, outstanding organizational performance must be constantly aware of the cult trap. Enron has given us important lessons about the dangers of this that go beyond the issue of suspect accounting and financial reporting techniques. Enron is a sad tale that illustrates how an organization can descend into a cult-like behavior pattern, encouraging its employees to act in illegally.[1] The case represents one of the most spectacular failures in business history. Enron was once ranked by its corporate peers, in the annual *Fortune* magazine poll, as the most innovative company in America. It was seen as a new-economy, paradigm-shifting organization. But in reality, it turned into a get-quick-rich cult enabled by digital technology, deregulation, and globalization.

Enron's craziness was propagated by two charismatic leaders, Kenneth Lay (Enron's founder and chairman) and Jeffrey Skilling (its CEO), who promoted a messianic vision of the future. They nurtured a quasi-religious belief in the company's mission and its leaders' greatness. (Lay would convince the

---

[1] Bethany McLean and Peter Elkind (2003). *The Smartest Guys in the Room: The Amazing Rise and Scandalous Fall of Enron*. New York: Penguin.

world that he had mystical business genius.) The consistent message to employees was that they were the brightest and the best; that they were greatly favored by being selected to work at Enron; and that they were now charged with an evangelical mission to transform the way business conducted itself throughout the world.

Lay and Skilling were masters in self-promotion, encouraging hagiographic accounts of their accomplishments, including in an influential book written by the management guru Gary Hamel, entitled appropriately enough *Leading the Revolution*.[2] The faculty of the Harvard Business School produced no fewer than 11 case studies about the company, applauding its innovativeness and recommending its business model to others. The Enronites were seen as the new "revolutionaries." Meanwhile, journalists who dared to criticize Enron could expect to receive piles of angry mail from within the Enron ranks.

Skilling was sometimes also known as "The Prince," after Machiavelli's famous study. In fact, new recruits were encouraged to read *The Prince* from beginning to end as part of an indoctrination method, to prepare them for what was coming.[3] The wealth that could be made within Enron encouraged employees to feel that they faced a much more exalted destiny than people who worked for other, more humdrum companies. Given these kinds of expectation management techniques, excessive working hours were seen as normal, and 84-hour weeks were the norm. Clearly, Enron employees were prepared to sacrifice today in the hope for a better tomorrow. Many of the people hired were very young, and more malleable, better placed to work to these excessive demands. Dissenting behavior was not tolerated. Giving bad news would hurt people's careers.

The carrot of being able to make lots of money enabled Enron's senior management to establish a harsh internal culture. Those who achieved the agreed objectives were eligible for huge bonuses. But the opposite was also the case. Anything gained could be taken away at the whim of senior management. The organization's HR appraisal system became known as "rank and yank," as people were graded on a scale of 1 to 5, and then divided into one of three groups—"As", who were to be challenged and given large rewards; "Bs", who were to be encouraged and affirmed; and "Cs", who were told to shape up or ship out, the latter the most likely outcome. Anyone who didn't put body and soul into the job would get fired.

---

[2] Gary Hamel (2000). *Leading the Revolution: How to Thrive in Turbulent Times by Making Innovation a Way of Life*. New York: Plume.

[3] Niccolò Machiavelli (2014). *The Prince*. Scotts Valley, Cal: CreateSpace.

Enron's cult-like practices, fueled by greed, ultimately led to the slippery slope of unethical, criminal behavior. Ironically, to the outside world, Enron continued to present a heavily promoted code of ethics, known as RICE, standing for Respect, Integrity, Communication, and Excellence. Also, it ran elaborate motivational sessions, where moderators would distribute inspirational rocks bearing the words "Integrity," "Respect," and "Enron." But the reality was quite different. Enron's leadership discarded RICE completely, in favor of misinformation and deception, and the company became a glaring example of the use of double standards. Eventually, the bubble burst, showing that the emperor had no clothes and that its top management had been engaged in criminal accounting practices. Several of Enron's executives were charged with conspiracy, insider trading, and securities fraud. Skilling served 12 years in Federal prison, while Lay died of a heart attack prior to sentencing. Enron's shareholders lost $74 billion in the four years leading up to its bankruptcy, and its employees lost billions in pension benefits.

## Resist the Siren Call of Cult-like Behavior

Some still argue that it is good business practice to look for cult-like devotion from employees but, apart from asking for commitment and cheerleading, most companies will benefit from a dose of skepticism and dissent. An organizational culture where people don't push back when asked to act in cult-like ways, or where they aren't engaged in robust debate, always leads to serious problems. Employees should never be afraid to rock the boat. They should feel safe to speak their mind. There should be two-way dialogue. If not, the company will end up stuck and its growth will be stifled. Thus, although it is commendable to overtly promote a culture where employees understand and buy into the company's goals and expectations, it's not a good idea to enforce a company's cultural practices through fear and intimidation. Ideology always kills creativity. Some business leaders pick this up. Memorably, William Clay Ford Jr., the former Executive Chairman of the Ford Motor Company, said: "Nobody's irreplaceable, including me. I think for too long we've had a cult of personality in this company and in this industry, and frankly, I'd like to see that diminish."

A healthy workplace culture is based on shared values that team members genuinely believe in and which are expressed in their day-to-day work. It is a place where employees show up to do good work, not to pledge undying allegiance. It is also a place where people are expected to give their talent, not their soul. Instead of introducing cult-like practices, companies should encourage individuality and non-conformism—key ingredients for innovative breakthroughs. We need to be vigilant to resist the siren call of cult-like organizations. Everyone, who works in an organization should be able to distinguish demagoguery from fact. The acid test of good leadership is the ability to unlock the potential of followers and get the best out of them, not to create a corporate culture that enslaves them. A great organizational culture is about learning from the past, aligning teams with their core values, finding people who both complement and challenge their thinking, where there is open communication, where people have fun, and work constructively together. In these team-oriented organizations, people should feel free to share ideas, opinions, and criticisms. In such cultures, as the dramatic case of Enron shows, staying quiet is not an option. Everyone should have the courage to speak their mind, when needed. Everyone in the organization should have voice, not become one among many in an echo chamber. An organizational culture where people know that they will have voice will provide the ultimate competitive advantage.

# 26

## Creating Best Places to Work

*Don't part with your illusions. When they are gone, you may still exist, but you
have ceased to live.*
—Mark Twain

I have always had concerns about organizational health—not just how organizations are designed, the appropriateness of an organization's strategy, structure, and other processes—but also, and in particular, the wellbeing of its
employees. A major goal in my life is to create healthy organizations with
people who feel good in whatever they are doing, places of work where people
can be the best that they can be.[1] To me, the acid test of this kind of organization is when employees enthusiastically recommend working there to their
family and friends. When that happens, it's a clear sign that the organization
has its employees' wellbeing at heart. Unfortunately, in my experience, very
few companies pass this wellness test.

## Authentizotic Organizations

Many years ago, as a way of describing these more enlightened organizations,
I created the term *authentizotic*. These kinds of organizations should be seen
as ideal types—something executives could strive toward. I see it as an end

---

[1] Manfred F. R. Kets de Vries (2001). Creating Authentizotic Organizations: Well-Functioning Individuals
in Vibrant Companies, *Human Relations*, 54 (1), 101–111.

M. F. R. Kets de Vries, *The CEO Whisperer*, The Palgrave Kets de Vries Library,
https://doi.org/10.1007/978-3-030-62601-3_26

position of a scale of best places to work. (Of course, reaching the final position on the scale would be pretty much Utopian.) The term itself is made up from two Greek words: *authenteekos* and *zoteekos*. The first conveys the idea that the organization is authentic. In its broadest sense, the word authentic describes both something that conforms to fact and is therefore worthy of trust and reliance and being true to oneself or an identified person. As a workplace label, authenticity implies that the organization has a compelling connective quality for its employees in its vision, mission, culture, and structure. The organization's leadership has communicated clearly and convincingly not only the *how* but also the *why*, revealing meaning in each person's task. Its leadership walks the talk; they are genuine; they are being what they claim to be; they are real.

The term *zoteekos* means "vital to life." In the organizational context, it describes how people are invigorated and energized by their work and experience a sense of balance and completeness. These organizations meet the human need for exploration, implying that continuous learning is an important element in its corporate culture. Over and above this, the *zoteekos* element of authentizotic organizations addresses the concept of self-assertion in the workplace, which makes for a sense of effectiveness and competence, autonomy, initiative, creativity, entrepreneurship, and industry.

Many years ago, I was in Copenhagen to visit a well-known pharmaceutical company that had asked me for advice. At the airport, I flagged a taxi to take me to its address and the taxi driver asked me enthusiastically if I was visiting that particular company. When I said I was, he started spontaneously to sing its praises. He couldn't stop expressing his admiration for the company. He said his father used to work for there, his uncle was still working there, and just recently, his sister had started to work in the same place. It was clear that the taxi driver's greatest wish was to be offered a job at this company. Talk about enthusiasm. What better public relations can a company have? Obviously, there was no need for this company to hire a PR firm. How great is that, to have that kind of fan club!

This level of enthusiasm is heartwarming, but more pragmatically, having that sort of reputation is very good for the bottom line. After all, if you have happy employees, they are not likely to leave, meaning your recruitment costs will be lower. Also, it's reasonable to assume that happy employees, unless they are masochists, work harder. Happy employees are also likely to be nicer to customers, which can make all the difference. There is a lot to be said for customer satisfaction. The sum total of all these factors contributes to a healthy bottom line.[2]

I have been told that my concept of authentizotic organizations and my arguments about the need for them are idealistic and unrealistic. Dystopias are more likely to occur than Utopias. Perhaps they're right. Maybe I am too idealistic. Maybe I am alluding to places of work that exist only in my imagination. I do think, however, that it doesn't hurt always to have something to strive for. Reaching Utopia may not be realistic but reaching for it can't do any harm, even if realistically an organization is likely to fall short of the goal. Working in an organization with a great corporate culture is only to be recommended. It is nice to be surrounded by committed people who like what they are doing, and who have a sense of ownership. Of course, it is easy to list a set of great cultural values on the company's website, as the example of Enron shows, but what differentiates mediocre from great companies is whether or not the people in the organization live those values. If they don't, there will be consequences.

## How to Get There?

As I have suggested before, one way to create authentizotic organizations is to use group (team) coaching, which can become an ideal trust-building exercise and deepen the connections among executives and between executives and their organizations. Team coaching, using the life case study methodology, can liberate people from the hidden intrapsychic forces that prevent them from changing and from assuming a more meaningful, authentic life within an organization. In Chap. 2, I described how this intervention technique can be a great antidote to organizational silo formation and thinking. It is also a very effective way to help leaders become more adept at sensing the hidden psychodynamic undercurrents that influence team behavior.

In trying to create authentizotic-like organizations, leadership group coaching not only helps the people in the organization acquire greater understanding of their own behavior (and how they are perceived by others) but also helps them to make sense of what happens in their teams, that is, the interpersonal and transpersonal processes that are part and parcel of organizational life. For example, it encourages the members of the organization to recognize, examine, and understand prevailing group dynamics. It sensitizes them to other executives' conscious, but sometimes unconscious, preoccupations in

---

[2] James L. Heskett and John P. Kotter (2008). *Corporate Culture and Performance*. New York: The Free Press.

the here-and-now. At the level of hidden or meta-communication, it enables them to decipher unconscious communications—that is, what is really going on between people, the "snakes under the carpet" that are generally avoided in ordinary discourse. Group (team) coaching encourages participants to examine themselves, study their own dialogues, and their relationships to others, overcome their inner resistance to change, and apply and integrate their learning into concrete behavioral changes. It will also make them more skilled at coaching others.

To create best places to work, it is important that members of organizational teams are familiar with the mystery that is themselves—a major theme throughout this book. Only by studying human motivation from the inside (facilitated by a group coaching intervention technique) will they be able to truly understand what is happening on the outside. They need to know their own strengths and weaknesses before they can be helpful to others. If this kind of understanding occurs, however, all members of the organization are more likely to create alignment between their individual goals and those of the organization, creating greater commitment, accountability, and higher rates of constructive conflict resolution.

Effective leadership group coaching interventions not only help develop the coaching skills of each team member (through the process of peer coaching), they also accelerate an organization's progress by providing a greater appreciation of organizational strengths and weaknesses, leading to better decision-making. They foster trust-based teamwork, and in turn, organizational culture is nurtured, as the leadership becomes used to creating teams in which people feel comfortable and productive. When they work well, team-oriented coaching cultures are like networked webs within the organization, connecting people laterally in the same departments, across departments, between teams, and up and down the hierarchy.

To sum up, when creating the kinds of high-performance teams that are part and parcel of authentizotic organizations, you need to consider not only the structures and processes that facilitate teamwork but also the messier aspects of team dynamics. You need to go beyond what is happening on the surface, and become aware of what lies beneath, including your ability to navigate your own unconscious world. To get the best out of each member of the organization, you need to be comfortable with the worlds of fantasy and illusion that each of us carries inside. You should never forget that the human world would not be what is without fantasy, as fantasy transforms reality.

A number of years ago, to help me in my work toward identifying the characteristics of authentizotic organizations, I conducted a survey of corporate values. I wanted to create a tool that would help executives identify the values that were important to them. To create a sense of urgency, I thought that some kind of gap analysis could be useful. I wanted the members of an organization appreciate the gap between their desired values, and values-in-practice. Closing the gap would be another way to arrive at the authentizotic organization.

My survey, which I turned into a Culture Audit (OCA™),[3] revealed that some of the most important values were trust, fun, empowerment, respect for the individual, social responsibility, teamwork, entrepreneurship/innovation, competitiveness, result orientation, customer centricity, responsibility and accountability, continuous learning focus, and being open to change. I believe that if these values are in the DNA of organizational members, they will go a long way toward creating authentizotic organizations.

Of course, if you want to get the best out of your people—if you want to create an ambiance in which people feel inspired and give their best—you need to go one step further than simply referring to organizational values. You also need to *create a vision* of the organization's fundamental purpose. What will provide meaning to the people that work in the organization? A vivid description of what your organization is trying to accomplish is essential to its viability. But if your organization is imbued with meaning, this characteristic will play a connecting role, contributing to the creation of a group identity.

Paying attention to vision and values is critical but it is not enough. In Chap. 5 of this book, I discussed self-actualization, and identified essential features of the self-actualizing "package," such as meaning, belonging, control, and competence. I strongly believe that the best companies to work in have a set of meta-values that closely echo the ingredients of the self-actualization package. I simplify these as "love," "fun," and "meaning." In other words, these firms create a *sense of belonging* (a feeling of community that comes from being part of the organization, addressing basic attachment and affiliation needs); a *sense of enjoyment* (creating a sense of playfulness that will enhance creativity); and, of course, a *sense of meaning* (providing the people in the organization with a reason why they do what they are doing).

Unfortunately, most organizations are not like this. Far too many have gulag-like qualities, where people feel disengaged, demotivated, and drained— negative feelings that are an important barometer of personal wellbeing. Lack of engagement with the job is a serious problem, if you look at the figures presented by Gallup. For example, over nearly two decades, the annual percentage of engaged U.S. workers has ranged from a low of 26% in 2000 and

---

[3] https://www.kdvi.com/tools/20

2005, to a high of 34% in 2018.[4] On average, 30% of U.S. employees have been engaged at work during the past 18 years—worldwide, the figure is only 13%.[5] Too many organizations are permeated by fear and paranoia; the organizational fear-safety axis is completely out of sync. When this happens, creativity disappears—and so does wellness.

---

[4] https://news.gallup.com/poll/241649/employee-engagement-rise.aspx?utm_source=link_wwwv9&utm_campaign=item_245786&utm_medium=copy

[5] https://www.gallup.com/workplace/236495/worldwide-employee-engagement-crisis.aspx

# 27

## Can Organizations Provide Wellness?

*The trouble with always trying to preserve the health of the body is that it is so difficult to do without destroying the health of the mind.*
—G. K. Chesterton *Come to Think of It* (1930) 'On the Classics'

*If you don't take care of yourself, the undertaker will overtake that responsibility for you.*
—Carrie Latet

The dismal Gallup figures about job engagement I cited in Chap. 26 provide ample reason to be concerned about wellness in organizational life. And we are right to be troubled by lack of engagement—it is extremely costly for organizations to have demotivated employees. When people are demotivated, they will not give their best. So, as a countermeasure and attempt to improve morale, many large corporations have introduced wellness programs: the yoga at Goldman Sachs and communal sleep logs at JPMorgan Chase & Company are widely cited. Apple launched medical clinics to better serve the needs of its staff;[1] Microsoft, Intuit, and SAP have dedicated wellness programs, while Google's campus offers a wide range of wellness programs, including onsite healthcare services (medical, chiropractic, physiotherapy, massage), access to fitness centers, classes, and community bikes. The leaders in these organizations have realized that they need to do something to have engaged employees. They take major efforts to prove Gallup wrong. And I agree that for reasons of motivation, it may

---

[1] https://www.cnbc.com/2018/02/27/apple-launching-medical-clinics-for-employees.html

© The Author(s), under exclusive license to Springer Nature Switzerland AG 2021
M. F. R. Kets de Vries, *The CEO Whisperer*, The Palgrave Kets de Vries Library,
https://doi.org/10.1007/978-3-030-62601-3_27

be much more beneficial to see people happily meditating on a beach rather than hunched over in their cubicles eating fast food.

## Our Attraction to Fads

When asked what surprised him most about humanity, the Dalai Lama answered: "Man. Because he sacrifices his health in order to make money. Then he sacrifices money to recuperate his health. And then he is so anxious about the future that he does not enjoy the present; the result being that he does not live in the present or the future; he lives as if he is never going to die and then dies having never lived."[2] This perception explains why the wellness industry is thriving. All these yoga classes, meditation retreats, mindfulness programs, spas, aromatherapy oils, crystals, juice cleanses, and other wellness-focused practices has helped to make the wellness industry a formidable force to be reckoned with around the world. Interestingly enough, in recent years, it has grown a healthy 12.8% in the U.S., becoming a $4.2 trillion market.[3] Wellness has become a major global industry that includes wellness tourism, alternative medical treatments, many anti-aging interventions, upscale wellness studios and spas, yoga, and numerous mindfulness programs. Some of the executives in my programs have described high-end programs, like tours proposed as healing and spiritual journeys to the Amazon, where people go in search of psychedelic, hallucinatory insights by sampling ayahuasca[4] (a traditional plant medicine), under the guidance of indigenous or self-styled shamans. Some experts, or more accurately pseudo-experts, suggest that these wellness programs not only help individuals manage stress, depression, and anxiety, but also enhance productivity, creativity, and concentration—you name it.

You don't have to look far to see that many celebrity figures have joined the wellness movement, a good example being Oscar-winning actress Gwyneth Paltrow, the founder of the highly successful Goop empire that has advocated, at times, questionable products based on pseudoscience.[5] This particular wellness company, however, has become a full-blown organization with a podcast, magazine, and shop filled with Goop-branded beauty products and supplements, specifically directed toward the female market. As this example shows, entire industries have popped up around our need to cleanse, detoxify,

---

[2] https://www.goodreads.com/quotes/885801-the-dalai-lama-when-asked-what-surprised-him-most-about

[3] https://globalwellnessinstitute.org/press-room/statistics-and-facts/

[4] https://www.businessinsider.nl/how-ayahuasca-went-from-healing-ritual-to-global-wellness-trend-2020-8/.

[5] https://www.inquirer.com/health/goop-gwyneth-paltrow-pseudoscience-netflix-jade-egg-20200204.html

meditate, be mindful, eat clean, and so much more. Obviously lala land has room for more than the gurus of the helping profession who promise miracle cures.

## Faddism

The business community has always been the willing victim of fads. The anxiety of many executives about missing out—of having a competitive disadvantage—makes them gullible. Like the apparently endless streams of books advocating psychological self-help, there is a similar stream of business publications that offer pie-in-the-sky solutions to knotty corporate issues. In reality, however, much of this comes down to a lot of verbal fluff without any grounding in reality. Consultant-speak only adds to the confusion. Consultants pour more oil on the fire of anxiety about whether or not you have done the right thing or are missing out. All in all, it is no surprise that management babble increases executives' anxiety level, resulting in a propensity to buy the prescribed "medicine" without any scientific evidence that the "cure" will be successful. The result is that many C-suite executives, who otherwise seem to be insightful human beings, turn into idiots when faced with some management fads.

Many of wellness entrepreneurial types have created health-oriented empires without any real proof that their remedies work, especially as many don't have any serious medical education or nutritional qualifications themselves. More often, their wellness philosophies are purely impressionistic, powered by erroneous assumptions: for instance, that natural products are superior to synthetic ones, and Eastern philosophies better than decadent Western ones. Large numbers of people are naïve enough to fall for this, notwithstanding the large body of empirical or scientific evidence that denounces the claims of these people.

Much of Eastern alternative medicine falls into this category of charlatanism as it lacks biological plausibility and has been untested. Many of its claims about wellness created by esoteric "potions" are based on anecdotal evidence. Of particular concerns are the "wet" or wildlife markets held in many of these countries, tapping animals or their body parts for these kinds of traditional medicines. Unfortunately, numerous diseases, including HIV and Ebola, had their origins in close contact between humans and wild animals. And given its disastrous impact, the present coronavirus pandemic can be seen as an extreme example.

I have learned from many people in the medical profession that they are highly frustrated by the claims made by practitioners of alternative medicine and the wellness movement, given the shady, shallow science behind them. The scientific community has repeatedly expressed its view that much of what is presented in the wellness cult is completely ridiculous, on every level.[6] Many medical doctors and other health professionals are adamant that the wellness trend is nothing more than another groundless fad, detrimental to both physical and mental health. Many are concerned that real specialists in the field will have to spend more and more resources disproving snake-oil wellness programs as opposed to testing viable interventions. The most positive commentary is that, at times, all these wellness programs and products show the benefits of the placebo effect. Given all the hype—and given all the money that organizations spend on creating wellness experiences for their employees—I think it is wise to step back and ask yourself: Do these wellness cures make a tangible difference or are they a transient marketing fad? And of course, we can also ask ourselves how will the coronavirus pandemic influence our future outlook on more esoteric wellness treatments, especially the use of animal parts?

## Going Beyond the Wellness Illusion

Returning to organizational life, are you really doing yourself a favor pursuing mindfulness training in the evening while being forced to endure daily stress at work? Is it possible that workaholic you, who spends lots of money on "detoxifying" treatments, crystal readings, expensive retreats, and mindfulness programs, are being taken for a gigantic ride?

Don't get me wrong, it makes sense to strive for wellbeing and a healthier lifestyle, at home or at work. It makes sense to look for some kind of balance in life. However, true wellness is a state of mind. You shouldn't feel compelled to pursue it in the form of external and often unfounded magical cures. Living a positive and healthy lifestyle should be a given, rather than something packaged and forced-fed to you as a product you need to purchase, experience, and consume. When hard-driving corporations with Darwinian-like cultures where everyone is out for themselves, institute wellness programs, you have to question their real goal. Do they want to change employees' lives or are they designed to prevent overworked individuals from totally burning out? In companies where people experience real wellness, it is part of the corporate DNA and not just another trend applied to squeeze the most out of their people.

---

[6] https://www.wrvo.org/post/health-and-wellness-myths-spread-trust-reliable-science-wanes

Returning to my concept of the authentizotic organization described in Chap. 26, many things need to be put in place before real wellness prevails. As I suggested before, organizations that truly enable wellness will have flat, organic structures that make it easy to share information, ideas, and feelings between people at all levels. In these places of work, communication flows freely between senior executives and their subordinates, so that the latter feel listened to and empowered. Frequently, flexible work arrangements are a reality, giving people greater control of their personal and professional lives. For wellness to flourish, trust is a key dimension of corporate culture, implying that people treat each other with mutual respect, behave with integrity, and fair process is a given. In my experience, trust and a coaching culture go hand in hand. When a coaching orientation becomes part of the organization's DNA, wellness is likely to follow. As I have also mentioned before, team coaching can be a highly effective way of creating these authentizotic organizations.

I am not saying that we should throw all wellness programs out the window. However, as a standalone agenda, wellness devoid of the other essential ingredients, such as trust and a coaching culture, will just turn into another management fad. Sadly enough, the world doesn't need more imagined quick-fix solutions. It's already full of them. Executives better realize that if the organizational basics are not in place, their expensive wellness programs will just be a waste of time and money. The whole point of wellness should be that it becomes so ubiquitous that you forget about pursuing it; that living a positive and healthy lifestyle is a given rather than something singled out as a phenomenon.

# 28

## Old Age Is Not for Sissies

*It's paradoxical that the idea of living a long life appeals to everyone, but the idea of getting old doesn't appeal to anyone.*
—Andy Rooney

*Growing old is like being increasingly penalized for a crime you haven't committed.*
—Pierre Teilhard de Chardin

Somehow, many of us have a fantasy that wellness will help us to live longer. It may be one of the reasons for all the contemporary brouhaha about wellness. But haven't we always had difficulty facing the fact of our own mortality? Can we really accept that our existence on this planet is only limited? Just think about Woody Allen's statement: "I am not afraid of death. I just don't want to be there when it happens." For many of us, death is the ultimate narcissistic injury. In whatever way we deal with it, it is a reality that touches all of us. There are going to be endings. And in real life, these endings aren't necessarily going to be neat.

The statesman Benjamin Disraeli once said astutely, "Youth is a blunder. Manhood a struggle. Old age a regret." In spite of our tendency to push death away, most of us have a pretty good idea how things will play out. We have experienced the deaths of our parents. We know—paradoxically, it being the preferred scenario—that we are next in line. But do we truly realize what growing old means? Have we thought seriously about it? Do we realize what life will be like? And is there anything to look forward to? Will old age bring happiness? Unfortunately, while a good way to summarize happiness is as

M. F. R. Kets de Vries, *The CEO Whisperer*, The Palgrave Kets de Vries Library, https://doi.org/10.1007/978-3-030-62601-3_28

"something to do, someone to love, and something to hope for," these views are less relevant as we get older. Perhaps we've reached retirement age, which for some of us means we have less to do. The people we love may no longer be around, which is very hard to take. And as our careers have come to an end—like many other endings—there is much less to hope for.

I sometimes ask myself whether our ancestors weren't much better off. They went out with a blast at an early age. There's something to be said for dying in your prime—when you are full of life. When you think about it, do you really want to live beyond 80? Would you really enjoy doing more of the same? When young, there were all these new experiences. But how are things now? What are we to do when we reach an advanced age? Are physical complaints the only new experiences to look forward to? Do you enjoy conversations about what part of your body is going wrong? For many people, old age can be tedious, monotonous, and painful, although there are, of course, some who argue that you are never too old to set yet another goal or to dream a new dream.

Recently, I talked to a very old client of mine. I asked him how he was doing. These are his comments:

> I feel like an old car that's running down. I'm not as strong as I used to be. Also, I'm starting to forget things. And to me, forgetting people's names can be quite embarrassing. Looking ahead, I can pretty much envision what life is going to be like—diminishing capacities, shrinking expectations, and being increasingly restricted in what I can do—even when those changes will only happen gradually. My body is slowly but surely starting to fall apart. I don't like how I look, particularly when I see pictures of myself when I was younger. And I certainly don't like what I can see ahead. When I look at old photographs of myself, I wonder where that person went. I would like things to be different. But I am not fooling myself. I know that there's no going back. When I was younger, I worried about dying when my children were still young. But now they're grown up. They can manage very well without me. They can take care of themselves. In the stage of life where I am now, I can see myself becoming a burden to them all. Heaven forbid they may have to take care of me. Of course, it sounds funny when people say getting old is better than the alternative—that every good day is another day you are above the ground. But that's just the difference between crappy and crappier. That's the reason I don't like birthdays anymore. At every birthday I get one step closer to death. What difference does it make to die at 65 versus 75 or 85? What's the good of all those extra years? Is anything new really going to happen? Do I want to hang around when I can't walk or think for myself any longer? Do I want to see all my contemporaries die off? Do I like going to funerals every couple of weeks? Do I want to spend what's left of my

life parked in front of a TV set or doing crossword puzzles, presuming that enough of my brain's still functioning? To look forward to all that, you have to be completely delusional. What's also depressing is that all the people I have known are gradually dying off. Soon, there will be a time that there's no one alive left who has ever known me. That's when I will be truly dead—when I exist in nobody's memory. What was it the movie star Bette Davis once said? "Old age is no place for sissies?"

## Do We Live Too Long?

This might not be the sort of question that would enliven polite dinner conversation. Nevertheless, it warrants our attention. Subliminally, we are all concerned about the quality of life in our later years, but we tend to push these painful thoughts away. Notwithstanding our talents in repression, however, we can't help but worry about the loss of physical independence and possible financial hardship that's up ahead. In fact, we probably worry more about the potential downsides of aging than about dying. Few of us look forward to old age. It doesn't fit the image of self-reliance, autonomy, and independence that we all like to embrace. I sometimes wonder if humankind as a whole doesn't participate in a silent conspiracy to repress or suppress the depressing future that we can look forward to when aging.

These depressive thoughts make me think of the Greek myth about the goddess Eos, an immortal given to falling in love with mortal men and suffering serial heartbreak. According to the myth, Eos begged Zeus to grant one of her lovers, Tithonus, immortality. However, she forgot to ask for him to have eternal youth as well. Tithonus duly lived forever but turned inexorably into a helpless old man. Eos eventually became so disgusted with his condition that she locked him away in a chamber, where he could be heard begging for death. The moral of this tale is that we should be careful what we wish for. Aging is the only available way to live a long life. Old age, however, can seem like the ultimate tragicomedy.

## The Decline of the Body

Although the idea of immortality is a mainstay of mythology, it loses its appeal if eternal youth and good health aren't part of it. In our efforts to deny reality, we want to live as long as possible without getting old. This may also be the main explanation for the current wellness craze. As I mentioned in the previous chapter, we search frantically for treatments that claim to slow the aging process—diets, exercise programs, plastic surgery. At the same time, we know very well that they're just patch-up solutions. In the end, they may do little more than prolong our pain and suffering.

Let's take a look at some hard evidence about aging. By the age of 75, creativity, originality, and productivity have declined for the vast majority of us. And then there is our physical condition. Although we are tending to live longer than our parents, we are likely to be more incapacitated. Half of people aged 80 and older have several functional limitations.[1] As we age, our muscular strength, reaction time, stamina, hearing, distance perception, and sense of smell are increasingly compromised. Our immune system weakens, meaning that we are more susceptible to deadly diseases like cancer, pneumonia—and of course the coronavirus.[2] A third of people aged 86 and older have Alzheimer's disease[3] and even if we don't become demented, our mental-processing speed, long-term memory, and problem solving deteriorate. It is salutary to remind ourselves that the average age at which Nobel Prize-winning physicists make their discoveries—as opposed to the age at which they receive the prize—is 48.[4] For nearly two millennia, the average length of a human life was 30 years and infant mortality was endemic. But over the last 200 years, life expectancy has more than doubled, largely because of improved personal hygiene, effective treatments for childhood diseases, and safer working environments. Now we live much longer than we ever did, largely because we don't die of things we used to, like infections. But we still wear out. Of course, modern medicine can keep us going, postponing the dying process as we sink to further depths of infirmity and dementia. Without it, we would probably die sooner and with more dignity. Some scientists have argued that we're now hitting the upper end on life expectancy, on the grounds that the most basic determinant of aging is the natural limit on somatic cell division. The theory is that the cell division that drives human life will eventually come to an end; in other words, there is a fundamental limit within the human body itself.[5] Even if science

---

[1] Guralnik, J.M., A.Z. LaCroix, L.G. Branch, S.V. Kasl, and R.B. Wallace (1991). "Morbidity and Disability in Older Persons in the Years Prior to Death." *American Journal of Public Health,* 81, 443–447; Wilcox, V. L., Kasl, S. V. and Idler, E. L. (1996). "Self-Rated Health and Physical Disability in Elderly Survivors of a Major Medical Event," *Journal of Gerontology: Social Sciences,* 51B, (2), S96–S104.

[2] Morrison, S. & Newell K. M. (2012). "Aging, neuromuscular decline and the change in physiological and behavioral complexity of upper-limb movement dynamics," *Journal of Aging Research,* 2012:891218 10.1155/2012/891218

[3] Alzheimer's Association (2012). *Alzheimer Association Report, Facts and Figures,* New York.

[4] Guterl, F. (2012). *The Fate of the Species.* New York: Bloomsbury; http://www.nobelprize.org/nobel_prizes/lists/age.html

[5] Kenyon, C. (2010). The genetics of aging, *Nature,* 464 (7288), 504–512.

eventually eradicates cancer, heart disease, and stroke, we would add only a limited number of years to our current life expectancy. The consequence of this is that we can look forward to an increase in the absolute number of years lost to disability as our life expectancy rises. We may have assumed greater control over the biological arc of death, but the general effect of better health is not to have slowed the aging process so much as to slow the dying process. And as we live too long, apart from death due to cancer, we have a greater probability of dying from neuro-degenerative diseases like Alzheimer's and Parkinson's—not an attractive proposition. We know all too well that diseases of the brain have great stigmas attached. Sufferers are seen and treated as mentally challenged.

All in all, if there is such a thing as graceful aging, it requires a hefty dose of optimism and effective coping styles. Happiness in old age may have more to do with attitude than health. The point some people make is that although we can't help getting older, we don't have to behave old. This is not a recent observation: centuries earlier, Plato wrote, "He who is of a calm and happy nature will hardly feel the pressure of age." Denial can be a marvelous defense. For example, I recall a comment once made by Mark Twain: "Age is an issue of mind over matter. If you don't mind, it doesn't matter." Don't worry about getting old, worry about thinking old. Wouldn't the successful prescription be to just live your life and forget your age? Personally, I think that knowing how to age—and not being afraid of aging—should be seen as a good sign of mental health.

Once, in a workshop I was facilitating, I asked one of the participants what she would wish for if she could wish for anything in the world. Without any hesitation, she replied, "A quick death." She knew what she was talking about, having nursed her mother for many years through a deadly cancer. No wonder so many people think that physician-assisted suicide should be legalized, and why such a large percentage of them say they would seriously consider that option if their physical health deteriorated sufficiently.

In our heart of hearts, we may feel that we are living too short and dying too long. It begs the question whether it isn't it better to live life to the full and look forward to a timely death? What's good about stretching life out indefinitely, doing more (or less) of the same; or worse, finding yourself totally helpless and dependent on the care of others? Although none of us wants to die young, none of us wants to live the last years of our life physically vulnerable and mentally handicapped. There is a great difference, however, between what people say and what they actually do, when it comes to the obvious alternative.

Nevertheless, living too long can be extremely depressing because aging is a process of decline that puts serious constraints on the quality of our experiences and the nature of our interaction with the world around us in the last phase of life. Living can become dominated by pain and suffering, including the loss of dignity. And we may also face age discrimination. In our youth-oriented culture, the younger generation may start to demean and patronize us, treating us like the children we once were. This is particularly true for Western societies. Mahatma Gandhi once said, "A nation's greatness is measure by how it treats its weakest members." Unfortunately, our century is not an age of Abraham, Jacob, or Methuselah, who were revered for their wisdom. On the contrary, we live in an age where the external signs of aging are avoided at all costs. Youth is worshipped, and immortality is sought through plastic surgery.

## Another Narcissistic Injury

Aging may even more difficult for people in a leadership position. They have always liked the power and status that come with the position. Thus, letting go doesn't come without a struggle. After all, what do they have to look forward to, when they leave their job? Things will be very different. Of course, for a while they could step into the position of non-executive director or do some volunteer work. But to these people, these options don't promise the same degree of gratification. Given their narcissistic disposition, what grates on many of them is the loss of public exposure, the loss of public contacts, and, in particular, the loss of influence, attention, and admiration. The challenge of spending more time at home with a partner who may have become a virtual stranger adds to their unhappiness. Thus, realizing what's to come, some executives cling desperately to power rather than confront painful realities. They will do anything to postpone the day of reckoning. To be treated as a "has been" by the younger generation is very hard to take.

## Living Beyond Our Productive Self

In the Western world at least, most of us live long past our productive self, having fulfilled our major evolutionary task and brought up a number of children. And as we have prepared the next generation for what needs to be done, is there any purpose or meaning left to life? Some of us might start a bucket list by way of response—usually a number of enjoyable things or things that physical incapacitation will rule out if we don't take action. Some of us try to spend as much time as possible with our grandchildren, if we have them. Others take courses or even teach part-time at a university, take up semi-artistic activities (like pottery or painting), or better our golf game. Others may be more ambitious and try, as I suggested, to do something for the community or mentor the next generation.

Playing the role of mentor, particularly in an organizational setting, can be hugely important as well as very satisfying. Unfortunately, mentoring is very frequently undervalued. It can be perceived as a convenient way for senior executives to hang on—in short, to resist retirement. I suspect that this perception is also colored by the fact that the younger generation of executives might not want a daily reminder of the aging process and that they are next in line. As with so many things in life, it's a case of out of sight, out of mind.

In spite of these activities—satisfactory as some of these might be—I come back to the existential question, asked by many, why do we hang on? Do we hang on for ourselves or do we hang on for others? It is a very relevant question. People who are close to us, and love us, dread the inevitable heartbreak and sorrow our death will bring. They don't want to deal with the fact that we are mortal. Generally speaking (although there are always exceptions), they don't want us dead, despite the stressful experience of having us hanging on.

But what if we spin these concerns another way? Being cynical, deep down unconsciously, do the people that are close to us really want us to hang around? If incapacitated, aren't we going to be a real pain in the neck? Actually, if they really do want us to hang in there when we aren't well, I'm tempted to ask what's wrong with them? Don't they want to move on with their lives? While children can never fully escape the parent-in-mind (even after their death), once we're gone, there will be much less pressure to conform to parental expectations. Children need to live out of their parents' shadows. When we live too long, the burden on our children can become excessive: think about the challenge of having to take care of themselves, their own children, and us as well.

Listening to the stories of some of my clients, I have come to believe that living too long entails another serious loss. It transforms how we are experienced and changes how people remember us. Most of us want to be remembered as creative, competent, and vibrant individuals. I'd like my children, grandchildren, and other significant people in my life to remember me as vigorous, engaged, animated, astute, competent, enthusiastic, funny, warm, and loving. I don't want to be remembered as an ineffective, incontinent, drooling shell of my former self.

## Socio-economic Concerns

Quite apart from these personal considerations, from a social policy perspective living too long has negative societal implications. Japan, which has the world's fastest-aging population, is a case in point. The Japanese, with their healthy diet, good healthcare, and advanced medicine, have the highest life expectancy in the world. Presently, more than a quarter of the population is over 65. By 2030, one out of three Japanese will be senior citizens.[6] But in this aging society a large number of Japan's citizens suffer from depression. The signifier of this is the dramatic rise in the number of senior citizens who take their own life. And what's happening in Japan might be a harbinger of things to come in other societies. If too many people live too long—whatever the state of their physical health—it could lead to an epidemic of loneliness and ennui. We can even make economic arguments against extending life. Regardless of what science makes possible, or what individual people desire, having an aged population is a public policy issue that has grave social consequences. Most Western societies currently spend the majority of their health resources on the elderly. This population group is constantly at the doctor's surgery needing treatment for what's essentially old age—a very costly proposition. This situation looks likely to get worse, as a generation of infirm and demented baby boomers will need increasingly expensive care.

From a socio-economic perspective, we know that there is a widening differential between the young and the old, a ratio too low to finance the various social security systems in developed societies. This adds new pressures to the world's already strained political and economic resources. If things stay as they are, people working today and contributing to social security systems will be keeping their elders secure with no guarantee that those systems will be able to support their own old age.

Of course, one obvious solution would be to keep the elderly employed for longer. The mandatory retirement age was introduced at a period when people didn't live very long. Retirement was generally a brief interlude of rest before death. Today, it simply lasts too long. However, the resistance to changing existing retirement policies is very high. Given the political implications, politicians prefer to deny the facts. They are extremely reluctant to deal with this issue as it is sure to create social unrest. And heaven forbid—given their short-term outlook—they will not be re-elected. Also, in stationary economies, the presence of the elderly can impede the upward social and economic

---

[6] http://www.u-tokyo.ac.jp/en/utokyo-research/feature-stories/toward-active-living-by-a-centenarian-generation/

mobility of the workforce. The old give less thought to preparing their successors, and the young see before them only layers of their elders blocking their career paths.

## Endings

It is a truism that endings are not very appealing. In *As You Like It*, Shakespeare described the seventh of the seven ages of man as "sans teeth, sans eyes, sans taste, sans everything." Sigmund Freud divided human development into oral, anal, phallic, and full-genital stages[7] but had no description for the final stage. Carl Jung devised a powerful image of life as split into two great phases: the rising sun of early years, coming slowly to its zenith in our late thirties, then its gradual setting in the years following.[8] My old teacher at Harvard, Erik Erikson, referred to eight stages of life, described as a series of polarities.[9] The last stage is the polarity of integrity versus despair. Erikson said our final developmental task should be retrospection, and that we should be able to look back at our life and accomplishments with satisfaction. If we can consider that we have led a happy, productive life, we develop feelings of contentment and integrity. Conversely, looking back on a life of disappointments and unachieved goals can result in despair. I have been told that in the Hindu tradition, the fourth and final stage of life is *sannyasa*, which is reached after the age of 72. The keynote of *sannyasa* is asceticism, detaching from life, renouncing material possessions, and spending what time is left in meditation and contemplation. Presently, I struggle with many of these ideas. Just how relevant are they to the last phase of life? How realistic is it to suppose that old age is accompanied by a substantial accumulation of knowledge and wisdom? If you have been a fool all your life, don't you just turn into an old fool? Why should the old be assumed to gain spiritual insight as their eyesight declines? I'm more inclined to think that to make a success of being old, you have to start young.

Perhaps we should split the last stage of life into two phases: early and extreme old age. During early old age we can still make a contribution to society but extreme old age, as Schopenhauer put it, is "like the end of a masquerade party, when the masks are dropped." The life of the "oldest

---

[7] Sigmund Freud (1991). *On Sexuality: Three Essays on the Theory of Sexuality and Other Works*. New York: Penguin Books.

[8] Car Jung (1989). *Memories, Dreams, Reflections*. New York: Vintage.

[9] Erik H. Erikson (1950). *Childhood and Society*. New York: Norton.

old"'—those over 85—is marked by what gerontologists call the "dreadful Ds"—decline, deterioration, dependency, and death.

It remains a debatable question whether we should help the old to become indefinitely older. Might our higher duty be the reverse, to let death have its day? I can bring personal experience to bear on this. My parents' last years were not their best. When they couldn't really laugh any more, when I couldn't have a proper conversation with them, I realized that their time was up. Seeing these once-lively people in that condition was deeply saddening.

Death is tragic but it can also bring peace and relief. My father died in my arms on Christmas night, in his own home, with all his children by his side. I think that was a nice way to go and I am signing up for it myself. However— and this is why I have touched on this subject—in their last decade my parents' quality of life was not good, and my father was very much aware that was the case. At 101, he decided he had had enough and stopped eating and drinking. Medical care could have kept him alive longer but, as his children, we decided to respect his wishes.

People who are important in our lives, and who die, teach us about the value of living. Keeping this in mind, I remind my clients remind not to take our life for granted, but to live each moment to the fullest. I also explain to them the importance of creating happy moments. At the same time, I think of the words of the writer Kurt Vonnegut: "You had your children. You wrote your book. Now don't be greedy." Or as the Buddha said, "Everything that has a beginning, has an ending. Make your peace with that and all will be well."

# Epilogue

*If it is true that good wine needs no bush, 'tis true that a good play needs no epilogue.*
—William Shakespeare

*And in real life endings aren't always neat, whether they're happy endings, or whether they're sad endings.*
—Stephen King

Recently, I had lunch with a musicologist. Somehow, our discussion drifted to the differences in the composing style of Mozart and Beethoven. She told me that Mozart would get a complete composition in his head without writing it down. Often, it meant he had to hurry home to be able to put his composition on paper before he forgot it. Beethoven's composition style seems to have been very different. His compositions would emerge as he went along.

Not that I want to compare myself to these two giants of the musical world, but her comments made me reflect on my own writing style. Often, when writing, I have a general idea about a topic but never know where that idea will end up. I free-associate while I meander along. However, there have also been many times when I would write a short note to myself, as I was afraid that I would forget what I wanted to say.

I admit that when I began writing this book, I had no idea about its structure—what its composition was going to be. The chapters weren't neatly arranged in my head. Each chapter emerged only gradually. To some extent, I was following the psychoanalytic tradition—I was free-associating. While writing, the only Leitmotiv that I had was that I wanted to explore various

© The Author(s), under exclusive license to Springer Nature Switzerland AG 2021
M. F. R. Kets de Vries, *The CEO Whisperer*, The Palgrave Kets de Vries Library,
https://doi.org/10.1007/978-3-030-62601-3

aspects of CEO "whispering." I wanted to give my readers an idea of the way I work with executives and what it means to embark on a journey of change. I came to realize that while free-associating in responding to knotty questions presented to me by executives, I had to deal with micro, meso, and macro issues—which is reflected in the various chapters in this book. Also, I didn't want to write yet another general textbook on leadership, coaching, or organizational transformation. I wanted to write a book that would be simple and personal. I also wanted to include some of my personal reflections on life, as I did many years ago, when I wrote a book called *Sex, Money, Happiness and Death*. With these ideas in mind, I began to write, not knowing where it would end. It was an interesting exercise, as over the last few years I have practiced writing mini articles for the *Harvard Business Review* and *INSEAD Knowledge*. Compared to writing a full-fledged book, you are constrained by the number of words when writing these kinds of articles.

I also wanted to point out that CEO whispering isn't easy. Although, at times, the work seems magical, doing it well takes a lot of practice. And making it really work takes its toll. Playing the role of the "wise" fool, in other words the morosophe, can be difficult. To be a truthsayer to executives when they seem to derail can be stressful. Playing psychological judo with executives—to nudge them toward taking action steps to change—isn't always easy. It has sometimes been a challenge keeping my sanity when faced with the many resistances that come my way. At the same time, I always remind myself of the stress experienced by my clients. I always ask myself how I would feel if our roles were reversed.

In this book I have tried to give you a snapshot of what it means to take on the role of whisperer. In addition, I have made a number of observations about the challenges leaders face. I have also made some personal reflections on what it means to live a fulfilled life. To help my readers understand why I do what I do, and how I do it, I have included various conceptual schemes but, as I wrote at the outset, I don't want to be ideological. I prefer to be practical. As I always say, I will do anything that works. Nevertheless, I do realize that concepts taken from the clinical paradigm loom large in this book, with reason. I have seen how, all too often, out-of-awareness behavior has derailed executives. Failing to recognize the rationale of the irrationalities of life will have serious drawbacks. We need to have the courage to go from the known to the unknown. We need to be prepared to explore our inner theater. We need to be willing to identify the various scripts that drive us—that make us who we are.

Throughout this book, keeping this thought in mind, I have emphasized the importance of self-awareness. I have suggested that we shouldn't be strangers to ourselves. We need to have an understanding of the reasons of why we are what we are today. We also should appreciate our differences. Although we all belong to the Homo sapiens community, there will always be differences in character and culture, creating different needs and wishes. It is the reason why a fulfilled life will be different for every person; why we have different dreams and goals in life.

Without dreams and goals, we are merely existing, not truly living. Therefore, as I mention repeatedly in this book, you the reader shouldn't just wait for life to happen; you shouldn't expect opportunities to just knock at your door. It is up to you to make it all happen. It is up to you to take the kinds of actions that suit your needs. As has been said many times over, the purpose of life is a life with a purpose. Purpose helps you to stay the course. Purpose helps you to transcend the absurdities of life. Without purpose, however, you will be unable to deal with the various psychological challenges that life has to offer. Without purpose, you are just living to die.

Living a full life means finding your true potential—to search out new experiences. It means getting out of your comfort zone. To quote the Russian novelist Fyodor Dostoevsky, "The mystery of human existence lies not just in staying alive but in finding something to live for." And if you really want to be really challenged, you shouldn't just push the boundaries to better yourself; you should be prepared to take up larger issues. To transcend narrow self-interests, you should consider the question of how you can make a difference in the world, even if only in a small way. And this thought reminds me of the parable of the starfish.

One early morning an elderly man was taking his dog out for a walk on a near-deserted beach. The day before there had been a terrible storm. Due to the high tide, thousands and thousands of starfish had been washed ashore. While walking on the beach, the man came upon a young woman who was picking up these starfish one by one and throwing them back into the sea.

Puzzled, the older man looked at the woman and asked, "What are you doing?"

Her response was, "I'm throwing these starfish back into the water. I'm trying to save them. They cannot get back by themselves. When the sun gets high, they will die, unless I throw them back into the water."

The man laughed. "But there are thousands of these starfish and there is only one of you. How can you make a difference?"

Holding one of the starfish in her hand, the young woman turned to the man and, tossing the starfish far into the sea, said, "It will make a difference to this one!"

Often, we find great things in little things. Often, small things are steppingstones to giants' causeways.

I have been extraordinarily lucky to have been able to help many people deal with the questions that really matter most, to help them lead more fulfilling lives. And doing so, I have very much appreciated the power of education. As an educator, I have seen how education can be the most powerful means through which we can change the world. Thus, it is only proper to end this book with the words of the philosopher John Dewey: "Education is not preparation for life; education is life itself."

# Index[1]

---

[1] Note: Page numbers followed by 'n' refer to notes.

© The Author(s), under exclusive license to Springer Nature Switzerland AG 2021
M. F. R. Kets de Vries, *The CEO Whisperer*, The Palgrave Kets de Vries Library,
https://doi.org/10.1007/978-3-030-62601-3